Spirituality and Psychotherapy

PCCS Books — publishers of counselling, psychotherapy and critical psychology texts

CRITICAL PSYCHOLOGY DIVISION

Commissioning Editors: Craig Newnes and Guy Holmes

This is Madness:
A Critical Look at Psychiatry and the Future of Mental Health
Services
Edited by **Craig Newnes**, **Guy Holmes** and **Cailzie Dunn**
ISBN 1 898059 25 X £16.00 1999

This is Madness Too:
Critical Perspectives on Mental Health Services
Edited by **Craig Newnes**, **Guy Holmes** and **Cailzie Dunn**
ISBN 1 898059 37 3 £14.00 2001

Personality as Art:
Artistic Approaches in Psychology
Peter Chadwick
ISBN 1898059 35 7 £18.00 2001

Spirituality and Psychotherapy
Edited by **Simon King-Spooner** and **Craig Newnes**
ISBN 1898059 39 X £15.00 2001

Spirituality and Psychotherapy

edited by
Simon King-Spooner
and Craig Newnes

PCCS BOOKS
Ross-on-Wye

First published in 2001

PCCS BOOKS LTD
Llangarron
Ross-on-Wye
Herefordshire
HR9 6PT
UK
Tel +44 (0)1989 77 07 07
email contact@pccs-books.co.uk
www.pccs-books.co.uk

Spirituality and Psychotherapy

ISBN 1 898059 39 X

Cover design by Denis Postle
Printed by Bookcraft, Midsomer Norton, Somerset, UK

Contents

PART FOUR: Practice

The following chapters are revised versions (many are substantial revisions) of papers first published in *Changes* Volume 18, Number 3 Autumn 2000. (PCCS Books.)

Chapter 1.   Previously published as: 'Counselling, Psychotherapy and Religion', *Changes* (18) 1: 146–52

Chapter 2.   Previously published as: 'Searching to do Justice to the Human – The Case of Religion in Psychology', *Changes* (18) 1: 180–90

Chapter 3.   Previously published as: 'Spirituality and Psychotherapy', *Changes* (18) 1: 163–71

Chapter 5.   Previously published as: 'On Not Being Able to Eff the Ineffable', *Changes* (18) 1: 172–176

Chapter 7.   Previously published as: 'The Transpersonal Relationship in Counselling, Psychology and Psychotherapy', *Changes* (18) 1: 191–207

Chapter 8.   Previously published as: 'Immanence and Transcendence in Psycho therapy', *Changes* (18) 1: 215–25

Chapter 9.   Previously published as: 'Psychosis and Spirituality: Finding a language', *Changes* (18) 1: 208–14

Chapter 13.   Previously published as: 'Tara Rokpa Therapy', *Changes* (18) 1: 153–162

Dedication

For Miller Mair

Introduction

Craig Newnes

Someone less suited to it would be hard to imagine.
                                    Kenyon, 1973

There is great wisdom to be found in the simplest of sayings: haiku are not solely popular because they fit neatly onto coffee mugs and T-shirts. When I told my school friends that I was off to study psychology at university they were bemused, and David Kenyon duly intoned the above. How he might have shuddered at the prospect of his mate turning up almost 30 years on as co-editor of a work featuring both psychotherapy and spirituality.

The book began as a debate between Simon King-Spooner and David Smail, one of a series of encounters organized by the Psychology and Psychotherapy Association (PPA). The association has survived since 1973 (how apt) as one of a very few places in the (post-) modern world of psychological enquiry where it is acknowledged that people are just too complex to be realistically defined and are just too involved, as people, to claim much expertise in defining others. Humility, rather than ambition and pride, should be the stance of those attempting to understand what it is to be human. From those claiming success for the genome project to those who believe that counselling is the answer to our ills. From those tasked with helping children to those pursuing the implications of the idea that conditions such as dementia are primarily physical. From experimental psychologists to editors. The basic premise of the PPA is that professional psychologists, therapists, counsellors, teachers, priests and the like are first and foremost people and only secondarily theorists, technicians and healers. This premise can be disconcerting for many and quite terrifying for some. It means that we shall all struggle with a conscience when asked to act in our professional capacity, we shall make mistakes, be subject to fits of passion, betray people, let some down and will face our own daemons. The evidence we use in our work will be flawed, come from personal experience as well as the laboratory and might be better expressed by other disciplines; art, poetry, literature, anthropology, politics and economic theory. If our task is to attempt an understanding of ourselves and others, then we need to reach out in ways that respect the widest possible range of experience and ways of describing that experience.

The experience of spirituality has not been much respected by a conspicuous majority of modern psychotherapists and psychologists. Estimates of religious belief amongst psychotherapists in the US suggest that about 5% have a God while 95% of their clients are theists. My own profession, clinical psychology, has been almost mute on the subject with only a very few papers in its UK newsletter mentioning spirituality or religion as of any concern at all; and this despite numerous articles dealing with terminal illness, mental health, the experience of anxiety, the assessment of a huge range of cognitive abilities, termination, managing people and so on as if the religious persuasion and spiritual positioning of the psychologists and their subject matter (people) were utterly irrelevant. Spirituality, of course, is but one facet of being human which clinical psychologists have tended to ignore; politics, poverty and social class haven't had much of a look-in either. The PPA, for one, has done its best to embrace these last three; in its conferences, its seminar series, its journal (*The Journal of Critical Psychology, Counselling and Psychotherapy* — formerly *Changes*) and in the enduring popularity, as lecturers, writers and public speakers, of many of its earliest members: Miller Mair, Jenny Firth-Cozens, Glenys Parry, Dave Pilgrim, Phil Salmon, David Smail and Dorothy Rowe. Spirituality has not been entirely absent from the PPA agenda: it featured, albeit briefly, at the Death and Dying conference in 1990 and *Changes* published papers on mindfulness-meditation (Claxton, 1994), Sufism (Kramer and Dawood, 1993; Kemal, 1994), New Age healing (Edwards and Dalton, 1992), Zen and Tibetan Buddhism (Handley and Kirkland, 1993; Brandon, 1996), the psychology of religion (Belzen, 1992), shamanism (Bates, 1993), traditional healing (Moodley, 1998), morality and virtue (Forsyth, 1991), religious counselling (Duffy, 1998; Len, 1997), even clairvoyance (Baxter, 1991). A drop in the ocean of all the papers published in the last 15 years, but not bad for a journal and association which continues to encompass those aspects of humanity beyond the narrowly defined notions of psychology and psychotherapy. Not bad also for an editor who took over the journal after working for a year in a therapeutic community for religious (Newnes, 1988) despite a degree of scepticism for all matters religious and ill-definedly spiritual which would make David Smail's ineffability (Chapter 5) look like Catholic dogma.

The debate between David and Simon led to a special issue of *Changes* (King-Spooner and Newnes, 2000) and, ultimately, to this book. Contributors to the special issue were either asked to update and re-edit their papers or write new pieces. Additional chapters from a sceptical stance (Rowe, and Williams and Irving) were sought alongside a section on practical aspects of working with spirituality (Loewenthal, Len, Maguire and Temaner Brodley).

William West starts by questioning the nature of spirituality and truth. He urges therapists to be open to the spiritual roots of their profession's own history as well as their clients' difficulties. Jacob Belzen (Chapter 2) questions the tools by which the discipline of psychology might define spirituality and suggests that psychologists have only modest means at their disposal to investigate meaning and have much to learn from historians. If truth be told, Jacob's reference section is, in itself, something of an education.

All the authors struggle with some kind of definition of spirituality, even if, as Dorothy Rowe says in her own contribution (Chapter 4), these definitions look, to the uninitiated, like ordinary experience; no more spiritual than yawning, laughing at a Woody Allen one-liner or getting drunk. David Smail prefers to leave the subject matter amorphous and indefinable while Clarkson, Loewenthal and Irwin and Hensey place spirituality in specific religious contexts. Chapter 6, by Williams and Irving, started as a spoof, but it is a position with a notable history. As clinical psychology trainees, we were acutely aware that in our counselling work we were the new, secular, priests granting absolution through behavioural rituals or Kellyan investigation. It is a position explored by previous writers (Halmos, 1965; Brazier, 1993) and one which Freud must have found both ironic and uncomfortable, given his scathing opinion of the 'black tide of mud of occultism'. Freud's refusal to give in to the black tide led to his split with Jung. Freud may not be a God, but, as Williams and Irving point out, this does not prevent his worship.

Chapters by Clarkson, Still and Clarke all attempt to make theoretical aspects of spiritual belief and mystical experience pertinent to the counselling relationship. Arthur Still (Chapter 8) sees spirituality as inherent in one-to-one therapy encounters rather than a transcendent, other-worldly, reality. Clarkson (Chapter 7) defines five relational modes in psychotherapy, of which the transpersonal is seen as referring to the spiritual and inexplicable dimensions. She examines these aspects with reference to both western and non-Eurocentric approaches to help. For both Clarkson and Clarke (Chapter 9), the language of experience is critical. In the world of psychosis in particular the language used to describe unusual and often unwelcome visions or voices is all. It can mean the difference between acceptance and incarceration. This divide too has a long history. There are many accounts of nineteenth-century women being carried away with religious ecstasy before being consigned to psychiatric hospitals while only 200 years previously such women were simply one subgroup of numerous others drawn to the religious life. In twenty-first century western society the medical frame is dominant; visions and voices are hallucinations, sensing God is mania.

In the last section the five contributors directly relate their experience of religion and spirituality to their work. Kate Loewenthal (Chapter 10) struggles with the reality of the supposed spirituality of motherhood in Judaism while Kate Maguire (Chapter 12) finds spirituality in the darkest recesses of her work with victims of torture. Michael Len (Chapter 11) wonders at the unchristianity to be found in Christian counselling practice while Edie Irwin and Lorna Hensey (Chapter 13) revisit the world of Buddhist therapy and training. Finally Barbara Temaner Brodley (Chapter 14) steps through the minefield that can be religion in her work as a person-centred therapist. She emerges unscathed. Better yet, her clients may find respect in her probing and compassion in her challenges.

None of these contributors attempt a clear definition of psychotherapy. Tom Szasz said it was a conversation between someone pretending to be an expert therapist and someone else pretending to be a patient. Of course this was before the days of co-counselling and deliberately ignored the numerous types of body-oriented, non-verbal therapies around at the time, but the point was well made. In a world of suffering, pretending to be an expert can get you far, and pretending to be ill may be your only defence. There is a risk that combining the ill-defined world of spirituality with the economic moral mission that psychotherapy can be will lead us down the road of American TV evangelism. Sheldon Kopp (1972) reminds us what to do if we meet the Buddha on that road.

References

Bates, B. (1993) Visions of reality in shamanic psychology. *Changes, 11*,3, 223–8.

Baxter, J. (1991) Clairvoyance and clairvoyants. *Changes, 9*, 3, 154–61.

Belzen, J. (1992) The rise of Dutch psychology of religion. *Changes, 10*,3, 190–6.

Brandon, D. (1996) Mind dancing: Humour and psychotherapy. *Changes, 14*, 4, 259–67.

Brazier, D. (1993) The faith of the counsellors revisited. *Changes, 11*,1, 13–19.

Claxton, G. (1994) Psychology in retreat: 'Pooh' therapy. *Changes, 12*,2, 81–6.

Duffy, T. (1998) Spirituality, the counsellor and the Church: can they journey together? *Changes, 16*, 4, 309–17.

Edwards, G., and Dalton, P. (1992) Living magically. *Changes, 10*,1, 64–7.

Forsyth, R. (1991) Towards a grounded morality. *Changes, 9*,4, 264–78.

Halmos, P. (1965) *The Faith of the Counsellors*. London: Constable.

Handley, N., and Kirkland, K. (1993) Healing: beyond ego and scientific materialism. *Changes, 11*, 4, 337–42.

Kemal, A. (1994) Sufism: a prevention and cure. *Changes, 12*,2, 87–91.

King-Spooner, S., and Newnes, C. (2000) Spirituality and Psychotherapy (Special issue) *Changes, 18*, 3, 145–225.

Kopp, S. (1972) *If You Meet the Buddha on the Road . . . Kill Him.* Palo Alto: Science and Behaviour Books Inc.

Kramer, G., and Dawood, S. (1993) 'This lunatic sphere and how to survive it' (Sufism, a gentle way with psychosis). *Changes, 11*,2, 99–102.

Len, M. (1997) Counsellor in the cloister. *Changes, 15*, 2, 124–33.

Moodley, R. (1998) Cultural returns to the subject: traditional healing in counselling and therapy. *Changes, 16*,1, 45–56.

Newnes, C. (1988) When God is not enough: Therapy with clergy and religious. *Changes, 6*,2, 1-5.

Counselling, Psychotherapy and Religion

1

William West

> *It is now common for people to present themselves to therapists with concerns that they themselves have categorised as specifically spiritual in nature.*
>
> Thorne, 1998, p. x

Recently, on a psychology and therapy email discussion list to which I belong, one of the participants said that whenever an email mentioned spirituality she would delete it without reading. This is someone whose contributions to the list I usually find of great value. I was left wondering what happened to her when one of her clients talked about spirituality. This article explores the often problematic relationship between therapy and spirituality and invites therapists to be open to the client's exploration of spirituality.

Counselling and psychotherapy, like psychology, have a problem with religion and spirituality that goes back to the foundation of modern therapy in the Victorian era in which there existed a deep antagonism between science and religion. The new disciplines of psychotherapy and psychology were determined to prove themselves 'scientific' and hence defined themselves largely as secular, an attitude that remains dominant to this day:

> Psychotherapy, many would argue, is scientifically informed . . . With this frame of reference, religion or spirituality is the enemy. (Heelas and Kohn, 1996, p. 294)

Freud kept returning to the question of religion which he spoke of as at best a 'crooked cure' and insisted:

> The derivation of religious needs from the infant's helplessness and the longing for the father aroused by it seems to me incontrovertible. (1963, p. 9)

Why the longing is for the father, and not the mother, Freud does not make

Acknowledgement

This chapter is based upon a paper delivered to a joint BPS North West/Department of Psychology and Speech Pathology Spirituality Day at Manchester Metropolitan University, 26 February 2000.

clear. He further states:

> The whole thing [i.e. Religion] is potentially so infantile, so foreign to reality… it is painful to think that the great majority of mortals will never be able to rise above this view of life (Freud, 1963, p. 11).

Despite the spread of counselling and psychotherapy and western ideologies in general, the vast majority of the world's population stubbornly insists on clinging to a reality that includes the spiritual. Indeed, David Hay's studies (Hay and Morisy, 1978; Hay, 1982) into religious experience showed that one-third of people replied 'yes' to the question, 'Have you ever been aware of being influenced by a presence or power, whether referred to as God or not, which was different from your everyday self?'. When he posed the question in qualitative interviews in people's own homes two-thirds replied yes. This points to the taboo that still exists in talking about religious and spiritual experiences; as Hay comments, 'Putting words to religious experience is notoriously difficult' (1982, p. 157). Hay, drawing on other research in the USA and elsewhere, concluded that religious experiences occurred in every culture and did not correlate with attendance at church or other religious institution.

Of course there have always been dissenting voices from the received scientific position, most significantly perhaps that of Jung who emphasised the value and the need for people to pursue an authentic spirituality:

> A psychoneurosis must be understood ultimately as the suffering of a soul which has not discovered its meaning. (1958, p. 330–1).

Indeed, Jung controversially insisted that:

> Among my patients in the second half of life — that is over 35 years of age — there has not been a single one whose problem has not been in the last resort that of finding a religious outlook on life. (1933, p. 164)

From the pastoral context there have been many voices challenging the psychologising of human spirituality including Leech (1994) and most notably Lyall (1995) who states:

> In the pastoral and spiritual context an understanding of what it means to be human cannot be contained solely within psychological models. (p. 80)

The same point is made by John Rowan (1993) writing from a transpersonal therapeutic perspective.

What is spirituality?

Religion is now seen by many people as the organisational structure for spirituality, whilst spirituality is more usually identified with one's personal beliefs and practices. Indeed it is common in Britain for people to maintain that they are spiritual but not religious or, as Davie (1994) suggests, it is a matter of 'believing but not belonging'. It is this focus on personal beliefs and experience that makes spirituality a plausible part of the therapeutic encounter. Indeed there is an ever increasing literature around the therapeutic encounter having a spiritual element to it (further explored in West, 1998; 2000a).

Within this context the work done by Elkins et al. at Pepperdine University in defining spirituality from a humanistic-phenomenological perspective is valuable. They developed a definition of spirituality that focuses on the human experience of spirituality:

> Spirituality which comes from the Latin *spiritus*, meaning 'breath of life', is a way of being and experiencing that comes through awareness of a transcendental dimension and that is characterized by certain identifiable values in regard to self, others, nature, life, and whatever one considers to be the Ultimate. (Elkins et al., 1988, p. 10)

What is truth?

There is a key assertion in the Freud quote above that people's religious beliefs are 'foreign to reality'. What is reality and whose reality is superior or more healthy? There is plenty of research evidence correlating spiritual beliefs and practices with well-being — well summarised in Richards and Bergin (1997) — despite the small minority whose religious faith is bound with unhealthy mental states. In our post-modern world, Freud's view is no longer tenable. Indeed it is much safer for therapist and client if the therapist respects the client's reality and perhaps follows Rogers' dictum:

> I, and many others, have come to a new realisation. It is this: the only reality I can possible know is the world as *I* perceive and experience it at this moment. The only reality you can possibly know is the world as *you* perceive and experience it at this moment. And the only certainty is that these perceived realities are different. There are as many 'real worlds' as there are people! (Rogers in Kirschenbaum and Henderson, 1990, p. 424)

Such a phenomenological viewpoint has profound implications for the practice of therapy and for mental health services that are beyond the scope of this article to fully explore, but are considered briefly below under point 4.

Some key issues that therapists could usefully address around spirituality

If we expect therapists to be able to be present to their client's spirituality in whatever form that takes within the therapeutic encounter, then the following is a list, by no means exhaustive, of some of the crucial training issues involved:

1. It is crucial that therapists examine their own prejudices and biases — both positive and negative — around spirituality and religion as advocated by Lannert (1991). For example many therapists are pro spirituality but anti organised religion, which may reflect unresolved painful childhood experiences. However, this position might not at all reflect the experience of a client who regularly attends church, mosque or synagogue. Therapists in training and beyond need to address themselves to issues around sexuality, gender, class, race and culture; it is time spirituality and religion were included.

2. There is a developing literature around spiritual experiences (e.g. Hay, 1982) that goes back to the pioneering research work of James (1901) one hundred years ago.

3. There is a great value and insight to be obtained in exploring a religion, including attending a religious service, from a different culture to that in which one was brought up. Indeed attending a religious service from within one's culture may well prove valuable.

4. There are assessment issues to be faced, including the possibility that a spiritual experience might have psychotic elements to it. Not all spiritual experiences are totally healthy nor are they all signs of madness despite the prejudices of therapists revealed in Allman et al.'s (1992) research. (The whole issue of spiritual assessment is discussed at more length in West (2000a).) There are times when a client will need a spiritual referral. There are times when what is happening to a client might be best viewed as a 'spiritual awakening' (Assagioli, 1986) or a 'spiritual emergency' (Grof and Grof, 1989). Richards and Bergin (1997) advocate asking spiritual questions as part of an initial assessment with a client. This both gives the client permission to speak of their spirituality as part of their therapy but also enables the therapist to consider what spiritual interventions could be used to benefit the client.

5. Many if not most of the theories of human development used within counselling and psychotherapy omit any mention of spirituality, e.g. Erikson's (1977) eight stages of man. However, there are a number of models that do include the spiritual including those from a transpersonal perspective put forward by Ken Wilber (1979; 1980) and John Heron (1998).

6. The implicit and explicit forms of spiritual counselling are worthy of study (e.g. Jung, 1933; Richards and Bergin, 1997; Rowan, 1993; Thorne, 1991; 1998).

7. It is important to clarify the differences and overlaps between spiritual direction and therapy (see Lyall, 1995; West, 2000a).

8. John Rowan (1993) rather controversially suggests that all therapists should be engaged in some form of spiritual development. It is my view that the disciplined practice of being a therapist is itself implicitly spiritual and akin to the Buddhist practice of mindfulness (Tart and Deikman, 1991) so that spiritual development will likely result. I do not think that we can insist therapists pursue a spiritual path, though perhaps we can insist they become aware of any unhealthy resistance to such an idea.

9. There are profound issues around supervision when working actively with clients around their spirituality which can lead to supervision difficulties, especially with those supervisors who take a negative or dismissive attitude to spirituality. I have researched and discussed this elsewhere (West, 2000b).

Conclusion

As we move into the twenty-first century it is clear that spirituality and spiritual experiences, unlike perhaps some outdated religious forms, are not dying out. There seems to be a continuing development of informal Do-It-Yourself forms of spirituality which many clients and their therapists are involved in. The forerunners of modern therapists, whether priests, shamans or witches, were always spiritually based (Ellenberger, 1970; McLeod, 1998). Therapy has for too long been in denial of its spiritual past and spiritual roots. As Colin Feltham states:

> Religious, and especially mystical, experience has had a profound impact on psychotherapy, and in many ways the therapists' agenda to induce radical transformation of the personality can be equated with just such religious states. (1995, p. 99)

Therapy sessions can and should be a safe and open space within which clients can explore all aspects of their lives and being, including the spiritual, if their therapists are willing to rise to the challenge.

References

Allman, L. S., De La Rocha, O., Elkins, D. N., and Weathers, R. S. (1992) Psychotherapists' attitudes towards clients reporting mystical experiences. *Psychotherapy*, 29(4), 65–69

Assagioli, R. (1986) Self-realisation and psychological disturbance. *Revision*, 8(2), 21–31

Davie, G. (1994) *Religion in Britain since 1945*. Oxford: Blackwell.

Elkins, D. N., Hedstorm, L. J., Hughes, L. L., Leaf, J. A. and Sanders, C. (1988) Towards a humanistic-phenomenological spirituality. *Journal of Humanistic Psychology, 28*(4), 5–18

Ellenberger, H. (1970) *The Discovery of the Unconscious*. New York: Basic Books.

Erikson, E. (1977) *Childhood and Society*. London: Paladin.

Feltham, C. (1995) *What is Counselling?* London: Sage.

Freud, S. (1963) *Civilization and Its Discontents*. New York: Basic Books

Grof, S. and Grof, C. (1989) (Eds.) *Spiritual Emergency*. Los Angeles: Tarcher.

Hay, D. (1982) *Exploring Inner Space: Scientists and Religious Experience*. Harmondsworth: Penguin.

Hay, D. and Morisy, A. (1978) Reports of ecstatic, paranormal, or religious experiences in Great Britain and the United States — a comparison of trends. *Journal for the Scientific Study of Religion, 17*(3), 255–68

Heelas, P. and Kohn, R. (1996) Psychotherapy and techniques of transformation. In G. Claxton (Ed.) *Beyond Therapy: The Impact of Eastern Religions of Psychological Theory and Practice*. Dorset: Prism.

Heron, J. (1998) *Sacred Science: Person-centred inquiry into the spiritual and subtle*. Ross-on-Wye: PCCS Books.

James, W. (1901) *The Varieties of Religious Experience*. London: Collins.

Jung, C. G. (1933) *Modern Man in Search of a Soul*. London: Routledge and Kegan Paul.

Jung, C. G. (1958) *Psychology and Religion*. London: Routledge and Kegan Paul.

Kirschenbaum, H. and Henderson, V. (1990) *The Carl Rogers Reader*. London: Constable.

Lannert, J. L. (1991) Resistance and countertransference issues with spiritual and religious clients. *Journal of Humanistic Psychology, 31*(4), 68–76

Leech, K. (1994) *Soul Friend*. London: Darton, Longman and Todd.

Lyall, D. (1995) *Counselling in the Pastoral and Spiritual Context*. Buckingham: Open University Press.

McLeod, J. (1998) *Introduction to Counselling*, 2nd edn, Buckingham: Open University Press.

Richards, D. S. and Bergin, A. E. (1997) *A Spiritual Strategy for Counselling and Psychotherapy*. Washington DC: American Psychological Association.

Rowan, J. (1993) *The Transpersonal, Psychotherapy and Counselling*. London: Tavistock/Routledge.

Tart, C. T. and Deikman, A. J. (1991) Mindfulness, spiritual seeking and psychotherapy. *Journal of Transpersonal Psychology, 23*(1), 29–52.

Thorne, B. (1991) *Personal-Centred Counselling: Therapeutic and spiritual dimensions*. London: Whurr.

Thorne, B. (1998) *Person-Centred Counselling and Christian Spirituality: The secular and the holy*. London: Whurr.

West, W. S. (1998) Therapy as a spiritual process. In: C Feltham (Ed.) *Witness and Vision of Therapists*. London: Sage.

West, W. S. (2000a) *Psychotherapy and Spirituality: Crossing the line between therapy and religion*. London: Sage.

West, W. S. (2000b) Supervision difficulties and dilemmas for counsellors around healing and spirituality. In: B. Lawton and C. Feltham (Eds.) *Taking Supervision Forward: Dilemmas, insights and trends*. London: Sage.

Wilber, K. (1979) A developmental view of consciousness. *Journal of Transpersonal Psychology, 11*(1), 1–21

Wilber, K. (1980) *The Atman Project*. Boulder CO: Shambhala.

Methodological Reflections on Spirituality from the Perspective of the Human Sciences

2

Jacob A. Belzen

To some, an essay on spirituality from the perspective of the human sciences may raise questions. What kind of meaningful statement about meaning could one possibly propose from within the human sciences? Psychology is not, any more than any other special discipline, authorized to make pronouncements about something like 'meaning', whatever it may be; and it loses its credibility when it succumbs to the temptation to make statements of this sort, since in so doing it loses sight of the boundaries of its (modest) professional competence. On the other hand, this by no means implies that the practitioners of the human sciences could not in some fashion deal with the question of meaning; on the contrary, one needs only to consider *how* they could do this. Just as philosophy is not called to answer the question of meaning but rather to reflect on it and to determine what kind of question this is, so the human sciences need to ask themselves how this question and the answers to it were arrived at; what it means for people who raise, or do not raise, this question. After all, in the empirical science which is psychology the object of inquiry is the human being. It always has its point of departure solely in flesh and blood and does not deal with theoretical abstractions. Also, it does not deal with people in general but with the specifically psychological properties of — always historico-culturally situated — human conduct, cognition, and experience. It will have to try to discover how meaning relates to the whole of human life and structures it.

Even when one starts one's reflections with the so-called 'experiences of meaning' one is struck by a transcendent component: it turns out that one cannot organize or produce experiences of meaning; they do or do not come over a person; they remain dependent on or show something of that which a human being has no control over and is in that sense transcendent. In the experience of meaning, a human being is reminded of the boundaries of autonomy. However, this heteronomous character not only applies to possible, incidental and transient experiences of meaning. In reflecting on meaning and spirituality it will be advisable, alongside of this heteronomy, to take account of participation as a second limitation of autonomy. For every act and for all of life it is the case, after all, that its meaning or significance does not exist of or by itself but derives from being inserted into a meaningful whole, whether this 'being inserted' is conscious or not.

As to this latter possibility, it may be assumed that there is much more meaningful life around than that which, sometimes all too loudly, advertises itself as such. There are good reasons even for a healthy measure of scepticism toward such excessive articulation and reflection. It was not for nothing that Freud made the comment that where the meaning and value of life is explicitly questioned one has to deal with a symptom of pathology (Freud, 1968b, p.452).

Having said this, I want to comment further, not on incidental or exceptional experiences of meaning, but on life as it is lived concretely every day, and more particularly on a subcategory of potentially meaningful living, in connection with which we are dealing with some more or less conscious insertion into a greater whole which makes life appear as meaningful. Although, by definition, it is impossible for us to get a grip on the transcendence which gives human life its meaning, that is not to say that human beings are completely unfree in relation to it or can only be taken by surprise by it. To categorize that subcategory of human life which, more or less consciously and articulately, enters upon a relation with transcendence and gives shape to it, one could use the term 'spirituality'. I will not here attempt to define spirituality as my answer to the obsolete essentialist question, 'what is . . . ?', for, depending on the time, place, and individual, spirituality has many changing forms. I will merely suggest a minimal description: spirituality as operationalization of commitment to transcendence.

Note the modesty of this circumscription. It does not postulate that humans are by nature spiritual; on the contrary, not everyone will want to acknowledge transcendence and certainly not everyone will want to observe the possibility of cultivating the relation that is intended here. Further, the circumscription leaves completely open the question whether it may perhaps be assumed that every human being — even when not conscious of it or refraining from giving content to it — has a relation to something denoted with terms like 'the absolute', 'the unconditional', 'the sum of reality'. In the proposed circumscription the reference is precisely to those cases in which we are in fact dealing with a more or less consciously realized relation. Note, too, that the word 'transcendence' is not defined, nor is it assumed that maintaining a relation to it is a superior form of being human. Over against the imperialism of many definitions and systems this circumscription attempts, as it were, to put into words that which can be observed over and over: the maintenance and cultivation of a relation to what is recognized as transcendent *can* be a form of living meaningfully, while it is not stated that this is the only form of living meaningfully, nor do we claim that this form of living meaningfully is always filled with the experience of meaning. Included in this minimal circumscription is the idea that the (desired) manner of realizing the relation and conceptionalizing transcendence differs or may differ depending on tradition, culture, and period. The circumscription aims at securing spirituality against being monopolized by a religious content; spirituality is by no means synonymous with religiosity — one could in fact write a long disquisition on the similarities and differences.

Included in the characterization of spirituality as 'living meaningfully' there is the note of dissociation from instrumentalist or even hedonist views. The idea is not to present or recommend spirituality as a means to make life more pleasant, to catch a vision of or to get a grip on the meaning of life, to raise the level of (public) mental health, or the like. Spirituality is a certain mode of life with possibilities, difficulties, and aberrations of its own. Based on what many mystics say, for example, spirituality could presumably have more to do with Heidegger's *Entschlossenheit,* with the readiness to abandon the way 'man in general' lives and to suffer the anxiety attendant on this abandonment, than with Marx's opium of the people. By the phrase 'as living meaningfully' I further hope to divest spirituality of mysterious and ethereal connotations: spirituality is very concrete. It is a possibility of *living* and refers to a life-form in the Wittgensteinian sense. The term suggests a framework of interpretation which sustains and makes possible a certain way of thinking, feeling, perceiving, and acting, but it does not offer a code of conduct which can be exhaustively spelled out in accordance with a given system of classification. Although spiritual life-forms are not necessarily religious, it has to be granted that many of them are religious in character and, conversely, that religions always present forms of spirituality.

Spirituality, being specific to human beings and fully human, as a possible form of human life can be approached in terms of the human sciences. If a person is or has become in some way spiritual, this involves her entire humanity, hence also her subjectivity, which is the object of psychology par excellence. As this is true of all that is human, so also spirituality has a psychological aspect. But since there are so many kinds of psychology (Vroon (1992) recently compared it to an exploded confetti factory), we will have to consider in more detail which form of psychology is best-suited for approaching spirituality, religious or otherwise.

Psychology in the plural

The character of the concrete operationalization of commitment to transcendence — something which is always variable in terms of time, culture, and the individual and sometimes highly variable — can yield an initial screening of the many divergent psychologies and mini-psychologies. In theoretical psychology, or in the philosophy of psychology, the diverse domain of theory formation in psychology is usually subdivided into two or three groups. People refer to mechanistic, organistic, and hermeneutic theories which exhibit successive levels of mounting complexity as a result of the increasing historico-cultural determinacy of the object and results of the research (see Sanders and van Rappard, 1982). While in mechanistic and organistic theories the tendency is as much as possible to disregard the historico-cultural determinacy of human reality, in hermeneutic psychologies this is deemed both impossible and undesirable.

These and other philosophy-of-science divisions of the different psychologies stem from an older but not entirely dated bipartite division.

The distinction between the natural and the human sciences, a distinction put forward around 1900, in its rigorous form is admittedly no longer adhered to today: the related distinctions between explaining and understanding, between nomothetic and idiographic research, could no longer be very strictly maintained. Virtually nobody today, for example, professes belief in the value-free character of the natural sciences. Still, in these terms there was and is a reference to a problematic which played a large role in psychology, in its history as much as in the present. The question is: must psychology be conceived and practised in the manner of the natural sciences or should it study its object in the manner of the human sciences?

Wilhelm Wundt, who is regarded as the founder of the natural-scientific approach in psychology, stated that psychology would have to be plural. Psychology can only turn to experiment as an auxiliary method if it seeks to examine the 'elementary psychic processes'; but if it seeks to study the higher psychic processes it has to consult other sciences for orientation. His own suggestion was that psychologists should consult history. Since Wundt's days, psychology has been fractured by a fault line which no one wants and which any number of theoreticians have repeatedly tried to bridge. Perhaps it must even be acknowledged that much theory formation in psychology occurs today at western universities, outside of the so-called psychological institutes. In striving for scientific objectivity and prestige, mainstream psychology has mostly concentrated on the one pole of Wundt's research programme: it naturalizes its object of study; its *modus operandi* is marked by de-subjectivization and de-contextualization. Admittedly the study of the reasonably constant psycho-physical constitution has its legitimate place. For by far the largest and most specific part of human functioning, however, it is true to say that it is neither determined by this constitution, nor can it be understood in terms of it. Decades ago, already cultural psychologists like Vygotsky pointed out that the higher psychic functions have a double origin: first a cultural and, after appropriation, an individual one. All concrete phenomena belonging to the reality of the psychic are culturally determined. All knowing, experiencing, action, wanting and fantasizing can only be grasped in light of the individual's historico-cultural situatedness and mediation. Emotions, for example, are not irrational eruptions of purely natural and unavoidable reactions. In contrast with what is currently thought, they turn out rather to be characterized by convictions, evaluations, and wishes, whose content is not given by nature but determined by systems of convictions, values, and mores of particular cultural communities. Emotions are socio-culturally determined patterns of experience and expression which are acquired and then expressed in specific social situations (Armon-Jones, 1986). The various behavioral, physiological and cognitive reactions which belong to the syndrome which is a specific emotion are not necessarily emotional in and of themselves. Ultimately emotions are based on the same physiological processes which underlie all other behavior. What makes a syndrome specifically emotional is the way in which the different responses are organized and interpreted within a certain context. To put it succinctly, emotions conform to pre-existing cultural paradigms: they are socially-construed syndromes, temporary social roles, which encompass an assessment of the situation by the person in question and are interpreted as passions instead of actions (Averill, 1985). Further, in the course of the so-called civilization process (Elias, 1976) which can be described for Western society, certain emotions, it turns out, are not only regulated but even created (see Foucault). Human subjectivity in its totality is always subject to specific culture-historical conditions: there is no meaningful conduct that is not culturally constituted. It has to be understood in the light of cultural contexts; and this not to find out how the postulated constant articulates itself again and again in different contexts ('cultural variation') but to trace how a specific cultural context made the specific action, knowledge, and experience possible. Accordingly, psychology, like history, anthropology, and linguistics, is an interpretive science: it focuses its attention on meanings and searches out the rules according to which meaning originates in a cultural situation. A psychology which seeks to study something as specifically human and entirely culturally determined as spirituality will therefore be well advised to orient itself to various hermeneutic psychologies and consult, say, narrative theory through which attempts are made to explore the relation between culture and the human subject. Narrative psychology, for example, directs one's attention to the role which available leading stories play in the construction and articulation of identity. It tells us that humans think and act, feel and fantasize in accordance with narrative structures and shape their lives in conformity with stories (see Sarbin, 1986). In this connection some psychologists, inspired or not inspired by Ricoeur (1977), go so far as to view the 'self' — the object of much discussion in anthropology and psychology — as a 'story' (Schafer, 1983).

In the historical-hermeneutic school of psychology now evolving there is plenty of room for the body which is a human being. In line with such divergent thinkers as Gehlen, Portmann, but also Lacan, the physical is here conceived as a complex of potentialities which, in order to become the basic material from which the psychic can originate, need a complement of cultural care and regulation. Further, it is pointed out in this psychology — along the lines of Merleau-Ponty — that the body, belonging as it does to a certain life-form and shaped by its practices, possesses an intentionality of its own (see van der Merwe and Voestermans, 1995). One must not underestimate the cultural-psychological perspective referred to here; it is still tricky enough to think through its implications. It cuts across numerous ideas which in the last few centuries have come to be the common understanding of the West.

The point is not only that human action, cognition, and experience, have consistently assumed variable forms in different cultures. Its viewpoint is more radical than that. It stresses that human subjectivity *as a whole* is culturally constituted. Somewhat aphoristically this perspective can be found articulated in the work of Clifford Geertz, an anthropologist who has had considerable influence in the psychology of culture: 'There is no such thing as human nature independent of culture' (1973, p. 49). The implications of this position are *inter alia* that psychology must attempt, much more forcefully than it has tried up until now, to recover and understand how by their culture, human beings have become who they are. A psychology which does not study human beings through the analogy of a mechanism but seeks to understand the almost infinite plasticity of human subjectivity, inquires into the effects of culture. It seeks to find out how a given culture incarnates itself, how it takes possession of the subject and shapes his (second) (De Boer, 1980) nature.

In other words, whenever a person wishes to undertake a psychological study of a specific spirituality, she will have to situate it again in a specific (sub-)cultural segment which, by a certain mode of treatment, i.e. by the way it speaks to and treats people, passes down the frameworks for individual experience and expression. In contrast to what is usually done in the natural sciences, the investigator, if he or she wants to make a psychological study of any form of meaningful life whatever, must as much as possible approach the subjects in their ordinary everyday reality (Voestermans, 1992). In contemporary research, common techniques like experiments, tests, and questionnaires are ill-adapted to this reality and are abandoned in the psychology of culture in favour of so-called 'experience-friendly' methods like the interview, participatory observation and self-confrontation. Cultural psychology argues for modesty: 'the search for stable patterns and long-range predictions in human psychological phenomena would probably not be the proper goal of the science. The role of the psychologist as a knowledgeable person would be to help in understanding, reading and interpreting behavioral episodes within the culture, and informing people about the potentialities of action within the range of possibilities in the culture. Thus the research would be a co-participant in the joint construction of reality, rather than an authority to control and predict the future of a person' (Misra and Gergen, 1993, p. 237; for a similar argument, see Hermans and Kempen, 1993).

The historicity of the subject

A hermeneutic psychology always meets the subject at an intersection of corporeality and a complex of cultural meaning. Usually it encounters a human being at a time when the latter has already completed a certain stage of his or her life's journey. When it asks the traveller about identity, the person he or she is, it inquires into his or her history, into the maturation process the individual has undergone to become that person. The relation between a human being and (his or her) culture, after all, is not a natural but a historical one. A hermeneutic psychology is continually confronted by history, since, on the one hand, a human being is shaped by a culture which has reached a certain (historical) stage of its development and, on the other, every individual is the outcome of a process of becoming, of a history within a particular culture-historical context. To function as a human being and not to become a Kaspar Hauser, the individual after all must more or less harmoniously fit herself into a specific culture. Also in the case of the study of contemporary subjects it is of lasting importance to conceptualize this historical character of the relation between culture and the body which every human being is.

In so doing, one can take either the culture or the individual body as starting point. Thus structuralist-inspired psychologists of culture have tried to grasp the way in which the culture took possession of the individual subject. In the history which every human being undergoes, socialization is set in motion by social definitions which already existed prior to the birth of the individual and which assign him his place in the human cultural order into which the subject, saying 'I', will later insert himself. These definitions are continued, strengthened and confirmed by the corresponding (social) treatment of the individual and are transformed into a quasi-naturalness. The 'habitus' (Bourdieu), which thus originates as product of a history, itself then again produces its own history and that in conformity with the schemes engendered by history. In that way it ensures the active presence of past experiences which have crystallized in the form of schemes of perception, thought, and action. The past, thus present, guarantees that a person becomes the bearer of the culture which produced him.

Psychoanalysis is of course another and perhaps more familiar example of a thinking through the relation between culture and individual which takes its starting point in the body. Its reflection on the fortunes of the 'drive', this boundary concept between soul and body, offers important contributions by fixing its attention on the very earliest experiences of the human child and by reminding us that our subjectivity, in all of its manifestations, also inevitably bears the marks of vulnerable moments in the individual's life history, of a relation to dynamic tension implying the possibility of failures which may later, in an extreme way, come to expression in the various forms of pathology known to psychology. With respect to every act and experience, therefore, one can and must raise the question concerning the place it occupies in the individual life story, in the life history of the person in question (see Jütteman and Thomae, 1987). In psychotherapy and other practical psychologies which, in contrast to academic psychology, were never devoid of hermeneutic bias (see Van Strien, 1986), the authors accordingly usually understand by 'meaning' the individual significance which can only be grasped from within the history of the individual. Thus Freud defines the meaning of a psychic process as 'the intention it serves and its position in a psychical continuity. For most of our researches we can replace "sense" by "intention" or "purpose"' (1971/1917, p. 40), that is to say, by terms which convey an intentional connection.

In such a historicizing approach, whether one takes one's point of departure in the culture or the body is a difference in accent. Ultimately psychology's aim is to understand something that has taken shape at the point of intersection between the two. For a psychological understanding of meaningful action and experience it is therefore necessary to apply a double perspective: the perspective of the meaning shared by a cultural community in general as well as that of the personal meaning which can only be understood in terms of the individual life history. Even a deviation, understood as symbol (in the sense of Lorenzer, 1977), can be thus interrogated as to its meaning, since in deviating from the surrounding order it can be a manifestation of the psychic conflict underlying it. I deliberately say 'can be' since not every deviation points to disturbance and, on the other hand, the (apparent) absence of conflict need not indicate psychic health. Psychology cannot say anything in advance about a person's health and sickness and will only make statements about them after it has examined a concrete individual against the background of culture and life history.

To a very large extent, therefore, psychology is a historical science. Also, in the concrete ways in which they operate, hermeneutical psychologists and historians frequently resemble each other: they favour attending to the concrete and specific, the individual and qualitative aspects of the person. In his exposition of the so-called 'indication paradigm', Ginzburg (1986) puts both groups of practitioners of the *ars individualisandi* in the same category as Sherlock Holmes. Psychology and history, however, not only follow a frequently similar way of working but may also go hand-in-hand materially. On some of the ways in which this may happen I want to comment in just a moment. I will leave aside possible combinations like 'a psychology of history' and 'the history of psychology'. I consider a psychology of history problematic: psychology can no more make history as such the object of investigation than it can explain religion or culture. Psychology does not explain history; the reverse, rather, is true. The history of psychology is a natural place of encounter between psychology and historical science. It has, however, grown into a special discipline all by itself.

Variants of a diachronic cultural psychology

Leaving out of consideration the synchronic variant for now, I want to try to expand a little more on the preceding with the aid of the diachronic variant of cultural psychology. I wish to call attention briefly to historical psychology, to psychological historiography, and to so-called psychohistory. All three can be regarded as belonging to a continuum between psychology and history or to an area where psychology and historiography overlap. Historical psychology is still mainly the business of psychologists; psychological historiography the business of historians; while psycho-history is a kind of natural cross between the two. Historical psychology is not 'dated' psychology: that kind of psychology belongs to the history of psychology. Historical psychology is a modern psychology: it comes into being when the cultural-psychological perspective is expanded diachronically, not synchronically or cross-culturally; it is a natural part of cultural psychology. Just as subjects differ to the extent they live in different cultures, so they also differ in their subjectivity in each successive historic era of the same culture. But in psychology people in general still consistently proceed on the assumption that 'in reality' or 'in essence' human beings were always and everywhere the same. In the meantime a sufficient number of studies have been made which invalidate this assumption. In historical psychology it has been adequately demonstrated that, even if one remains within a single culture, the phenomena which psychologists so eagerly study — phenomena like cognition, emotion, personality, identity, mental illness — are historically determined (Peeters, 1974, 1993; Hutschemaekers, 1990). And this is true not only in the trivial sense that in earlier times people thought, desired, or felt somewhat differently than they do today, but in the more radical sense that in earlier times people thought, desired, or felt in a different way. The course of life, cognitive development, the memory — each of them was different and used to function differently in earlier times (Olbrich, 1986; Ingleby and Nossent, 1966; Huls, 1986; Sonntag, 1990). For a psychology which considers itself scientific to the degree it attempts to uncover unchanging laws, this is hard to swallow. For this psychology, culturally and historically determined variability in human conduct and experience is actually only disturbing, an error in measurement for which compensation must be made in the analysis. It is fearful of the conclusion which Gergen (1973) drew from these considerations for his own discipline: social psychology, according to him, is the historiography of the present, the recording of how a thing is at the moment of investigation. The facts with which it operates are historical and do not permit generalization. Historical psychology for that reason calls for relativization and modesty: it raises the question whether present-day psychological concepts can be at all applied in a context different from that in which they were developed. It may be considered characteristic for historical psychology that it has its starting point in present-day psychology. It has a mild as well as a critical variant: the mild variant believes it is able, by means of historical research, to arrive at an additional validation of (present-day) psychological knowledge (see Runyan, 1982; 1988). The critical variant, in contrast, continually points to the limited validity of such knowledge. Like a bug in the fur of established psychology it seeks to keep alive the critical awareness that, as academic enterprise, psychology is just as much a historical product as the object for which it wants to be the science. Its point of entry reminds the historiography of psychology that it describes the construction of psychological objects, not the history of discoveries.

Clearly related, of course, but still different is the already somewhat older psychological historiography or the history of human consciousness (Vouelle, 1985). Being as a rule but little concerned about the systematics and nomenclature of any twentieth-century psychology whatever, historians like Huizinga, Ariës, Fèbvre, Le Roy Ladurie, and Le Goff focus their attention on psychologically relevant phenomena like anxiety, hate, smell, hearing and perception (see Anders, 1956; Ariès and Béjin, 1984; Corbin, 1982/1986; Delumeau, 1982; Kamper, 1977; Lowe, 1982; Schivelbush, 1979). They describe and analyze how in earlier times these phenomena were different both in form and in content and how in the course of centuries they have changed. If these authors were read more by psychologists, they would continually remind them of the 'hodie-centric' character of present-day psychological investigation. This psychological historiography has been the primary source of inspiration of historical psychology. Since the psychology of religion is a part of (more) general psychology it is understandable that there exists no historical psychology of religion: the theoretical and methodological tool-box of the psychology of religion, after all, is that of psychology in general. Other than in the view of so-called 'religious psychology' — a view now generally regarded as antiquated and passé — there are no specifically religious psychic functions, nor specifically psychology-of-religion concepts or methods. (A project like the publication, even recently, of the *Wörterbuch der Religionspsychologie* is therefore in this respect an anachronistic misunderstanding.) A psychology-of-religion historiography, on the other hand, does in fact exist, though hardly under that name: fine studies have in the past been published on the psychological aspects of spiritual and religious themes. Just think of works like those of Fèbvre (1942/1962), Keith Thomas (1973), Demos (1988), King (1983), Cohen (1986).

Concerning so-called psychohistory, the third and most interdisciplinary form of a possible relation between psychology and history, there are any number of prejudices and misunderstandings, not least due to bad examples. To focus on these examples in forming a judgement seems a little unfair. Let me try to correct a couple of these misunderstandings. In general, psychohistory can be defined as the systematic use of scientific psychology in historical investigation. In all its unpretentiousness this definition nevertheless already calls attention to a potential advantage of the psychohistorical *modus operandi*: one who turns to the past, after all, always uses one or another psychology, and certainly when reviewing themes relevant to this field. Now, instead of doing this altogether uncritically, or of mindlessly applying the homegrown common sense one happens to have inherited, psychohistory is an attempt to do it in a carefully thought-out manner. Though not a guarantee of infallibility, such a considered attempt is nevertheless preferable over unreasoned psychological dilettantism. Just as disciplines like sociology or economics can be integrated with historiography (see e.g. Burke, 1980) and yield an additional perspective, so this can also be done with psychology. Here, too, it is the case that psychohistory and the psychology of religion share a similar fate: they are accused of reductionism; they are said to step forward to explain history or religion in terms of psychology. This representation of the state of affairs is self-evidently incorrect; it has already been sufficiently refuted above. Contrary to what could still recently be stated in a professional journal of psychology, psychohistory is *not* 'the most extreme representative of the assumption that much of culture is shaped by the psychodynamics of the individual psyche' (Gadlin, 1992, p. 888). Far from being reductionistic, psychohistory, as presented for example by Erikson, may be considered exemplary in its attempt to recognize the individual intertwinement of an instinct-driven body and symbolic order. A good psychobiography requires triple-entry bookkeeping. The individual under study needs to be understood on three complementary levels: (a) the body and all that constitutionally comes with it; (b) the ego as idiosyncratic synthesis of experience, and (c) the social structures within which the individual life history is realized and whose ethos and mythos shapes the subject and, in the case of exceptional individuals, is shaped by the subject.

Psychohistory, for that matter, in no way needs to limit itself to the genre of biography and to the utilization of psychoanalysis. These are additional misunderstandings which need to be rejected. Although the lion's share of psychohistorical production is still made up of biographical and psychoanalytical studies, there is no logical necessity for this. It does have to be recognized, however, that psychoanalysis in its reflection on the interpretive process in therapy offers a valuable tool-box for helping in the analysis of the interpretive work of the historian (Röckelein, 1993). The number of studies in which an attempt is made with diverse forms of psychology to conduct other than exclusively biographical investigation is growing. In two ways, heuristically as well as hermeneutically, one can also employ, say, personality theory, social or developmental psychology, in historical investigation. The views developed in these branches of psychology can draw the attention of historians to certain themes which would probably otherwise remain un- or underexposed. In the second place, psychological theories or viewpoints may furnish additional possibilities for the interpretation of sources. I should be the last to sing the praises of the attainments of academic psychology, but it seems to me hard to deny that it has produced some knowledge of motivation and emotion, social interaction, decision behavior, human development and personal life stories which, for all their limitations, exceed the level of common sense. To deny that all such and many other psychologically nameable processes play and have played a role in the history of groups, organizations, institutions, also in the spiritual domain, would seem a rejection of historical science as such because the latter, being only partial as well, adds no knowledge either to what we already know about the past.

On the other hand, we must indeed practise modesty and not forget Fèbvre's critical question: what could a psychology developed in and in response to the twentieth century contribute to the study of the past? As sketched earlier, this is a question which historical-psychological research raises. Between psychohistory and historical psychology, both of which assume the historicity of the psyche, there exists therefore a tension-filled relation of which psychohistory can in any case take account and from which it can profit. Historical psychology can keep psychohistory continuously alert to the boundaries of its competence. Just as psychohistory can keep a historian (of human consciousness) from an unreasoned application or assumption of an equally anachronistic common-sense psychology, so historical psychology can keep psychohistory from flatly applying present-day psychological categories — categories which though scientifically developed are nevertheless often of only limited validity — to phenomena in the past. Historical psychology prompts hermeneutic reflection. The history of human consciousness, furthermore, remains important for psychohistory by calling attention to some things like folk culture and ordinary people. Why, after all, would we study only the lives of the mighty and noble? Are there so many mystics among them? From the perspective of spiritual development, for example, those who remain under psychiatric care could be just as interesting as or even more interesting than the inhabitants of an equally all-encompassing institution like a home of so-called 'religious'.

Numerous attempts at exploring spirituality have already been made from a psychohistorical viewpoint. There is even striking historical kinship between the psychology of religion and psychohistory. Stanley Hall, one of the founders of the present-day psychology of religion and founder and publisher of the first professional journal in this field, attempted to make a psychohistorical study of Jesus Christ, an attempt which did not gain a following. Usually, however, psychohistory is viewed as having started with Freud's study of Leonardo da Vinci. And it may be well known that Freud was also considered the patriarch of the psychoanalytic psychology of religion. The era of steady growth in the new-look professional psychohistory begins with a study which has at the same time become one of the most read classics in the psychology of religion, viz. *Young Man Luther* by Erik Erikson in 1958. It would seem there is some sort of psychic kinship between the psychology of religion and psychohistory: both great and small in the psychology of religion have made psychohistorical contributions. Consider Pfister's studies on Zinzendorf and Sadhu Sundar Singh; the work of Sundén (1966, 1987); his pupils (Källstad, 1974, 1978, 1987, Wikström, 1980; Holm, 1987) and many other Scandinavian colleagues (Geels, 1980, 1989; Åkerberg, 1975, 1978, 1985; Hoffman, 1982); Vergote's (1978) study of Teresa of Avila and other mystics; Meissner (1992) on Ignatius, and the many psychological studies of Augustine (Capps and Dittes, 1990). As examples of the psychohistorical psychology of religion which does not confine itself to the study of one individual, we can mention Freud (1913), Pfister (1944), Carroll (1986) and Belzen (2000), while Festinger et al. (1964) and Belzen (2001) offer examples that also employed other than a psychoanalytic method.

To conclude, then: for psychology there seems to be no systematic rationale nor methodological reason to neglect history. On the contrary, psychology would do well to take into consideration the cultural and historical dimensions of the psychic life it is investigating. Just as it collaborates with or incorporates techniques used by physiologists, sociologists, mathematicians, computer scientists and anthropologists, psychology might make a serious and systematic effort to integrate viewpoints and techniques of historians. Such will enlarge its foundations, competence and applicability, and will — after so many complaints on the 'boredom' of much of academic psychology — make its results relevant and interesting to a much broader audience of scholars and general public. Psychology of religion has — probably more than psychology in general and probably because of its often being localized in a department with historians, anthropologists and philosophers — usually been aware to some extent of the cultural and historical make-up of the phenomena it investigates. In this regard, therefore, it might serve as a model to psychology in general.

References

Åkerberg, H. (1975) *Omvändsele och Kamp: en Empirisk Religionspsykologisk Undersökning av den Unge Nathan Söderbloms Religiösa Utveckling 1866-1894 [Die Bekehrung Nathan Söderbloms: eine psychologische Studie]*. Lund: University of Lund (Doktorarbeit).
Åkerberg, H. (1978) Attempts to Escape — A Psychological Study on the Autobiographical

Notes of Herbert Tingsten 1971–1972. S. 71–92 In: T. Källstad (Ed.): *Psychological Studies on Religious Man*. Stockholm: Almqvist & Wiksell.

Åkerberg, H. (1985) *Tillvaron och Religionen – Psykologiska Studier Kring Personlighet och Mystik [Psychologische Studien über Persönlichkeit und Mystik]*. Lund: Studentlitteratur.

Allport, G.W. (1950) *The Individual and his Religion – A Psychological Interpretation*. New York: Macmillan.

Anders, G. (1956) *Die Antiquiertheit des Menschen – Über die Seele im Zeitalter der zweiten industriellen Revolution*. München: Beck.

Ariës, Ph., and Béjin, A. (1984) *Die Masken des Begehrens und die Metamorphosen der Sinnlichkeit – zur Geschichte der Sexualität im Abendland (Übers. M. Bischoff)*. Frankfurt am Main: Fischer (Original veröffentl. 1982).

Armon-Jones, C. (1986) The Thesis of Contructionism. In: R. Harré (Ed.) *The Social Construction of Emotions*. Oxford: Blackwell.

Averill, J.R. (1985) The Social Construction of Emotion – With Special Reference to Love. In: K.J. Gergen and K.E. Davis (Ed.) *The Social Construction of the Person*. New York: Springer.

Badinter, E. (1981) *Die Mutterliebe – Geschichte eines Gefühls vom 17. Jahrhundert bis heute (Übers. F. Griese)*. München: Piper (Original veröffentl. 1980).

Bairoch, P. (1988) *Cities and Economic Development: From the dawn of history to the present*. London: Mansell.

Bairoch, P. (1993) *Economics and World History: Myth and paradoxes*. New York: Harvester Wheatsheaf.

Batson, C.D., Schoenrade, P., and Ventis, W.L. (1993) *Religion and the Individual: A social-psychological perspective*. New York: Oxford University Press.

Belzen, J.A. van, (1996) Die blühende deutsche Religionspsychologie der Zeit vor dem Zweiten Weltkrieg und eine niederländische Quelle zur Geschichte der deutschen Psychologie. In: H. Gundlach (Ed.) *Untersuchungen zur Geschichte der Psychologie und der Psychotechnik*. München-Wien: Profil.

Belzen, J.A. (1998) Errungenschaften, Desiderata, Perspektiven – Zur Lage der religionspsychologischen Forschung in Europa, 1970–1995. In: C. Henning and E. Nestler (Eds.) *Religion und Religiosität zwischen Theologie und Psychologie*. Frankfurt: Lang.

Belzen, J.A. (1999) Paradoxes – An essay on the object of psychology of religion. In: J. Platvoet and A. Molendijk (Eds.) *The Pragmatics of Defining Religion: Contexts, concepts and contests*. Leiden: Brill.

Belzen, J. A. (2000) Religion, culture and psychopathgology: Cultural-psychological reflections on religion in a case of manslaughter in the Netherlands. *Pastoral Psychology, 48*, 415–35

Belzen, J. A. (2001) *Psychohistory in Psychology of Religion: Interdisciplinary studies*. Amsterdam/Atlanta: Rodopi.

Boer, Th. de, (1980) *Grondslagen van een Kritische Psychologie*. Baarn: Ambo.

Bourdieu, P. (1987) *Socialer Sinn (Übers. G. Seib)*. Frankfurt am Main: Suhrkamp (Original veröffentl. 1980).

Brown, L.B. (1987) *The Psychology of Religious Belief*. London: Academic Press.

Brown, L.B. (1988) *The Psychology of Religion: An Introduction*. London: Society for Promoting Christian Knowledge.

Bucher, A.A. und Oser, F. (1988) Hauptströmungen in der Religionspsychologie. In: D. Frey, C. Graf Hoyos und D. Stahlberg (Eds.) *Angewandte Psychologie*. München: Psychologie Verlags Union.

Burke, P. (1980) *Sociology and History*. London: Allen & Unwin.

Capps, D. (1994) An Allportian analysis of Augustine. *International Journal for the Psychology of Religion, 4*, 205–28

Capps, D., und Dittes, J.E. (Ed.) (1990) *The Hunger of the Heart: Reflections on the confessions of Augustine.* West Lafayette (IN): Society for the Scientific Study of Religion.

Carroll, M.P. (1986) *The Cult of the Virgin Mary: Psychological Origins.* Princeton: Princeton University Press.

Carruthers, M.J. (1990) *The Book of Memory: A study of memory in medieval culture.* Cambridge: Cambridge University Press.

Cohen, C.L. (1986) *God's Caress: The psychology of puritan religious experience.* New York: Oxford University Press.

Corbin, A. (1984) *Pesthauch und Blütenduft: Eine geschichte des geruchs (Übers. G. Osterwald).* Berlin: Wagenbach (Original veröffentl. 1982).

Crapps, R.W. (1986) *An Introduction to the Psychology of Religion.* Macon, Georgia: Mercer University Press.

Delumeau, J. (1982) *La peur en Occident (XIVe–XVIIIe siècles): Une cité assiégée.* Paris: Fayard.

DeMause, L. (1982) *Foundations of Psychohistory.* New York: Creative Roots.

Demos, J. (1988) Shame and Guilt in Early New England. In: C.Z. Stearns and P.N. Stearns (Eds.) *Emotion and Social Change: Toward a new conversion in America from puritan conscience to Victorian neurosis.* New York: Holmes & Meier.

Deusinger, I.M. und Deusinger, F.L. (1981)Untersuchungen zur Religionspsychologie. In: H. Haase und W. Molt (Ed.): *Handbuch der angewandten Psychologie, Bd. 3.* Landsberg: Verlag Moderne Industrie.

Dörr, A. (1987) *Religiösität und Depression: Eine empirisch-psychologische Untersuchung.* Weinheim: Deutscher Studien Verlag.

Dunde, S.R. (Ed.) (1993) *Wörterbuch der Religionspsychologie.* Gütersloh: Mohn.

Elias, N. (1976) *Über den Prozeß der Zivilisation: Soziogenetische und psychogenetische Untersuchungen.* Frankfurt am Main: Suhrkamp.

Erikson, E.H. (1958) *Der junge Mann Luther: Eine psychoanalytische und historische Studie (übers. J. Schiche).* München: Szczesny (Origininal veröffentl. 1958).

Fèbvre, L. (1942/1962) *Le Problème de l'Incroyance au XVIe Siècle: La religion de Rabelais,* Paris: Michel (Original veröffentl. 1942).

Festinger, L., Riecken, H.W., and Schachter, S. (1964) *When Prophecy Fails.* New York: Harper Torchbooks (Original veröffentl. 1956).

Foucault, M. (1976) *Überwachen und Strafen: Der Geburt des Gefängnisses (Übers. W. Seitter).* Frankfurt a.M.: Suhrkamp (Original veröffentl. 1975).

Fowler, J.W. (1991) *Stufen des Glaubens: Die Psychologie der menschlichen Entwicklung und die Suche nach Sinn (Übers. A. Foellenblech, H. Streib, U. Fischer).* Gütersloh Mohn (Original veröffentl. 1981).

Fraas, H. J. (1990) *Die Religiösität des Menschen: ein Grundriß der Religionspsychologie.* Göttingen: Vandenhoeck & Ruprecht.

Freud, S. (1910) Eine Kindheitserinnerung des Leonardo Da Vinci. In: *Freud-Studienausgabe, Band X: BildendeKunst und Literatur* (Eds. A. Mitscherlich, A. Richards und J. Strachey). Frankfurt: Fischer, 1982.

Freud, S. (1913) *Totem und Tabu: Einige Übereinstimmungen im Seelenleben der Wilden und der Neurotiker. Gesammelte Werke: Chronologisch geordnet. Band IX* (Ed. A. Freud u.a.). London: Imago, 1940.

Freud, S. (1917) *Vorlesungen zur Einführung in die Psychoanalyse. Gesammelte Werke : Chronologisch geordnet. Band XI* (Ed. A. Freud u.a.), London: Imago, 1940.

Freud, S. (1968) *Briefe 1873 – 1939* (Eds. E. Freud and L. Freud) Frankfurt am Main: Fischer.

Gadlin, H. (1992) Lacan explicated [Rezension J. Scott Lee: Jacques Lacan]. *Contemporary Psychology, 37,* 888

Geels, A. (1980) *Mystikerna Hjalmar Ekström 1885–1962 [Der Mystiker Hjalmar Ekström, 1885–1962]*. Malmö: Doxa.

Geels, A. (1989) *Skapande Mystik: En Psykologisk Studie av Violet Tengbergs Religiösa Visioner och Konstnärliga Skapande [Kreative Mystik — Eine Psychologische Studie Violet Tengbergs Religiöser Visionen and Artistische Kreationen]*. Löberöd: Plus Ultra.

Geertz, C. (1973) *The Interpretation of Cultures*. New York: Basic Books.

Gergen, K.J. (1973) Social psychology as history. *Journal of Personality and Social Psychology* 26, 309–20

Ginzburg, C. (1986) *Miti Emblemi Spie: Morfologia e storia*. Turino: Einaudi.

Grom, B. (1992) *Religionspsychologie*. München: Kösel.

Hermans, H.J.M., and Hermans-Jansen, E. (1995) *Self-Narratives: The construction of meaning in psychotherapy*. New York: Guilford Press.

Hermans, H.J.M. and Kempen, H.J.G. (1993) *The Dialogical Self: Meaning as movement*. San Diego, CA: Academic Press.

Hoffman, D. (1982) *Der Weg zur Reife: Eine religionspsychologische Untersuchung der religiösen Entwicklung Gerhard Tersteegens*. Lund: University of Lund (Studia Psychologiae Religionum Lundensia 3).

Holm, N.G. (1987) *Joels Gud: En religionspsykologisk studie [Joels God: eine religionspsychologische Studie]*. Åbo: Åbo Akademi.

Holm, N. (1990) *Einführung in die Religionspsychologie*. Basel: Reinhardt.

Hood, R.W., Spilka, B., Hunsberger, B., and Gorsuch, R. (1996) *The Psychology of Religion: An empirical approach*. New York: Guilford Press.

Huls, B. (1986) Historische Veranderingen in Geheugenprocessen bij Kinderen. In: H.F.M. Peeters und F.J. Mönks (Ed.) *De Menselijke Levensloop in Historisch Perspectief*. Assen/Maastricht: Van Gorcum.

Hutschemaekers, G.J.M. (1990) *Neurosen in Nederland: Vijfentachtig Jaar Psychisch en Maatschappelijk* Onbehagen, Nijmegen: SUN.

Ingleby, D., und Nossent, S. (1986) Cognitieve Ontwikkeling en Historische Psychologie. In: H.F.M. Peeters und F.J. Mönks (Ed.) *De Menselijke Levensloop in Historisch Perspectief*. Assen/Maastricht: Van Gorcum.

Jones, J.W. (1996) *Religion and Psychology in Transition: Psychoanalytic feminism and theology*. New Haven/ London: Yale University Press.

Jüttemann, G. und Thomae, H. (1987) *Biographie und Psychologie*. Berlin: Springer.

Källstad, T. (1974) *John Wesley and the Bible: A psychological study*. Uppsala: Acta Universitatis Upsaliensis.

Källstad, T. (1978) *Psychological Studies on Religious Man*. Stockholm: Almqvist & Wiksell.

Källstad, T. (1987) *Levande Mystik: En Psykologisk Undersökning av Ruth Dahlens Religiösa Upplevelser [Lebendige Mystik — Eine Psychologische Studie der religiösen Erfahrungen Ruth Dahléns]*. Delsbo: Åsak.

Kamper, D. (Ed.) (1977) *Über die Wünsche: Ein Versuch zur Archäologie der Subjektivität*. München/Wien: Hanser.

Kim, J.K. (1988) *Strukturelle Zusammenhänge zwischen Religiösität und Persönlichkeit: Theoretische und empirische Untersuchungen zu Zusammenhängen zwischen Religiösitäts- und Persönlichkeitsdimensionen im Rahmen einer psychologischen Diagnostik*. [unveröf. Dissertation, Universität Bonn].

Lorenzer, A. (1977) *Sprachspiel und Interaktionsformen: Vorträge und Aufsätze zu Psychoanalyse, Sprache und Praxis*. Frankfurt am Main: Suhrkamp.

Lowe, D.M. (1982) *History of Bourgeois Perception*. Chicago: University of Chicago Press.

Meadow, M.J. und Kahoe, R.D. (1984) *Psychology of Religion: Religion in individual lives*. New York: Harper and Row.

Meissner, W.W. (1992) *Ignatius of Loyola: The psychology of a saint*. New Haven: Yale University Press.

Misra, G. und Gergen, K.J. (1993) On the place of culture in psychological science, *International Journal of Psychology, 28,* 225–43

Moosbrugger, H. (Ed.) (1996) *Religiösität und Persönlichkeit.* Münster: Waxmann.

Much, N. (1995) Cultural Psychology. In: J.A. Smith, R. Harré ad L. van Langenhove (Eds.) *Rethinking Psychology.* London: Sage.

Olbrich, E. (1986)De Levensloop in de Moderne Tijd: Historische Perspectieven en Levenslooppsychologie. In: H.F.M. Peeters und F.J. Mönks (Ed.) *De Menselijke Levensloop in Historisch Perspectief.* Assen/Maastricht: Van Gorcum.

Oser, F., und Bucher, A.A. (1995) Religion — Entwicklung — Jugend. In: R. Oerter und L. Montada (Ed.) *Entwicklungspsychologie: Ein Lehrbuch.* Weinheim: Psychologie Verlags Union.

Oser, F., und Reich, H. (Ed.) (1996) *Eingebettet ins Menschsein: Beispiel Religion. Aktuelle psychologische Studien zur Entwicklung von Religiosität.* Lengerich: Pabst.

Paloutzian, R.F. (1996) *Invitation to the Psychology of Religion.* Boston: Allyn & Bacon.

Peeters, H.F.M. (1974) *Mensen Veranderen: Een Historisch-Psychologische Verhandeling.* Meppel: Boom.

Peeters, H.F.M. (1993) Mentaliteitsgeschiedenis en psychologie. *Nederlands Tijdschrift voor de Psychologie, 48,* 195–204

Pfister, O. (1910) *Die Frömmigkeit des Grafen Ludwig von Zinzendorf: Ein psychoanalytischer Beitrag zur Kenntnis der religiösen Sublimierungsprozesse und zur Erklärung des Pietismus.* Leipzig: Deuticke.

Pfister, O. (1926) *Die Legende Sundar Singhs: Eine auf Enthüllungen protestantischer Augenzeugen in Indien gegründete religionspsychologische Untersuchung,* Bern: Haupt.

Pfister, O. (1944) *Das Christentum und die Angst: Eine religionspsychologische, historische und religonshygienische Untersuchung.* Zürich: Artemis.

Popp-Baier, U. (1989) *Mythen und Motiven autoritären Handelns: Ein kulturpsychologischer Beitrag zur Autoritarismusforschung.* Frankfurt: Campus.

Popp-Baier, U. (1993) Die Stellung der Religionspsychologie in der deutschsprachigen Psychologie: Positionen, probleme, perspektiven. In: L. Montada (Ed.) *Bericht über den 38. Kongreß der Deutschen Gesellschaft für Psychologie in Trier 1992, Bd. 2.* Göttingen: Hogrefe.

Popp-Baier, U. (1996) *Das Heilige im Profanen. Religiöse Orientierungen im Alltag. Eine qualitative Studie zu religiösen Orientierungen von Frauen aus der charismatisch-evangelischen Bewegung (Habilitationsschrift)* Erlangen: Ms., (1996)

Raguse, H. (1993) *Psychoanalyse und biblische Interpretation: Eine Auseinandersetzung mit Eugen Drewermanns Auslegung der Johannes-Apokalypse.* Stuttgart: Kohlhammer.

Ricoeur, P. (1992) The Question of Proof in Freud´s Psychoanalytic Writings. In: *Hermeneutics and the social sciences* (Ed. & Übers. J.B. Thompson). New York (Original veröffentl. 1977)

Röckelein, H. (Ed.) (1993) *Biographie als Geschichte,* Tübingen: Diskord.

Rostow, W.W. (1960) *The Stages of Economic Growth: A non-communist manifesto.* London: Cambridge University Press.

Runyan, W. (1982) *Life Histories and Psychobiography: Explorations in theory and method.* New York: Oxford University Press.

Runyan, W. (1988) *Psychology and Historical Interpretation.* New York: Oxford University Press.

Sanders, C., und van Rappard, J.F.H. (1982) *Tussen Ontwerp en Werkelijkheid: Een Visie op de Psychologie.* Meppel: Boom.

Sarbin, T.R. (Ed.) (1986) *Narrative Psychology: The storied nature of human conduct.* New York: Praeger.

Schafer, R. (1983) *The Analytic Attitude*. New York: Basic Books.

Schafer, R. (1992) *Retelling a Life – Narration and Dialogue in Psychoanalysis*. New York: Basic Books.

Schafranske, E.P. (Ed.) (1996) *Religion and the Clinical Practice of Psychology*. Washington: American Psychological Association.

Schivelbusch, W. (1979) *Geschichte der Eisenbahnreise: Zur Industrialisierung von Raum und Zeit im 19. Jahrhundert*. Frankfurt am Main: Ullstein.

Schmitz, E. (1992) *Religionspsychologie: Eine Bestandsaufnahme des gegenwärtigen Forschungsstandes*. Göttingen: Hogrefe.

Schneider-Flume, G. (1985) *Die Identität des Sünders: Eine Auseinandersetzung theologischer Antropologie mit dem Konzept der psychosozialen Identität Erich H. Eriksons*. Göttingen: Vandenhoeck & Ruprecht.

Sonntag, M. (Ed.) (1990) *Von der Machbarkeit des Psychischen*. Pfaffenweiler: Centaurus.

Sonntag, M., und Jüttemann, G. (Ed.) (1993) *Individuum und Geschichte: Beiträge zur Diskussion um eine 'historische Psychologie'*. Heidelberg: Asanger.

Spilka, B., Hood. R.W. and Gorsuch, R.L. (1985) *The Psychology of Religion: An empirical approach*. Englewood Cliffs, NJ: Prentice-Hall.

Strien, P.J. van, (1986) *Praktijk als Wetenschap: Methodologie van het Sociaalwetenschappelijk Handelen*. Assen: Van Gorcum.

Sundén, H. (1966) *Die Religion und die Rollen: Eine Psychologische Untersuchung,* Berlin: Töpelmann (Original veröffentl. 1959).

Sundén, H. (1987) Saint Augustine and the psalter in the light of role-psychology. *Journal for the Scientific Study of Religion 26,* 375–82

Theißen, G. 1983: *Psychologische Aspekte paulinischer Theologie*. Göttingen: Vandenhoeck & Ruprecht.

Thomas, K. (1971) *Religion and Decline of Magic: Studies in popular beliefs in 16th and 17th century England*. London: Weidenfeld & Nicholson.

Utsch, M. (1995) *Grundmerkmale wissenschaftlicher Religionspsychologie und Entwurf einer Synopse*. [unveröffentl. Dissertation, Universität Bonn].

van der Merwe, W.L. und Voestermans, P.P. (1995) Wittgenstein´s legacy and the challenge to psychology. *Theory and Psychology, 5,* 27–48

Vergote, A. (1978) *Bekentenis en Begeerte in de Religie*. Antwerpen: Nederlandsche Boekhandel.

Vergote, A., und van der Lans, J.M. (1986) Two Opposed Viewpoints Concerning the Object of the Psychology of Religion: Introductory statements to the plenary debate. In: J.A. van Belzen und J.M. van der Lans (Eds.) *Current Issues in the Psychology of Religion*. Amsterdam: Rodopi.

Voestermans, P.P.L.A. (1992) Cultuurpsychologie – Van Cultuur in de Psychologie naar Psychologie in ,Cultuur'. *Nederlands Tijdschrift voor de Psychologie 47,* 151–62

Vovelle, M. (1982) *Ideologies et Mentalités*. Paris: Maspero.

Vroon, P. (1992) *Wolfsklem: de evolutie van het menselijk gedrag*. Baarn: Ambo.

Vygotsky, L.S. (1978) *Mind in Society: The development of higher psychological processes* Cambridge (Mass.): Harvard University Press.

Wikström, O. (1980) Kristusbilden i Kristinebergsgruvan: Historiska och Religionspsykologiska Aspekter [The vision of Christ in a cave]. *Kyrkohistorisk Årsskrift 80,* 99–112

Wulff, D.M. (1991) *Psychology of Religion: Classic and Contemporary Views*. New York: Wiley.

Zwingmann, C. (1991) *Religiösität und Lebenszufriedenheit: Empirische Untersuchungen unter besonderer Berücksichtigung der religiösen Orientierung*. Regensburg: Roderer.

The Place of Spirituality in Psychotherapy

3

Simon King-Spooner

'Spirituality' refers to what most matters; 'spiritual experience' is central to our lives.

Such experience is not a rare and all-or-nothing business, but pervades the whole of life in more or less occluded and diluted ways, so that a 'spectrum of enlightenment' can be proposed.

The — originally Buddhist — concept of mindfulness comes in here. Position on the spectrum of enlightenment is highly correlated with — is perhaps the same thing as — position on a mindfulness-mindlessness spectrum.

Mindfulness is implicit in, and promoted by, psychotherapy in a number of ways. The most foundational and perhaps the most 'therapeutic' of these is the I-Thou relation.

It can be argued that psychotherapy is ultimately a spiritual project. That the whole therapeutic enterprise, in its widest sense, needs to be restructured according to a kind of Maslovian layout: with foreground problems of emotion, addiction, relationship or whatever, seen as occurring against middle-ground existential and cultural-political frameworks, which in turn stand against a perennial, transcultural, higher-meaning-bestowing spiritual background.

These are the assertions I want to develop. (I don't of course claim any novelty for them, though they might not have been put in quite this way before.)

By 'spirituality', 'the spiritual', I mean something like this: an encompassing 'significance' or 'meaning' within which our lives are lived, wittingly or unwittingly; which surrounds us at every hand if only we let ourselves open to it; with which, anyway, our day-to-day experience is far more saturated than we realise; and against which all other significances and meanings are of a lower order, except insofar as they reach towards the greater significance that contains them. The term is a loose one, as is the term 'enlightenment' with which I alternate it more or less freely.

Inevitable features of the language we use in speaking about spirituality create two sorts of difficulty. First, evident in the assertions above, is that it is of the essence of spirituality that it cannot be 'pinned down' in language, but can only be hinted at, alluded to. Language, and our conceptual system, work by 'bitting' the world; the 'higher' perception of spiritual experience is what happens when that bitting is suspended (see Isabel Clarke's chapter in this volume for a version of this claim). Second, language, or at least naming, achieves such bitting through either-or distinctions, which are systematically misleading when the field to which language is applied is one of continuous variation — I will claim that the term 'spiritual experience' hives off and makes exotic the extreme end of a continuous spectrum, the lower reaches of which include, for example, the whole field of aesthetic response.

Perhaps a better way to try and convey spirituality is by describing my own main 'spiritual experiences', in the hope and expectation that they will chime in, in some way or other, with the reader's, with yours. Since such chiming in is the only real basis for persuasion here, as the subject matter by its nature slips between the cracks of reductionistic argument, I will give some space to this.

Enlightenments

I grew up a Catholic, in the days when the Mass and all other services were in Latin. Once when I was about 12 I served on the altar at Easter Midnight Mass. I remember it like this.

For something like an hour in the lead-up to midnight, when the Mass proper started, a long and complex ceremony took place, centring on the huge Pascal Candle. This, after various moves that I don't recall, and each member of the congregation having at some point picked up a standard-sized candle, was taken out of the church and the door closed, and after further ceremonial, during which the church was completely darkened, was lit with flint and steel and carried back in by the priest at the head of a procession of us altar boys. The priest was American, Father Gray: the quintessential quiet American, with a quiet, easy, serious but just-slightly-amused manner, his personality matched by a light and very pure tenor voice. The procession stopped three times as it passed up the aisle of the darkened church, and each time Father Gray held up the candle and sang, each time louder, the words 'Lumen Christi' — the Light of Christ. The third time he stood near the head of the church, with the single perfect flame held up high and every eye on it and every breath held. Then a light was taken from the Pascal Candle and passed down the pews and the whole church was lit up with candlelight.

A long, soaring moment, catching somewhere in the throat, lifting us all above ourselves; the most powerful instance of something I had the good fortune to grow up with: the stilling and uplifting, the widening of Blake's doors of perception, that goes with religious ceremony. (I have lost track of the subsequent changes in Catholic practice, but not all of that technology of the numinous can have been rationalised away. A few years ago, at the funeral of an uncle, maybe 20 years since I had last been inside a Catholic church, I was surprised and moved to see again what had once been too commonplace to notice: the expression of contained and concentrated devotion on the dour, lived-in faces of middle-aged and elderly working folk coming back from communion. It occurred to me I had not seen such an expression, on such faces, in all that time.)

One summer very much later I took part in a one-week 'Strict Practice', an intensive meditation retreat, in a quietly beautiful part of Gloucestershire. After the first few days, on the twice-daily walk we were permitted, once some of the muddiness and distractibility of everyday consciousness had settled out, I was (*we* were, you could tell by glancing at fellow retreaters in the silent passing) dropped into the paradise spoken of by so many mystics. For example by the eighteenth-century American theologian Jonathan Edwards:

> The appearance of everything was altered; there seemed to be, as it were, a calm, sweet cast, or appearance of divine glory, in almost everything; in the sun, moon and stars; in the clouds and blue sky; in the grass, flowers and trees; in the water and all nature; which used greatly to fix my mind. (James, 1958, p. 199)

I had been there before. As a child I had spent all the time I could in the woods, and had perhaps been unwittingly cued in to natural beauty. Howsoever, the meditation retreat was paralleled by a number of experiences, before and after, which were briefer but of even greater intensity — on LSD and psilocybin, in the woods where I grew up and on the Downs and by the shore in West Sussex, in the Leicestershire countryside, in the Peak District. I recall in particular the utterly absorbing beauty of the autumn woods, the beauty both astonishing and deeply familiar; and with it other qualities: a characteristic sense of security, an assurance (an inevitable banality creeps in) of an ultimate rightness in things — an inner equivalent, perhaps familiar to those engaged in spiritual practices, of a long sigh of relief.

There is another less congenial source of spiritual experience in grief at a loved one's death. Then, when the literally unthinkable has happened — when that which, before it occurred, could not be seen past, which formed a kind of horizon beyond which our own life could not be contemplated — when we are naked and stupefied before the weird, irredeemable goneness of the dead: then a peculiar solace can come. I remember a kind of pain-washed purity of spirit and vision in the aftermath of my mother's death: the well of despair in the sour, outrageously offhand functionary who made up the death certificate, seen as in a hyper-lit dream; the seasoned unctuousness of the funeral director, with its bad faith and comedy and its merciful smoothness; the busy, stunning sordidness of the streets of Woolwich. And the way the March wind blew and the forsythia and the daffodils bloomed their clean cold yellows had a kind of piercing reassurance: in with the knives of pain — as in the sweeter instances of such enlightenment — coming the conviction, against the manifest evidence, that it was all alright, in the end.

A final major source of spiritual experience in 'ordinary' life — though maybe I should have put it first — lies in the connection with and absorption in another. This is discussed below, in the 'I and Thou' section. In everyday life it is found most readily, perhaps, in two kinds of engagement: lovemaking, and the calmer spells in our engagement with our children. In both it is fleeting, quickly lost, easily sentimentalised or otherwise degraded, denied in memory; but in both — the silent enchantment of a sleeping child; the astonished mutual fascination that surfs the physiological surge — another world touches us, a greater possibility opens out. You might reflect on your own examples.

Such 'spiritual' experiences — of or through religious ceremony, the beauty of the natural world (with or without the clearing of vision through spiritual practice or drugs), traumatic loss, connection with another — are hardly unusual. I suppose I am not unusual, either, in having lived most of my life as if they never happened. But they retain their familiarity even when they are forgotten. When they return, and even when they astonish us, they come as no surprise.

And they contain diffuse but unarguable certainties. I have mentioned the incontestable sense of a rightness in all that exists, a rightness that transcends and contains its opposite. There is also a kind of aching benevolence: both a feeling and a conviction of the centrality of compassion, of what the Buddhists call 'human-heartedness', to reality; what the Sufi poet Rumi had in mind when he wrote that 'the astrolabe of the mysteries of God is love' (quoted in Huxley, 1946, p. 95).

But it seems to me that there is another disclosure in these experiences: that not only is what opens to us in them there all along, but that, at some level and in some attenuated and occluded way, we could see it all along. I have already said that our language, and behind it the oppositional principle by which concepts are formed, requires an either-or divide between spiritual and non-spiritual experience. But it isn't like that: the relation is not either-or, but more-or-less.

The spectrum of enlightenment

Topographical metaphors seem as inevitable here as those of illumination: from the lowlands of mindlessness, of self-regard, of frenetic pursuit and avoidance, to the cool heights of enlightenment, the country rises gradually. Moments of transcendence, falls from grace, are irregularities, even precipices, which divert attention from the generally moderate gradient. Much everyday experience is, as it were, shot through with spirituality, even though our language and our way of thinking gives us no purchase on this infiltration and, anyway, our mindlessness and our attachments continually obscure it from us.

Part of the difficulty here, as already mentioned, is that our conceptual system carves up a certain range of experiences in a way that obscures their close relation. Another part, perhaps, is a kind of exclusiveness in those who speak of spiritual experience, and who want to claim for it some esoteric distance from more plebeian states. However, I want to claim that a wide range of familiar modes of experience point in the same direction as more clear-cut spiritual or religious or mystical experiences and are bound in a family with them — in that the unquestionable but ineffable revelations of spiritual experience are there, though more weakly and less clearly, in these lesser and more compromised modes. All aesthetic experience, even the lowliest; all response to ceremony (maybe *any* ceremony); all serenity, calm, solace; any human relation that has a grain of authentic meeting — all these, and no doubt others (perhaps, say, the nub of childlike purity that lies within honest laughter, even at its most malicious) are marked, however lightly, with the claim of the numinous; are gesturing, however vaguely, however ambivalently, towards the higher ground.

So spiritual experience, thus broadly conceived, pervades the whole of life. (There is an interesting heap of issues here about the structure of complex and ambivalent experiences in which tacit elements play a defining part — about the whole notion of 'mixed' or 'diluted' experience.) I believe this contention can be supported — for the spiritual-in-the-aesthetic, for example, by a comparative phenomenological examination of what it is to be 'moved' spiritually or aesthetically, by an analysis of the use of those terms and their mutual boundary, by a deconstruction of materialist understandings of aesthetics and aesthetic experience — but for the present it will have to stand as a bare assertion (for further development of the point see Steiner, 1989).

Mindfulness

Mindfulness is the seventh element in the Noble Eightfold Path of Buddhism. It is, arguably, the main one, the one through which enlightenment is attained — the other seven (right conduct, right effort, right concentration and so on) clearing the way of impediments and acting as back-up.

Descriptions of mindfulness vary, but not in any important way. Three characteristics are generally given: the mindful state is described as reflective, present-centred, and non-judgemental. In traditional descriptions the last characteristic takes the form of an open, even-handed acceptance of *all* that enters awareness, without either grasping or rejection. (Less so in recent 'clinical' texts such as Kabat-Zinn, 1990, where there seems to be a tendency to see mindfulness less broadly — perhaps from pragmatic considerations, such as the stress on narrow-focus mindfulness exercises and the need to avoid an untimely opening up of difficult therapeutic material.)

With mindfulness, with centring in the here and now and the loosening of what the Buddhists call 'attachments', comes a progressive easing of the habitual restrictions on perception, our everyday state of blindness to spiritual reality. As already suggested, a case can probably be made that 'position on the spectrum of enlightenment' is *synonymous* with 'level of mindfulness'; at any rate the correlation is so high, between mindfulness and the spiritual experiences that open up through it, that the one can be taken as implying the other. Given this relation (or identity) an exploration of the place of spirituality in psychotherapy would be wise to take mindfulness as its vehicle.

Mindfulness and therapy

From the intruction to 'say whatever comes to mind', which might be claimed as its original and originating injunction, psychotherapy has promoted mindfulness. One of the forms this promotion has taken — the I-Thou relation — is discussed below. It is beyond the scope of this chapter to do much more than mention some of the others.

All here-and-now reflection — all 'bringing it into the room' and 'staying with it' and 'speaking from it' — elicits and promotes mindfulness.

Non-judgementalism, a core element of mindfulness, is the foundation for therapy's attempts to enable clients to prise free of the network of received evaluations which constitutes the means and the matrix for their invalidation.

'Resolute perception' has been persuasively claimed as a crucial common factor in effective psychotherapy — whether in facing supermarket queues, repressed trauma, ego-dystonic motives and emotions, or existential guilt (Hanna and Puhakka, 1991). Resolute perception in its widest sense — being open to whatever arises and is present, within you or without — is virtually synonymous with mindfulness. Even in its narrowest sense it requires a partial mindfulness, in the way that a focal mindfulness exercise does.

Resolute and mindful perception is also needed to examine our attachment to our reified and restricted sense of self. ('Attachments', of which this is the central one, are seen by the Buddhists as the main impediment to enlightenment.) Every therapy just about (as Alan Watts, 1951, might have been the first to point out), from Freud onwards, has systematically subverted this rigid self-concept — with the unconscious, with the breakdown of self into subpersonalities, with the encouragement of a letting go of conscious control in favour of spontaneity, and so on.

And therapy promotes the mindful subversion of a much greater range of attachments than this. Where it prods and massages and prises open obsessions — in the widest sense of that term — it both reveals their characteristic hollowness and allows the first tentative exploration of what it might be like to let them go.

But the 'I-Thou' relation, which is or should be at the heart of psychotherapy, can be taken as the central instance of the role of mindfulness in it.

I and Thou

A therapist's way of being with a client — the necessary qualities of what the Buddhists call 'human-heartedness' as well as mindful attention — have a spiritual dimension from the start, if the engagement is as it should be. I rely here on the understanding of what it is to attend properly to another that was developed by the Jewish theologian Martin Buber (1923).

Buber saw two ways of engaging with another person, or indeed with any living or even inanimate being — the I-It and I-Thou modes. I-It, for Buber, is the mode of objectification (in a very wide sense), of analysis and comparison and the cataloguing of qualities, of distance and manipulation, of making use. I-Thou is the mode of relation — the absorption in and engagement with the other, without calculation or tacit comparison, without any agenda of modification or manipulation. In other words in a reflective, non-judgemental, present-centred way (not a goal-directed and thus future-focused one): that is, mindfully.

I-Thou is the mode of relation — with the world, with others, and, for Buber, with God. We are only properly and fully ourselves in this mode. In the I-It mode — to which we will always inevitably return from I-Thou — we are both blinkered and diminished: diminished because we are in the lesser part of our dual possibility; blinkered, because we only know the other in a fragmentary and incoherent way when we relate to them as It (for which He and She are alternatives). Rogers' 'unconditional positive regard' catches something of I-Thou, though in a thinned-down and somewhat hollow way.

What is crucial here is that Buber sees I-Thou as a mode of relation which always enters, or has the potential to enter, a spiritual dimension, in the sense in which I am using that term. For Buber all I-Thou relation points towards God — in each Thou we catch a glimpse of the everlasting Thou. But there is no obvious necessity to follow him into a monotheistic belief system — or any other, beyond perhaps a kind of spiritually informed agnosticism (or even atheism) falling within the rough definition of 'spirituality' given above.

The situations in which most of us are most likely to find ourselves in I-Thou mode are, as already suggested, in our sexual relations, and with our children during their first four or five or six years (though in both cases, of course, we can have an intense and sustained absorption that is never other than I-It). But it seems to me that the I-Thou mode is also absolutely of the essence in any real therapy — 'therapy' as understood not just from the personal-humanistic-existential nexus, but from anywhere outside the most objectifying and scrupulously I-It sub-brands of psychodynamic and cognitive-behavioural intervention. Not that it is possible to hold to a pure form of the I-Thou mode for long. To do so would, I think, be to lose access to the informing matrix of experience and accumulated therapeutic understanding in which we must indwell, if our engagement is to offer anything more than could be offered by someone without that experience and understanding. But the I-Thou mode has to be the primary one; otherwise we lose the point.

Buber's I-Thou is a powerful spelling-out of what it is to be fully mindful of another. The more fully our engagement lies within this mode, the more spiritual it becomes. Three noteworthy ways in which this can take effect are these.

First, I'm sure Buber is right: all I-Thou relation does carry with it some greater or deeper sense of Thou which is essentially like that found in other forms of spiritual experience. Trying to find and stay within that mode is a spiritual exercise for the *therapist*; it is an act of devotion which will promote his or her spiritual development.

Second, the reaching for relation that is at the core of the I-Thou mode opens up and invites the same possibilities for the other, even if he or she is or seems completely blind to them. Part of what is implicit here is the foundation for a theory of listening: the opportunity opens for the client to listen to him- or herself being listened to; that opening is itself a revelation, irrespective of any informational content.

And third, I suspect the tone, the atmosphere, that goes with a non-objectifying openness to and acceptance of the other has a hint of the numinous about it — something of the small informal ceremony, of a world trying to open up which transcends the everyday, use-making one. It might be in its provision of such 'spaces' that the familiar assertion that therapy has taken over from religion comes nearest to the truth.

Therapy reframed

The implications of what I am arguing for are unclear. But if one possible understanding of them is correct, I don't think it is possible to overstate the role that might fall to psychotherapy.

It is banal to claim that the spiritual barrenness of modern secular society has thrown up some very strange gods, that an unmet hunger is all the time in evidence. That seems almost too obvious to mention. The greater part of what we are, individually and collectively, is given no place and no voice. Worse: materialism, a smug corrosive rationality, seem to leave no place for such a place. Into all this wanders psychotherapy, its many modes and attitudes strung out across the spectrum of enlightenment, affirming or denying the spiritual and the crypto-spiritual in innumerable ways, but more or less all sharing two things: the promotion of mindfulness, in one way or another; and the generation, demonstration and compassionate employment of it in the I-Thou relation. And by this, it seems to me, a kind of trick has been worked: from a starting point entirely within the spiritual wasteland of its culture, a locus has appeared with unknown potential for the development of structures for spiritual development; which, unlike most of the great religions — some forms of Hinduism and Buddhism might be exceptions — has it in its remit to encompass the whole range of our existence, and to give it all its proper and spiritual framing.

Such a developed 'psychotherapy' would, of its essence, be mindful of everything. From a careful and phenomenologically attuned disclosure of immediate, 'presenting' difficulties, to the progressive deepening of understanding of those difficulties, to 'upstream' reflection on the sources of those understandings, to the client's framing existential challenges, to the spiritual framing of that framing, to the therapeutic relationship and the culture and the wider world in which all this is going on. Its essentially personal focus would have similar mindful breadth: the person as centre and field of consciousness; as one half of a perpetual dialogue; as body-mind; as skills package; as individuated chunk of culture; as bearer of the imprint of political forces; as exhibitor of 'third chimpanzee' evolutionary dispositions; as product of reinforcement contingencies; as battleground for warring subpersonalities; as extracted region of a multidimensional relationship field; as bearer of the — Heideggerian — existential task of addressing the issue of her own being; as meeter and ducker of moral challenges; as treader of — or lounger on — or backslider down — a spiritual path. And first and last the person as person, which is the intermeshing of all of these.

It would transcend 'therapy' while staying rooted in therapeutic concern. Noone knows where it might end up — what spiritual structures might emerge on this new locus. Only its honest mindfulness, which perhaps always retains a sense of the ridiculous, would keep it from drifting into a Rajneesh-like cult.

All this might sound rather breathless, a kind of hyperventilative wishful thinking. There are people, for whom I have great respect, at the thought of whose reading these lines I cannot help but shrink. Breathless but at the same time familiar, given the spiritually informed systems of therapy that have been around since Jung split with Freud. But my suspicion is that the right moves still haven't been made, to open up the next step — that something is needed which is more fully rooted in the historical-cultural here-and-now than seem to be the various post-Jungian or faith-specific or transpersonal or New Age therapies that have spiritual agendas.

References

Buber, M. (tr. Ronald Gregor Smith — second edition 1958, first German edition 1923) *I and Thou*. Edinburgh: T & T Clark.

Hanna, F. J. and Puhakka, K. (1991) When psychotherapy works: Pinpointing an element of change. *Psychotherapy*, 28, 598–607

Huxley, A. (1946) *The Perennial Philosophy*. London: Chatto & Windus.

James, W. (1958 — first published 1902) *The Varieties of Religious Experience*. New York: Mentor.

Kabat-Zinn, J. (1990) *Full Catastrophe Living*. New York: Delta.

Steiner, G. (1989) *Real Presences*. London: Faber.

Watts, A. (1951) *Psychotherapy East and West*. New York: Pantheon.

What do You Mean by Spiritual?

4

Dorothy Rowe

Religion has always been one of my interests — what people believe and why, and the consequences of different beliefs. This was the subject of my second book. I called this book *The Construction of Life and Death* (1982) but when the publisher HarperCollins acquired it from the original publisher John Wiley my editor changed the title to something more upbeat, namely *The Courage to Live* (1991). The theme of this book was that our metaphysical beliefs are central to the way we live our lives because these beliefs always concern the nature of death and the purpose of life.

All religions try to bridge the chasm that death creates in the project of our life by teaching that some important part of ourselves will continue on after death. Actually, no one knows what death is. All we can say for certain is that a living person becomes strangely still. Nevertheless we each choose one of the two possible meanings we can give to death. Either death is the end of our identity or it is a doorway to another life. Whichever meaning we choose determines the purpose of our life. If we see death as the end of our identity we need to make our life in some way satisfactory, though there are a multitude of ways in which we might define 'satisfactory'. If we see death as a doorway to another life we have to live this life in terms of the next. For instance, if we see death as the doorway to either heaven or hell then in this life we have to strive to be good enough to go to heaven.

We are not likely to choose a meaning for death in a logical fashion by drawing up lists of the pros and cons of each meaning. Rather, one or other of the two meanings appeals to us because it confirms or strengthens that whole structure of meanings which gives us our sense of being a person. If seeing death as the end of our identity fits with how we see ourselves, that is the meaning we choose. If we cannot bear the thought of not existing we choose to see death as a doorway to another life. Whichever we choose, we go on to construct fantasies which elaborate the meaning we have given to death. With death as the end we might fantasise about the cessation of pain or about how we shall be remembered after our death. With death as a doorway to another life we might fantasise about that next life. The fantasies which we create to elaborate the meaning we have given to death all have this aim, the maintenance of ourselves as a person.

Such fantasies have little relationship to logic and reason and what we might call reality. In *Friends and Enemies* (Rowe, 2000) I speculated about a form of thought or a function of the meaning structure which I call 'primitive pride' which reacts immediately and ruthlessly to any threat to the meaning structure. This is not a new idea. It is implicit in the psychoanalytic concepts of defence mechanisms, particularly in rationalization. Karen Horney wrote about compensatory 'pride systems' (see Mace, 1999) while the American psychologists Daniel Gilbert and Timothy Wilson discovered what they called 'the psychological immune system, an army of rationalizations, justifications and self-serving logic' (Gilbert and Wilson, 1998).

Primitive pride operates without reference to reason and to what is actually going on. It protects our sense of being a person even in the most extreme conditions. Thus someone in the depths of depression and in danger of being completely overwhelmed by self-disgust can be implying in what he says to another person, 'I might be totally bad but I'm better than you because I know how bad I am while you don't know just how bad you are.'

Primitive pride can save us and it can destroy us. It is primitive pride which prevents people from seeing that in certain circumstances it would be in their long-term interests to compromise with their enemies. Thus primitive pride helps maintain the conflicts in Northern Ireland and in Israel. It is also primitive pride that reacts so strongly, even murderously, to anyone whose mere existence seems to threaten dearly-held fantasies. Down the centuries the infidel has been attacked and killed. Nowadays there might be ecumenical sweetness and light among the various religious groups, but a non-believer is still a threat. Even among those peace-loving people for whom spirituality is the highest good a dangerous person is one who asks, 'What do you mean by spirituality?' As I know only too well.

In 1997 BBC Radio 4 presented a series called *Devout Sceptics*. When I was invited to take part I was told that each programme would consist of an interview with someone who had no religious beliefs. In the weeks leading to the recording of my interview I persisted in thinking that the series was called *Passionate Sceptics*, a description that certainly applied to me. My error prevented me from thinking critically about who had set up this series and why.

Thus it was not until I was in the studio with the interviewer Bel Mooney that I discovered that the series was part of the 'God slot', that is, the period of airtime devoted to religious matters. I was quite cheered by the discovery that BBC religious broadcasting had adopted such a broadminded approach. It is only of comparatively recent years that *Thought for Today*, broadcast during the Radio 4 *Today* programme, has included spokespeople for Judaism, Hinduism, Sikhism and Islam, but all attempts by humanists to get themselves included have been adamantly rejected.

Bel began the interview by quoting from *The Courage to Live* where I wrote, 'Despite, or perhaps because of, my upbringing I have never been able to believe in a personal God and an afterlife'. Bel said, 'That was written in 1982. Is it still your position?' I replied that it had always been my position and that I had never had any reason to change. I felt that I had stated my position so clearly that it needed no amplification but soon Bel returned to the subject. She asked, 'You had a traditional Christian upbringing. Who was the God you believed in when you did?'

I replied, 'I didn't ever believe in God.' I explained that somehow the belief in God had never taken hold. I had been sent to Presbyterian church and Sunday school and attended scripture classes at school, and so acquired a detailed knowledge of Christianity, but I never acquired a belief in God. Rather, I acquired an intense scepticism about anyone who claimed to be in possession of some absolute truth. Such scepticism is often the outcome of a Presbyterian upbringing. Presbyterianism rests on the individual's conscience, and such a conscience will not allow lying to oneself. I could not pretend a belief that I did not have.

Moreover, my parents had not set me an example of belief. My father had no time for religion and was intensely sceptical of anyone who set himself up as a leader either religious or political. My mother sent her two daughters to church because she was frightened of what her mother would think if she did not, but she never attended church herself. She did not like people, and no man, whether earthly or heavenly, was going to tell her what to do. In my home there was no mention of God except as a rhetorical exclamation at times of crisis.

I thought my long answer had exhausted the matter but Bel was not going to let it go. I could now see that the interview was not going to be one of the Anthony Clare variety, a gentle yet penetrating exploration of how the interviewee saw herself and her world. Rather, it was an interrogation aimed at forcing from me the confession that really, underneath, like all right-thinking people, I did believe in God. Now I had a better idea of what the title of the series actually meant and what the aim of the series really was. Each person interviewed might begin by claiming to have no religious belief but, through skilful questioning Bel would elicit from them, or bring them to understand, that they did have some spiritual or religious belief in some great power.

This kind of interview has a long history. During the Spanish Inquisition the inquisitors sought to wring a confession of faith from their prisoners, and so they developed in their interrogation the contrasting themes of 'you poor wretch' and 'you have powers you know not of', themes which Bel was now employing. The 'you poor wretch' theme was there in the way Bel kept implying that, if I had no religious beliefs, I must live a barren, empty life in a world devoid of mystery, and with nothing ahead but death and eternal blackness. This is what many religious or spiritual people see as what we sceptics experience. I know it is a waste of time to say, 'No, not really, my life isn't like that,' because religious or spiritual people do like to feel superior to us sceptics, but if Bel had asked me I would have said that I find life enormously interesting and enjoyable. I like people. One of my favourite pastimes is to be in a public place and watch people go by. If anyone cares to tell me a story about themselves I am completely enraptured by what they say. People are to me infinitely interesting. Moreover, I love the world. I watch the sky. I gaze at flowers, fields, mountains, gardens, any stretch of water, and bliss is to be beside, if not in, the ocean. Trees are my passion, such creatures of beauty, truth, reliability and safety. As a child I used to escape into the bush to avoid my mother's dangerous temper, and there were the comforting, reliable trees. A woman — a psychologist colleague — once told me that she saw trees as alien and dangerous. I was shocked in a way that few things have shocked me.

I did not tell Bel all this but I did say that I especially loved eucalypts — gum trees as we call them in Australia — and that I had planted some in each of the gardens I had owned in England. I wondered whether Bel thought that at last I had confessed to a faith, albeit an arboreal one, and indeed she did, for she began to insist that all my beliefs were spiritual and I was most devout.

Alas for Bel, my love of trees does not amount to a religion. Though the bottom of my garden in London does bear a remarkable resemblance to the Australian bush, needing only a passing kangaroo to complete the picture, when I go there and give the solid trunks of these trees a pat, or even a hug, it is the pat or hug of friendship. I do not kneel down and worship them either actually or metaphorically.

Friendship is a relationship between equals. My trees and I are equals. We both exist. I find that so extraordinary and amazing that I do not need to add anything to it. To insist that all this had a Maker and that it was all part of some Grand Design would gild the lily so much as to destroy it. Admittedly, some of our experiences are so meagre and disappointing that they need to be polished up with various fantasies, but for me existence itself is not meagre and disappointing. It does not need fantasies about a Maker and other spiritual worlds. It is more than enough in itself.

Bel's insistence that I was both devout and spiritual was yet another example of religious colonization. The Christian Church has always done this. Christian colonizers took over the religious festivals of the people they wanted to convert and claimed them for Christ. All the human virtues are claimed to be Christian virtues, as if non-Christians cannot have a morality. In this way Bel insisted that must be devout because I had devoted my life to helping people. I assured her that this was not the case. I tried to explain that when I was born I was presented with a problem that I came to feel I had to solve in order to survive. It was, 'Why does my mother behave as she does?' Soon this question broadened to, 'Why do people behave as they do?' I now know the answer to that question. I arrived at this answer over many years of reading, listening to people, and writing to clarify my thoughts. The fact that a by-product of this intensely selfish activity was that some people found themselves helped by what I said is very pleasing to me because I would rather live in a world where people were happy than in one where people were sad and confused, but to claim that I had devoted my life to helping people would not only be a terrible lie but an insult to those many people, both devout and non-devout, who have spent their lives devotedly and unselfishly helping others.

What Bel did in this interview was to take the words 'spiritual' and 'devout' and stretch their meanings in order to prove the premises of her argument that, in fact, I held religious beliefs. Down the centuries Christian apologists have been adept at stretching and juggling the meaning of words, and at creating fuzzy meanings that mean one thing in one situation and something else in another but thus prove the apologists' arguments. However, in earlier centuries no one would be considered to be a member of a faith unless that person professed that faith and accepted without question the dogma of that faith. Where a church had great political power many people professed that faith because not to do so meant exclusion from public life and often great economic disadvantage. For instance, in Britain until well into the nineteenth century people who were not members of the Church of England were excluded from the universities and from public office, and even later Irish Catholics were excluded from all economic advantages.

As the political power of the church dwindled in the twentieth century so the language of the church changed. The language associated with hell-fire and a vengeful God disappeared except from the discourses of the evangelical/fundamentalist churches where sinners still had to be frightened into repentance. Even in these churches the emphasis was on the good news of salvation, which meant that those who had been saved were told that they were now part of a community which offered endless love and security. Meanwhile, the mainstream churches watered down the demands of their faith, while many westerners encountering the eastern philosophies created forms of Buddhism and Zen which eschewed the rigours of those practices and beliefs for something much more cosy. All these changes allowed people to indulge in what Simon Fanshawe (2000) called the individual personal religions of the 'pick and mix variety like a Woolie's sweet counter' with 'a nice cuddly God who leaves loopholes', something that the Gods of previous centuries never did. It was in this atmosphere that the word 'spiritual' came into its own.

All religions of whatever variety try to find words which imply virtue and special qualities and which are accepted without question. Politicians do the same. American politicians use 'America' and 'the American people' in this way, as does Tony Blair use 'family values'. The word 'spiritual' might once have meant simply 'relationship to God' but now it is a Humpy Dumpty word that means whatever the speaker wants it to mean. Thus, whenever someone uses the word 'spiritual' to me I have to ask, 'What do you mean by "spiritual"?'

The answers I have been given to this question are many and various but in general they fall into two groups. Both groups include the meanings 'beneficial' and 'virtuous' but they differ greatly in the extent of the territory they each cover. The first group covers only communing with nature while the second group covers power and magic.

The use of the word 'spiritual' to refer to the experience of feeling at one with nature often carries the connotation of feeling superior to others, and this comes from the vanity which is always grounded in primitive pride acting to defend the sense of being a person. Both individuals and nations have claimed superiority because they commune with nature. According to the psychiatrist and writer Takeo Doi (1986), the Japanese 'sometimes have feelings of superiority towards westerners who in their eyes cannot easily become one with nature' (p. 155).

However, Takeo Doi points out that there is a very big difference between how the Japanese see themselves in relation to nature compared to westerners. He wrote,

> In the Christian world view, God is the fountainhead of all existence. Nature may be a comfort for human beings, or even a companion, but it can never give human beings salvation. Human beings seek God and attempt to find peace with God. Even nature shares the anguish of humanity and awaits the salvation of God. In Japan, God, as a creator, is absent, and, therefore, human beings seek comfort by attempting to immerse themselves completely in nature. (p. 147)

Takeo Doi went on to speculate that in Japanese society where conflicts in society are hidden in the shadows:

> It may be more accurate to say that Japanese turn to nature because there is something unsatisfying in the way they deal with human relations, rather than to say simply that they escape to nature from human complications. Only this would explain why the Japanese feel able to breathe again when they confront nature. (p.151)

Whatever our nationality, an important part of our meaning structure, our sense of identity, is our feeling of belonging to the place where we were born. This never goes away no matter how many years we live elsewhere — hence the gum trees in my garden. A sense of belonging to a place is a sense of being at home there, of being part of that place and no other. Living in a place where we do not belong is very threatening to our meaning structure, but usually primitive pride comes to our rescue. When the white settlers went to America they were overwhelmed by the immensity and majesty of the land. To survive as a person they had to create an unquestioning belief in a personal God who watched over their every move, making a personal assessment of their virtues and vices and rewarding and punishing them appropriately. Thus they inflated their sense of their own importance and reduced the majesty of the wilderness to that of a servant provided by God to serve His and their purposes.

Their predecessors, the Native Americans, knew better than to believe in the rewards and punishments of a personal God in a land where the rewards may be unexpectedly easy (a readily captured buffalo) and the punishments inordinately harsh (an all-encompassing blizzard). Like the Australian Aboriginals, they saw that the best way to survive in an inhospitable vastness was to see themselves as one with it (Rowe, 1991; 2000).

Australian Aboriginal writers like Mudrooroo (1995) often use the word 'spirituality' when writing about their people, but they use it as a kind of shorthand to encompass many aspects of their life — their attachment to the land, the rules of their society, their history, how people should relate to one another, and the vast body of stories which inform them about the way everything in their land, human, spiritual, plant, animal, the land itself and its climate, behaves. White settlers in Australia despised the Aboriginals, but as the years went by many descendants of the settlers discovered in themselves an intense attachment to their land. Nevertheless, as Thomas Keneally (2000) remarked, 'If we are so enamoured of Australia after three or four generations, imagine what a sense of possession the Aborigines have after 12,500 generations?'

Alas, the Aboriginal people are now suffering the ill effects of spiritual colonisation in the same way they had suffered the effects of Christian colonisation which robbed them of their homes and their children. Many white 'spiritual' people, while expressing immense admiration for the spirituality of the Aboriginal people, take the view that, as the Aboriginal people have such a deep spiritual relationship to their land, they do not need unspiritual things like decent jobs, homes, health care and education.

When 'spiritual' becomes a Humpty Dumpty word what is lost is the specific reference to a very distinct and very important experience. This is what occurs when we cease to be wrapped up in our own concerns, cease to think about the past and the future, and attend only to the present and to what is before us. When we do this we reduce the number of our meanings or constructs that form a buffer between us and what is actually going on. We see what is before us with much more clarity and, in not concentrating on our personal concerns, we feel closer and even part of all that is around us. Such an experience can be the outcome of meditation or in what Buddhists call mindfulness, that is, close attention. It is an immensely important experience because it helps us keep our anxieties and wishes within reasonable limits, it ameliorates a painful sense of loneliness, and it helps provide the conditions whereby we can be happy. Happiness is not a goal we can achieve but is simply a by-product of what we do, and can be enjoyed only in the present.

Language cannot give a good account of what it is to be at one with our surroundings, just as language never gives a good account of all great emotional experiences. Being at one with our surroundings is a unique experience and thus might merit the word 'spiritual', but when this word takes on the connotations of superior virtue and contact with mysterious powers the experience itself with all its wonderment is degraded.

Throughout the history of the human race, people have explained certain events in terms of unearthly powers, and these explanations have often been turned into religions that confer, or appear to confer, particular magical powers on an elite who guard their privileges jealously. Belief is demanded from the rest of the populace, and in return the elite promise to use their magical powers for the benefit of the populace.

Justification for all this has been claimed in different ways at different times and places, but at present with genes and the genome so much in the news many apologists for religion are claiming that there must be a gene for religion or at least that a need for religious belief is an essential part of human nature. Such justifications usually ignore the situation in which all human beings find themselves. We are a puny species blessed and cursed with consciousness. We know how puny we are and how vast the universe. We try to predict and control, but the forces of nature, indifferent to our existence, go their own way.

It requires great courage to see our situation as it is and to try to look after ourselves using our intelligence and creativity without resorting to fantasies of magic. It is not surprising that many people turn to magical beliefs to give them the illusion of power and control. In the short-term such beliefs can help a person deal with fears and give hope, but in the long-term such beliefs prevent us from gaining the knowledge and understanding which we need both to survive as a species and to become fulfilled as the person we could be.

Describing religious belief in this way can be threatening to people with strongly held religious or spiritual beliefs because they do not wish to confront their own helplessness and limitations. To defend themselves they will protest that the non-religious attitude strips from our lives all that is best and reveals the world as a meagre, ugly, hateful place.

This indeed is how many religious or spiritual people see the world. Such a view has a long history in religions where all things material and physical are despised and only things of the spirit valued. Politically such a view keeps the rich rich and prevents the poor from protesting about their poverty. However, such a way of seeing the world can have its roots in earliest childhood.

When we are small children the adults around us use their power to persuade or coerce us into being good. Alas, being good means never being good enough, and so we can easily acquire a sense of being intrinsically bad and unacceptable. At times of crisis when we are being punished for being bad or we are punishing ourselves this sense of intrinsic evil can rise like a black tide and spill out over our surroundings. We are bad and the world around us is bad. Self-disgust becomes disgust with the world. A small child might destroy his toys; an adult might see trees as alien and dangerous.

Simultaneous self-hatred and world hatred make living impossible. Primitive pride comes to the rescue and suggests fantasies of a spiritual world outside the ordinary world, a place of redemption and salvation, and magical powers.

Such fantasies can enable a child to survive both physically and psychologically, but, if the child carries these fantasies into adult life and never subjects them to critical examination, that child's life is spoilt because he can never just be, accepting himself and his world. Happiness is impossible. He has to continue to elaborate his fantasies and resist, violently if necessary, anyone who suggests that his fantasies are just that, fantasies. From this way of thinking comes endless religious wars and, in a peaceful society, the sense of danger a non-religious person can feel when confronted by a religious or spiritual person.

This is how I felt when interviewed by Bel Mooney. Rather than simply explaining my views I was constantly being put on the defensive. There was the implied threat that unless I owned up to a religious belief I would be revealed as a much lesser person than I thought I was. I could have caved in, but the stubbornness of a Presbyterian conscience prevailed. I could not allow myself to be described as a spiritual and devout person with a religious passion for trees.

Curiously, in that same year, 1997, I came to the attention of a Buddhist monk, T. S. Abeywickrama from Sri Lanka and founder of the Wisdom Centre of the Universal Friendship Foundation. He wrote to me saying, 'I was amazed and delighted to see a self-enlightened westerner for the first time through your illuminating article on "Why Therapy Does Not Work" published in *The Times*. Your article is graphic evidence that through your own experience you are enlightened to the reality that we know only what we have constructed in our mind.'

In this article I had written:

> While the world we live in seems to be solid and real and shared with others, what we each experience is our own individual construction. We can imagine events that occur without any relationship to us, but what we have is not knowledge but theories. In fact, everything we know is a theory, a construction, and this construction is inside our heads ... Because all that we have are our interpretations, we are free to choose to acknowledge that what we have are theories and that we can use all means to test these theories, or we can insist that our theories are accurate representations of the truth. (Rowe, 1997)

Of course this is a statement in modern-day terms of the essence of what the Buddha taught. I already knew that, and I also knew that understanding the Buddha's teaching is enlightenment. Nevertheless, I was greatly amused and delighted to be told by a Buddhist monk that I was enlightened without my having to go through many hours of meditation in the sitting postures which I always found excruciatingly painful. However, the trouble with enlightenment is that it does not confer any magical powers. You just have to work at deconstructing your constructions in order to get as close as you can to seeing the world as it actually is, while all the time knowing that, constructed as we are physiologically, we can never see reality directly. There is nothing spiritual in that knowledge at all.

References

Doi, T. (1986) *The Anatomy of Self.* (trans. Mark A. Harbison) Tokyo: Kodansha International Ltd.

Fanshawe, S. (2000) *Simon Fanshawe Gets to the Bottom of All Things Spiritual* Radio 4, November 2.

Gilbert, D. and Wilson, T. (1998) *Journal of Personality and Social Psychology 75,* 617

Keneally, T. (2000) *The Guardian.* October 30

Mace, C. (1999) Socratic Psychotherapy. *Changes, 17,* 3, 164

Mudrooroo (1995) *Us Mob.* Sydney: HarperCollins.

Rowe, D. (1982) *The Construction of Life and Death.* Chichester: John Wiley.

Rowe, D. (1991) *Wanting Everything*. London: HarperCollins.
Rowe, D. (1991) *The Courage to Live*. London: HarperCollins.
Rowe, D. (1997) Why therapy does not work. *The Times*, January 3.
Rowe, D. (2000) *Friends and Enemies*. London: HarperCollins.

On Not Being Able to Eff the Ineffable

5

David Smail

Whereof one cannot speak, thereof one must be silent.
Ludwig Wittgenstein

There is much more to Wittgenstein's famous last sentence (of the *Tractatus Logico-Philosophicus*) than merely an obvious tautology, and I think we would do well to take it as a guide in any discussion of spirituality. That is to say, the place of spirituality in psychotherapy must remain, I think, largely unspoken.

This is principally because words are such an inadequate means of giving expression to experience (despite what the 'deconstructionists' say, there is a great deal beyond discourse and text!), but also because 'psychotherapy' is such a broad, inclusive and imprecise concept. We should stick to what we can be clear about.

I also put this view extremely tentatively. Therapy can be, and is, done in many different ways, and need not, for all I know, be spoken about at all in any systematic manner. Certainly, in trying to get my ideas together for this discussion, I have, as I'm afraid will be all too obvious, found it hard to arrive at a firm and consistent view. What I detect in myself *as a psychologist* is, so to speak, a prejudice for the material over the spiritual, the public over the private, and what follows is an attempt to explain that prejudice.

Inevitably, what I want to discuss here is *my* view of psychotherapy, i.e. the view of a psychologist who is concerned to analyse and make explicit understandings of psychological distress, how it comes about and how it may best be alleviated. From this point of view, there is an almost total dependence on words and the struggle, through them, for common understanding; what cannot be spoken of has no place in this undertaking (which is not the same as saying it is unimportant).

There is nothing especially difficult or unusual about finding oneself in this situation. As Michael Polanyi (1958) argued in his terribly neglected *Personal Knowledge*, ineffability is involved in every human undertaking. He showed that ineffable personal experiences and appreciations lie at the very core of scientific judgement itself.

But for psychotherapists there is perhaps a particular difficulty, since we are not only dealing *with* ineffable subjectivity more than most, but also *through* it. The very tools of our trade are inexpressible, not least because the therapeutic encounter is, first and last, intensely and irreducibly *personal*. We are constantly tempted to try to talk about the experience beyond language because that is where so much of our experience lies. And we *can't* talk about it! In this way the heart of psychotherapy can only be *alluded to* with a delicate discretion. There are very few writers who manage to achieve this. Peter Lomas (1999) is one; Miller Mair (1989) is one; Paul Gordon (1999) is one; in his inimitable way, Bob Hobson (1985) was one. Immediately psychotherapeutic writing does try to eff the ineffable — and it does so all too often — it becomes yet another cultural influence turning us inside-out, and the result is a kind of sickening intrusion; at best a seductive sentimentality, at worst a violation of interiority. The process impoverishes us by trying to turn our private riches into public capital: we are propelled into a kind of cultural stock exchange in which we lose title to our own souls.

All this presents those of us who try in our writing to convey something of the heart of psychotherapy with a familiar dilemma in which we tend either to fall into the kind of sentimentality or intrusiveness just mentioned, or to attempt to convey the nature of the therapeutic process through, for example, case examples that betray the confidentiality of our clients or distort, more or less subtly, the nature of our relations with them. The trouble is we *cannot* say what we do without falling into exactly the kind of bad faith Jean-Paul Sartre described so well in *Being and Nothingness*.

But even if we could say what we do there would be little point because nobody else would be able to do it. We, all of us, 'do' psychotherapy in our own way, and no two of us are the same. It's impossible to impersonalize the personal — in my view that is precisely the mistake of trying to form 'schools' of psychotherapy around the personal characteristics of one individual (e.g. Freud, Jung, Rogers, Perls, Ellis, et al.), or indeed to create a 'profession' of therapy and counselling with registers, systems of 'training' and accreditation, etc.

Some things that can be said about the experience of the spiritual

As a psychologist I am a materialist. My core belief is that the experience of being a body in a world gives rise in each of us to a unique subjectivity. But there still *is* nothing other than bodies and worlds. Selves and subjectivities are not self-creating and self-moving *things* and spirit has no intrinsic substance through which it can act on the world.[1] However, privately, like everyone else, I live within my subjectivity. I have a soul too. The behaviourists and positivists try to rob us of our subjectivity, they rape and trample on it.

---

1. This view is elaborated in my book *The Origins of Unhappiness*, Constable, 1999. See also *Power, Responsibility and Freedom* at:
http://www.djsmail.com/intpub.htm

But to take a materialist stance does not imply insisting in a totalitarian manner that subjectivity is mere illusion, that the whole notion of souls or spirits is *meaningless*: only that there's very little point in trying to talk about them in anything other than an essentially theological context. I've nothing against theology — but it is, or at least in my view should be, different from psychology.

As psychologists trying to say something in public about the causes and cures of human distress, we have to stick to the effable, even though the effable never tells the whole story.

I *would* say, though, that there is nothing necessarily 'higher' about the ineffably subjective: it is a mode of experience we all know and which as much informs the clumsy, banal and destructive as it does the rare, sublime and healing.

Take the example of writing (I'm quoting here from a previous talk[2]):

> Many professional writers speak with awe of the magical experience of writing, of the way it seems to take place through them, almost as if their words were being written by the hand of God. Portentous accounts of creativity have been grounded on this experience. Indeed, I have experienced it often myself and can vouch for its capacity to leave one feeling deeply moved.

It wasn't until a man I knew told me how his short stories came to him that I began to get an idea of what this experience might be about. Eyes misting with emotion, he told me how his stories seemed eerily to write themselves, how they poured themselves from the end of his pen faster than he could control the muscles of his hand. He positively glowed — humility and pride in equal proportions — that the mystery of the creative act should have been vouchsafed to him.

The trouble was, his were without question the worst short stories I have ever seen committed to paper. Chaotically constructed, banal, misspelt and ungrammatical, they were in fact barely literate.

What this reveals, I suspect, is merely that for anyone, creatively gifted or not, writing tends often to carry with it a different kind of experience from talking, without the same kind of illusion of control: one is more aware, with writing (rather perhaps as with dreams), that the ego is not as central as we often take it to be.

A lot of our subjective experience is like this: it comes with an overwhelming force of conviction, revelation even, un-sicklied-over with the pale cast of words in such a way that it seems to possess us from outside, from 'above'. This, I suspect, is more or less what Freud meant by 'primary process'. It is the stuff of dreams, and in part no doubt also of 'peak experiences'. But in fact it's not really special; it's just the way subjectivity

---

2. Smail, D. (1999) 'Psychotherapy, society and the individual'. Talk given at the Ways with Words festival of literature, Dartington. This may be read at: http://www.djsmail.com/talk99.htm

feels, and *it* feels before *we* think. In this way, subjective experience is quite literally irresistible. But that doesn't mean that it's incorrigible, as the philosophers say (i.e. infallible).

Please note that I'm not belittling the sense of spirituality — I value it as highly as anyone. Nor (though in principle I have nothing against reductionism) am I reducing it to anything. All I am doing is trying to demystify it. Mystification is a constant danger for psychological speculation and reflection, and one of the best ways we can protect ourselves against it is, precisely, to beware of trying to eff the ineffable.

So in my view our best bet as far as our vocational discourse is concerned is to focus on the public world in which we are embodied (and which we can discuss in a common language) and leave our privacy (and our souls) in peace.

As psychologists and psychotherapists writing and talking about psychotherapy we should aim as far as we can to tell the truth about it. This does entail staying within a universe of common discourse, where the currency is words more than feelings. In this respect I am happy with the notion of 'science'. Science still needs rescuing from scientism. Science, though hijacked for much of this century by various piratical groups (such, in our discipline, as the behaviourists), is not identical with positivism and should not be allowed to become the object of derision for so-called 'post-modernists'.

At its broadest, scientific truth is the ever-corrigible judgement of society, in which its members seek freely and unconstrainedly to understand and elaborate their relations with each other and the world. But it is partial, always and for ever incomplete. The ultimate nature of reality is a mystery. It really *is* a mystery, and we can't 'discover' it, 'establish' it or even talk about it meaningfully. But that doesn't mean that there is no reality or that nothing is real or that we can't do our best with what we've got.

There is, no doubt, a kind of discipline — at times perhaps quite an uncomfortable one — in restricting ourselves to the common currency of words as we try to understand and elaborate what goes on in our patients, between them and their worlds and between them and us. Parallel with our necessarily incomplete attempts to do this, and to elaborate a common set of (linguistic) concepts which will facilitate our understanding, there runs all the time a deep stream of inexpressible private experience, an ebbing and flowing of feeling and relationship, an unending seam of imagination, intuition and dream which form the most basic elements of our cognition and understanding as human beings.

There are places in the world for all these things — in religion, in art, in poetry. My only question is how much room they should occupy in our discussions about psychotherapy — discussions which I do really want to call scientific discussions. It would be absurd, certainly, if we tried to mix up the spiritual with the professional; if, that is, we not only tried to eff the ineffable, but also made it the object of degree courses, accreditation and registration procedures, etc.

As I indicated at the beginning of this piece, I do not want to be dogmatic about all this. Perhaps psychotherapy itself is more a spiritual calling than a scientific discipline. I could easily be persuaded of that. Some people, indeed, make out a very good case for it. My own inclination, though, from my point of view as a psychologist, is to persevere with scientific aspects of what causes human distress and what are the best ways of trying to do something about it. It may of course turn out that that is not much to do with psychotherapy at all.

References

Gordon, P. (1999) *Face to Face. Psychotherapy as Ethics*. London: Constable.

Hobson, R.F. (1985) *Forms of Feeling. The heart of psychotherapy*. London and New York: Tavistock.

Lomas, P. (1999) *Doing Good?* Oxford: Oxford University Press.

Mair, M. (1989) *Between Psychology and Psychotherapy*. London and New York: Routledge.

Polanyi, M. (1958) *Personal Knowledge*. London: Routledge & Kegan Paul.

Sartre, J.P. (1995) *Being and Nothingness: An essay on phenomenological ontology*. (trans. Hazel Barnes) London: Routledge.

Wittgenstein, L. (1992) *Tractatus Logico-Philosophicus*. (trans. C. K. Ogden and F. P. Ramsey) London: Routledge.

Counselling as Western Religion

6

David Williams and Judi Irving

Counselling has many of the facets of a religion — as a shared system of beliefs about the nature of mankind and of life. It has a spiritual dimension and many of its beliefs are founded on 'faith' rather than research evidence. It has its priests and prophets, its sects and gurus, and tries to convert others (including clients) to its beliefs. Even when presented merely as a technique that is non-directive and non-judgemental, counselling embodies a system of values which determine what statements are challenged. This bias is not always obvious because it concurs with the current western philosophy of life, which emphasises the rights and responsibilities of the individual. These meta-beliefs may only become apparent when used cross-culturally, where the values may be inappropriate to a particular society — as when the needs of the group are valued over those of the individual, or when clients speak of spirits, spells, and fate. Counsellors need to work with the beliefs of a particular culture and not to impose their implicit (religious?) values upon it.

Counselling as a new religious movement

It has been suggested that counselling is a new religious movement (Wallis, 1984). Yet there is no deity and no formal worship. But not all religions make reference to a higher non-human being. All are, however, characterised by a shared system of beliefs, which have implications for morality and ethics; invariably they are prescriptive of how to live, specifying aims and goals, usually with reference to rewards and punishments. In short, all religions say something about the nature of humankind, as in Christianity which teaches the doctrine of 'original sin'. They also emphasise our spirituality, and hold that belief is not a matter of logic but of faith. Believers commonly try to convert others to join the movement. Religion within society has a worldly structure which may include priests and prophets, and because

A short version of this chapter was presented at the International Association for Counselling conference, 'Counselling in the New Millennium: Meeting the Challenges of Diversity and Promoting Peace and Social Inclusion', Thessaloniki, Greece, May 2000.

religions tend to advocate particular rules for living they tend to be integrated within a particular culture.

Organised religion encompasses: (i) a shared system of beliefs, and (ii) a formal (social) structure. Counselling (as taught in the western world) fits this specification.

A shared system of beliefs

There is a meta-theory behind even the most pragmatic of counselling approaches. Crucial concepts, which are embedded and derived from western thinking, include client autonomy, self-reliance, and empowerment. The values of privacy, intimacy, and personal worth are similarly prized. Practitioners frequently assume that presenting issues are symptomatic of deeper ones, that current problems are to be resolved by exploring the past, or that it is necessary to move from the conscious to the unconscious. And apparently neutral statements relating to technique — for example, of confrontation or challenge — invariably carry implicit assumptions as to how a client needs to change.

Any definition of counselling invariably contains a social theory as to the nature of the problems people face. Some practices, like feminist counselling, are up-front in their assumptions and beliefs. Similarly, Transactional Analysis has been accused of being 'unabashed about its congruence with consumerist culture' (Kovel, 1988, p. 142). The capitalist ideals of the work ethic, personal effort, personal autonomy, and personal responsibility, are evident throughout the (western) counselling literature. It could be argued that the industrial revolution in the West resulted in emotional problems becoming medicalised, so opening the door to therapy.

The rise of industrial society corresponded with (one could say resulted in) the decline of organised religion. This left the existential questions as to the meaning of life open. Counselling theories perhaps emerged to fill this void. At the same time the acceptance of science as an explanatory force for nature and for living processes gave further legitimacy to other (apparently) secular, answers to life's dilemmas (see Nelson and Torrey, 1973). Meadow (1964) argues that counselling is a product of the American capitalist culture, with distrust of 'experts' and emphasis on method rather than theory. The phrase 'Cult of the Individual' can be applied equally to both capitalism and counselling.

Morality and ethics

Ethical principles in counselling derive either from some universal (religious?) principle — usually humanism — or reflect contemporary (western) morality/political correctness. Thus, in the UK, practitioners are expected always to challenge racial attitudes, but be tolerant of sexual orientation or of any religious belief (Ethical Guidelines relating to UK National Vocational Qualifications) no matter how bizarre.

Prescription of how to live

Religions invariably prescribe values for living, and embody social goals. Even the rather bland definition of counselling adopted by the British Association for Counselling and Psychotherapy at its AGM in 1996: 'to provide the opportunity for the client to work towards living in a more satisfying and resourceful way' has been criticised by Howard (1997) for its implicit values — of being hedonistic and individualistic. He argues that this definition focuses on 'growth (as opposed to growing up), satisfaction (as opposed to self-discipline), [and] resourcefulness (as opposed to "social responsibility")' (Howard, 1997, p. 90). It is clear to See how these (non-neutral) values become embedded in what counsellors See as their task. Such values are always present, no matter how much they are denied. For example, it is commonly held that person-centred counselling 'has no goals for the client beyond that which the client has for himself. This is of course nonsense' (Mearns, 1994, p. ix). This is because Rogerian thinking supposes that there is only one way to move forward, and that is to take the path of self-actualisation; these Rogerian goals are frequently implicit in the work of counsellors in the West regardless of the particular techniques they employ.

In approaches such as Rational Emotive Therapy, for example, there is much made of 'faulty thinking', but on what (and whose) grounds is any thinking categorised as being faulty? Challenge is a central concept in counselling, but who decides the perspective of the challenge, and how can challenges be neutral? Whether counsellors look at faulty thinking, an unexamined past, or ways of living more authentically, the impact of western ideas is apparent. For example, all approaches to counselling assume a positive valence for concepts such as client autonomy and place responsibility onto the individual. But not all cultures reflect such a philosophy. Foucault (1988) refers to this structuring of (culture-bound) goals as 'technologies of the self', and the framework within which any practitioner works can be seen as an 'aspirational model' (Stenner, 1999).

The counselling movement and individual counsellors in the West carry what Page (1999) calls the 'collective shadow' of their culture. In his case, being raised as 'middle-class English', he describes his own shadow as embodying 'xenophobia and racist beliefs'. Of course, clients will also have their (cultural) shadows; Jung (1959) suggested that under stress the veneer of civilisation is lost to expose what he called these 'folklore' beliefs.

Faith

Adherence to any religious belief is an act of faith. In counselling, many of the basic tenets are held as unquestioned beliefs, and practitioners eschew attempts to research the basis of their knowledge (Williams and Irving, 1999). It would be fair to say that allegiance to a particular way of working is a matter of faith rather than being based on formal comparative judgement.

Spirituality

Rogers (1980) wrote about the healing power of the spirit, although most counsellors play down this aspect of his writings (Thorne, 1997). Edwards (1992) is one who has made an explicit plea to encompass the spiritual. She draws the distinction between 'religion' which involves seeking for truth 'outside ourselves' and therapy/counselling which seeks truth 'inside ourselves'. This assertion is strongly contested by Ellis (1992) who sees no difference. Edwards, in her rebuttal, writes that 'therapeutic spirituality' is our own truth, not dogma — but clearly her meta-assumptions are as dogmatic as any religion.

Tillich (1952; 1963) saw counselling and psychotherapy as having the same agenda as religion in addressing existential questions of life, but while therapy embraced spiritual thinking only religion offered spiritual presence; the priest has access to God — counselling could help a client, but not make them 'whole' (Tillich, 1956). In this vein a clergyman colleague of ours used to say that he had the edge over us counsellors in that he could offer forgiveness. But this is merely a reference to a construct in a particular spiritual (Christian) model. Freud repeatedly made the point that the church was a refuge of the neurotic; curing neurosis therefore negated the need for religion, and therapy became a substitute for it. Thus the need for a God is obviated.

Converting others

In a very real sense counsellors seek to 'convert' their clients. The client may come with some specific practical problem only to find that this relates to their lack of personal development, some unconscious desires/denials, or an earlier (childhood) event (Williams, 1994). Counsellors sometimes teach clients a language in which to construe their problems and, along with it, a philosophy of life. For example, Transactional Analysis can help noone until they have absorbed the concepts, and neurolinguistic programming relies on the 'faith' the client has in the power of the practitioner.

Similarly students are indoctrinated into the profession. The allegiance to the course ethos demanded of trainee counsellors is not unlike that demanded of novices in a religious order (Wicklund and Eckert, 1992). In our experience, counselling 'trainers', when asked: 'Is the aim of counsellor training to produce competent professionals or a particular kind of person?' invariably specify the latter.

Priests and prophets

Can there really be, as is so frequently stated, over 400 different talking therapies? Are they so different? Or have there been 400 or so charismatic teachers — gurus? Counselling even has semi-religious trappings like the 'Counsellors Creed' (Mearns and Thorne, 1988, p. 18), and Thorne (1999) suggests that counsellors are priests for a new age. Szasz (1979) makes the most comprehensive case for therapist as priest: arguing that therapy 'is a modern, scientific-sounding name for what used to be called the "cure of soul"' (Szasz, 1979, p. 26). In this he is only reiterating earlier claims by Jung (1933) that therapists were the new priesthood. Similarly Freud (1927, p. 252) argued that analysis is 'pastoral work' and that analysts were 'secular pastoral workers', but conducted a campaign against Jung's view of therapy as religion (Freud, 1914). Yet Freud's dogmatic assertions that analysis was science did not stop Szasz (1979), amongst others, describing Freud as a 'great religious leader'; not just priest, but prophet.

Specific alliance to religion

It has often been noted that the origins of psychoanalysis are in Judaism and person-centred counselling in Protestantism. Thorne (1999) is more specific in pointing out the affinity between the teachings of Rogers and those of the Anglican Church. Paradoxically, Rogers departs from the doctrine of original sin and designates the self to be at core good, whereas for Freud it is bad. Both these theoretical positions go beyond psychology to say something about the nature of mankind and of life. This concurs with the views of Browning (1987) who argues that therapeutic psychology is 'filling the void left by the waning influence of religion in answering questions of ultimacy and providing moral guidance' (Jones, 1994, p. 192).

Although a religion, counselling is not yet a church. In its form it resembles the early days of Christianity with factions vying for the higher ground. Nevertheless, ceremonies and rituals are emerging. In training courses and conferences ceremonial hugs, or moments of 'hand-holding silence' are common; symbols, candles and aromas are creeping into practice. Also, counsellors are increasingly replacing the priest as the moral voice in the media and making a formal contribution in the community on life issues such as drugs, pregnancy, suicide and euthanasia — areas where formerly the church has been the sole authority. And, in the aftermath of a disaster, comfort and support to victims is now more likely to be offered by counsellors than the clergy.

(Religious) values in practice

It is a strong argument to say that counselling is nothing without values. The skills of the counsellor to evoke change in their clients are powerful; they could be used for good or bad — to help a man in distress, or to sell him a second-hand car. In short, it is ethical values which characterise counselling (in this respect it is not unlike spiritual guidance that may be offered by a priest). Without such a value base, counselling is clearly a dangerous enterprise. So the values have to be there; but they need to be explicit. For it is imperative that the value system of the counsellor is not imposed upon the client. Russell et al. (1992) make the point that giving direction to clients is not simply undesirable, but incompatible with helping clients make choices within their own value system.

We have argued that counselling is a 'western religion'. At one level this is just an interesting academic debate. But it is much more than this. For this analysis demonstrates that counselling in the West is underpinned by a particular set of beliefs and values. These are implicit in counsellor training and in the formal structure of the profession; they form the zeitgeist within which counsellors practise.

Imposing the zeitgeist

One of the paradoxes of a zeitgeist is that it is unknown to those it encompasses. Everyone once believed the earth was flat despite being surrounded by evidence to the contrary. It is suggested here that the zeitgeist of counselling (with its 'religious' belief system) is so much part of shared current western belief that it is not easily detectable. Note that the philosophy of Carl Rogers encompasses the American Dream of 'I can be what ever I want to be'. This is the doctrine of the human potential movement, which puts the needs and resources of the individual before those of society.

Such western thought fits ill with many cultures. For example, the philosophy of 'Shingaku', which still dominates thinking and behaviour in Japan, teaches that to have no self is the highest virtue — respect for the harmony of the group is all. In many parts of the world, personal happenings are to be explained in terms of the action of spells and spirits which may be dealt with by a witchdoctor or shaman. Rituals may be prescribed, or consultations with ancestors advised. Is the counsellor to challenge such 'solutions' and beliefs? If so, on what grounds? Being possessed by spirits is as real in one culture as an identity crisis in the USA. Counselling has no *a priori* access to 'truth'. Accepted explanations in one society, like the value of conversations with a genie, may to the western mind evoke notions of mental illness. All too often clients who assert their cultural belief as a reason for their behaviour — perhaps invoking 'fate' — may be adjudged by the counsellor as having a problem, and not taking responsibility (see Eleftheriadou, 1997).

Conclusions

Counselling does, it seems, have all the characteristics of a religion and, as such, embodies a system of beliefs which underlie practice. Its adherents will necessarily be committed to their philosophy of life, which will be implicit in their work such that they will inevitably seek, albeit unconsciously, to convert clients to their views. This conclusion is at complete variance with the publicly stated objectives of counselling organisations to allow clients to work within the clients' own values. How is this paradox to be resolved?

First, if counsellors really do believe that in their theories they possess the secret of the fulfilled life — as the majority undoubtedly do — then they should come clean about it. Let them publicly proclaim their faith — evangelise and propagate their gospel — whether it be according to Rogers or Freud. Let them go forth and convert their clients. This, we contend, would maintain the status quo. But we would make a plea for up-front honesty. Counsellors should not seek to inveigle their opinions into clients' lives under the pretext of problem solving or personal development.

The second, and for us the preferred, strategy is to fully recognise that counselling can never be truly neutral in terms of its values, and to recognise the western values implicit in current theory and practice. By making implicit beliefs explicit, they become less dangerous and more readily challenged. This approach is not merely moral, it is practical. Moreover, it conforms to the stated aim of counselling: to focus on the needs of the client within the client's own values.

Nowhere is the necessity of counsellors being clear and honest about their assumptions and beliefs more important than in cross-cultural work. Our own experience in the aftermath of the war in Kuwait and with Bosnian refugees demonstrated to us the importance of respecting the religious and social beliefs of clients, and recognising that our (western) notions of how issues were to be construed had constantly to be reassessed. Counsellors surely need to listen to and try to understand the culture of their clients (see Tribe and De Silva, 1999), and aim to work within these beliefs and not to impose their (western-religious) values upon them.

References

Browning, D. (1987) *Religion, Thought and the Modern Psychologies.* Philadelphia: Fortress.

Edwards, R. (1992) Does psychotherapy need a soul? In: W. Dryden and C. Feltham (Eds.) *Psychotherapy and Its Discontents.* Buckingham: O.U. Press.

Eleftheriadou, Z. (1997) Cultural Differences in the Therapeutic Process. In: I. Horton and V. Varma (Eds.) *The Needs of the Counsellor and Psychotherapist.* London: Sage.

Ellis, A. (1992) Response to Edwards. In: W. Dryden and C. Feltham (Eds.) *Psychotherapy and Its Discontents.* Buckingham: O.U. Press.

Foucault, M. (1988) Technologies of self. In C. Martin, H. Gutman and P. Hutton (Eds.) *Technologies of Self.* London: Tavistock.

Freud, S. (1914) *On the History of the Psychoanalytic Movement. Collected Works, Vol. XIV.* Hogarth Press: London.

Freud, S. (1927) *Postscript to the question of lay analysis. Collected Works, Vol. XX.* Hogarth Press: London.

Howard, A. (1997) Defining Counselling (letter). *Counselling, May,* 90–1

Jones, S. L. (1994) A constructive relationship for religion and the science and profession of psychology. *American Psychologist, 49,* 184–99

Jung, C. G. (1933) *Modern Man in Search of a Soul.* London: Kegan Paul Trench Trauber & Co.

Jung, C. G. (1959) *The Archetypes and the Collective Unconscious. Collected Works. Volume*

9, *Part 1*. London: Routledge Kegan Paul.

Kovel, J. (1988) *The Radical Spirit: Essays on Psychotherapy and Society*. London: Free Association Books.

Meadow, A. (1964) Client-centred therapy and the American ethos. *International Journal of Social Psychiatry, 10*, 246–60

Mearns, D. (1994) *Developing Person-Centred Counselling*. London: Sage.

Mearns, D. and Thorne, B. (1988) *Person-Centred Counselling in Action*. London: Sage.

Nelson, S. H. and Torrey, E. F. (1973) The religious function of psychiatry. *American Journal of Orthopsychiatry, 43*, 362–7

Page, S. (1999) *The Shadow and the Counsellor*. London: Routledge.

Rogers, C. R. (1980) *A Way of Being*. Boston: Houghton Mifflin.

Russell, J., Dexter, D. and Bond, T. (1992) *Differentiation Project: Summary Report*. Welwyn, Advice, Guidance & Counselling Lead Body

Stenner, P. (1999) Sincerity, authenticity and aspirational models. *Changes, 17*, 3, 249–64

Szasz, T. S. (1979) *The Myth of Psychotherapy*. Oxford: Oxford University Press.

Thorne, B. (1997) Spiritual responsibility in a secular profession. In: I. Horton & V. Varma (Eds.) *The Needs of the Counsellor and Psychotherapist*. London: Sage.

Thorne, B. (1999) *Person-Centred Counselling and Christian Spirituality*. London: Whurr

Tillich, P. (1952) *The Courage To Be*. London: Nisbit.

Tillich, P. (1956) *The New Being*. London: SCM Press.

Tillich, P. (1963) *Systematic Theology, Vol. 3*. Welwyn: Nisbit.

Tribe, R. and De Silva, P. (1999) Psychological interventions with displaced widows in Sri Lanka. *International Review of Psychiatry, 11*, 184–90

Wallis, R. (1984) *The Elementary Forms of the New Religious Life*. London: Routledge & Kegan Paul.

Wicklund, R. A. and Eckert, M. (1992) *The Self-Knower: A Hero Under Control*. London: Plenum.

Williams, D. I. (1994) Who (and what) is counselling for? *Counselling News, 13*, 3–4

Williams, D. I. and Irving J. A. (1999) Why are therapists indifferent to research? *British Journal of Guidance and Counselling, 27*, 367–76

The Transpersonal Relationship in Counselling, Psychology and Psychotherapy

7

Petrûska Clarkson

This chapter challenges counsellors and psychologists to embrace the transpersonal and the spiritual if they are to make the most of the most important factor in psychotherapy, the relationship.

Humankind has been engaged in the search for making meaning of our existential 'thrownness' (Heidegger, 1987) since the beginning of time. Frankl (1964), in *Man's Search for Meaning* phrases it thus: 'He who has a *why* to live for can bear with almost any *how*' (p. 76). There is so much that we cannot solve in life — loss, our bodies, time, other people, illness, bereavement, daily frustrations, life's catastrophes.

Although 'the proportion of British people involved in some form of organised religion dwindles as each year passes . . . there are now more than 600,000 Web sites associated with religion' (*Daily Mail*, Tuesday 30 May 2000, p. 53). There is a growing interest in all aspects of the transpersonal in our culture (parapsychology, astrology, feng shui, spiritual healing) and even in the most orthodox regions of our discipline. For example, Sterling (2000), writes that 'there is a growing body of literature that suggests that prayer reduce [*sic*] arthritis, heart rate and stress, and has a beneficial effect over and above relaxation. There is much evidence in brain research that prayer often alters brain wave patterns to synchronise with those involved in the praying. Meditation is known to have health benefits' (p. 3). The Mental Health Foundation's (1999) report 'Strategies for Living' (user-led research) also found that religion and spirituality play a major role in surviving the psychiatric system and getting and staying well.

The ecological connectedness of our world has been dramatically brought to our attention by the way in which, for example, BSE, GM foods, cloning, designer DNA, the damage to the ozone layer can affect people in all parts of the world. The development of technology and communications has led to a situation where 'For the first time . . . all humanity has the technological means to sit round the same planetary hearth and listen to each other's stories' (O'Hara, 1991, p. 73).

Language

Lyotard (1989) defined post-modernism as the 'collapse of the meta-narrative' (the story which explains everything). The emergence of post-modern thinking addresses our current, global mode of interaction and our need to attend to issues of diversity (McNamee, 1992). Rudkin (2000), a clinical psychology trainee, writes:

> There is often a sense that one Absolute truth is going to provide the answer to the numerous questions asked by trainees. A fantasy in which, graduating from clinical training, we shall be presented with an envelope inside of which The Secret will be written, and forever more we shall be sure we are doing the right thing. (p. 48)

The post-modernist turn has involved the abandonment of 'one of the deepest assumptions (and hopes) of Enlightenment thought; that what is "really" available for perception "out there" is an orderly and systematic world, [potentially] the same for all of us — such that, if we really persist in our investigations and arguments, we will ultimately secure universal agreement about its nature'(Shotter, 1992, p. 69).

Philosophers of language have shown how the world we perceive is inescapably structured by the language we inhabit. Polanyi (1958) has shown how the notion of scientific truth rests upon subjective and emotion-laden choices; Wittgenstein's social psychology also undermines any certainties we may have that individuals — psychologists or patients — can be construed separately from the language games ('forms of life'), norms and practices,of the social group to which they belong: 'What determines our judgement, our concepts and reactions is not what *one* man is doing *now*, an individual action, but the whole hurly-burly of human action, the background against which we see any action' (1967, p. 567).

As the Oxford philosopher Farrell also pointed out in 1979, participants, 'trainees' or clients are usually considered to be 'cured' or 'trained' or 'analysed' or 'qualified' by one single criterion — they have adopted the WOT ('way of talking') of the leaders, governing bodies, examination boards and others of perceived status or power (p. 108). Rarely if ever are *the clients* actually asked their opinion about what 'worked'. From David Winter's and my current 'Users' voices' research the therapist's theoretical orientation also does not appear relevant from the clients' perspective — but *the therapeutic relationship* does.

In their massive and scholarly overview of the last 40 years of psychotherapy outcome research, Hubble et al. (1999), write that:

> . . . rather than squeezing the client's complaint into the language and theoretic bias of the therapist's, the data suggest the exact opposite (p. 430) . . . Each client presents the therapist with a new theory to learn, a new language to practise, and new interventions to suggest . . . the process begins by listening closely to *the client's language*. (p. 431. My emphasis.)

Hubble et al. suggest that loyalty to a formal theory and its later impact on the way events are understood and handled in therapy can be understood as 'theory transference' (p. 430). For some years now I have termed this Babel phenomenon in counselling and psychotherapy as *'schoolism'* — defined as *'passionately held convictions of being right which fly in the face of the facts'* (Clarkson, 1997a; 1998a).

Levenson (1991), a psychoanalyst himself, comments on the current situation in psychodynamic and psychoanalytic approaches:

> Just because we are using the same words, we are not using them in the same way ... Any reader, not totally committed to one ideology or another, cannot fail to be impressed — and one might hope, dismayed — by the total conviction with which prominent analysts proclaim diametrically opposed clinical strategies for what they diagnose as the very same characterological category. (p. 244)

Or, as Rumi said some 800 years ago: 'There are Indians and Turks who speak the same language. There are Turks who don't understand each other' (Rumi, 1991, p. 18).

Too often we have a situation in counselling and psychotherapy where the client has to learn to speak our language — whatever that may be. (See also Silverman's 1997 research findings on 'localised rhetoric' in HIV counselling centres.) Remember that Foucault (1974) taught us that all stories (and disciplines) impose discourses of values and power. The professional, moral and ethical consequences of schoolism are further explored in Clarkson (2000).

> It is not simply that therapists and counsellors from a given 'school' will ensure that their clients come away bearing beliefs in their particular account. By implication (and practice) the ultimate aim of most schools of therapy is hegemonic. All other schools of thought, and their associated narratives should succumb. Psychoanalysts wish to eradicate behaviour modification; cognitive-behavioural therapists see systems theory as misguided, and so on (Hubble et al., 1999, p. 71).

Building on, and applying the wisdom of therapy's most influential scholars, Duncan et al. (1997) view the client's theory as containing most, if not all, of the trappings of any psychological theory. It encompasses aetiology, treatment, and prognosis and includes clients' thoughts, attitudes, and feelings about their problems and how therapy may best address their goals. They view the client's theory of change as not only having the values that most affect the client's participation in therapy but also as holding the keys to success despite the method or technique used by the therapist (Hubble et al., 1999). Yet,

> Sad to say, clients have not been highly regarded in most therapeutic systems. Called maladjusted, disturbed, regressed, neurotic, psychotic,

and character-disordered (to name just a few) . . . the practice of therapy is not about nosology. It is about change. (Hubble et al., 1999, p. 409)

The therapeutic relationship

In *Persuasion and Healing* Frank (1961) and later Frank and Frank (1993) surveyed Eurocentric psychotherapy outcome studies along with other cultural healing practices in the rest of the world. They identify four essential factors for psychological healing to occur: (1) the therapeutic relationship, (2) a dedicated space, (3) a prescription for action, and (4) a culturally congruent narrative.

There is no significant evidence that theoretical approach is relevant to the successful outcome of Eurocentric psychotherapies — no matter how measured. There is substantial evidence that it is in fact the *psychotherapeutic relationship* rather than theory, diagnosis or technique which potentiates the beneficial effects of psychotherapy (see Clarkson, 1998a for a review).

In l996 Shapiro concluded:

> Many, if not most, of the cherished beliefs of theorists and practitioners of particular methods of psychotherapy remain largely unsupported by the kinds of evidence preferred by those who control the budgets of health care systems across the globe . . . However . . . For most of the disorders reviewed here, there is little evidence to take us beyond the paradoxical 'Dodo bird verdict' of equivalent outcomes from very different treatment methods. (p. ix)

As in post-modernism, the 'new' physics makes it untenable to consider an objective or value-free scientific approach. It also postulates the co-existence of apparently contradictory views of reality, for example in the words of Sir William Bragg: 'Elementary particles seem to be waves on Mondays, Wednesdays and Fridays, and particles on Tuesdays, Thursdays and Saturdays' (in Zohar, 1990, p. 10).

Quantum Entanglement (Isham, 1995) indicates that, *scientifically*, self and other are inseparable. 'Experiments have provided strong evidence that this "non-local" linking of distinct parts of the world really happens' (Buchanan, 1999, p. 26).

Like Quantum physics, the science of chaos and complexity also highlights the importance of relationships. In this way, chaos theory has shown us that everything and potentially everybody is related in a kind of dance. Everything is in this sense connected with everything else. Any separation is therefore theoretical rather than actual.

Epistemologically also, the things we see (people, objects, etc.) exist only in relationship and, when analysed microscopically, they too are best viewed as relationships. It is no secret in physics (Capra, 1976; 1983) that the closer we analyse some 'thing' the less it appears as a thing and the more it appears as a dynamic process (things in relationship). Consequently, relationships become a primary source of our knowledge of the world. This can be taken to the ontological extreme by stating that things do not exist . . . that, in fact, things ultimately *are* relationships (Cottone, 1988, p. 360).

I suggest that classical notions of self and other, objective and subjective, individual and group, inside and outside, beginning and end, the very nature of psychological knowledge and what we as psychologists think we do with it, needs to come under very serious review.

From my own research (see Clarkson, 1996a) I came to the conclusion that psychotherapeutic psychology is 'the intentional use of relationship' (Clarkson, 1995a, p. 5). It has also been found that there are *different kinds of relationship* required for different kinds of patients. My study identified five modes of therapeutic relationship which are potentially present in any so-called 'pure' approach (from Klein to Rogers) as well as so-called 'integrative' approaches.

The *working alliance* is the aspect of client-psychotherapist relationship that enables the client and therapist to work together even when the patient or client experiences strong desires to the contrary.

The *transferential/countertransferential (biased) facet of the relationship* is the experience of wishes and fears which distorts the working alliance (otherwise referred to as resistance, non-compliance and similar concepts).

The *reparative/developmentally needed facet of the relationship* is the intentional provision by the psychotherapist of a corrective, reparative, or replenishing relationship or action where previous relationships were deficient, abusive or overprotective.

The *person-to-person facet of the relationship* is the real relationship or dialogic subject-to-subject relationship — as opposed to 'object' relationship.

The fifth relational mode I defined as the *transpersonal relationship*, which refers to the spiritual or inexplicable dimensions of relationship in all forms of applied psychology (Clarkson, 1990; 1995a; 1996a).

It is important to remember these are not stages but states in psychotherapy or psychoanalysis, often subtly 'overlapping', in and between which a client creates his or her unique experiences. Although one can see these five as separate therapeutic relationships for the purposes of analysis, research or teaching, it would be more precise to describe them phenomenologically as aspects, modes or facets of *one* intrinsically indivisibly whole relationship — not an integrative framework, but an integrated whole — a fractal (Mandelbrot, 1974).

The transpersonal relationship in psychotherapeutic clinical psychology

It can be used as (a) *a simple miscellaneous conceptual basket* into which we place all those aspects of the healing relationship which do not fit into any other category; (b) those *post-postivistic scientific aspects* of the healing relationship concerned with notions of chaos and complexity as well as quantum physics where modernist norms of causality and duality become redundant and (c) those universes of discourse concerned with what may be described *as spiritual, mystical or archetypal human experiences including the traditional healing practices of the two-thirds world.* (See Chapter 7 of Clarkson, 1995a for extensive discussion.)

The first physicians — medical doctors — have for centuries admitted: '"Je le pensay, et Dieu le guarit " . . . we treat them, but it is God who cures them' (Agnew in Berne, 1966, p. 63).

Examples of the transpersonal in counselling and psychotherapy discourses

Psychoanalysis
Freud (1986/1907) has clear negative views about religion: 'The formation of a religion, too, seems to be based on the suppression, the renunciation, of certain instinctual impulses . . . they are self-seeking, socially harmful instincts, even so, they are usually not without a sexual component' (p. 39).

Since Freud, psychoanalysis has been characterised by what Black (2000) calls an 'orthodoxy of atheism' (p. 13). Sadly he perpetuates the ideologically based distinction between 'mature' and 'primitive religions'. However, later in that paper he comments on how the Kleinian analyst Jacques (1988) speaks

> . . . . with great feeling of the possible serenity and confidence of old age, using the supreme imagery of Dante's Paradiso: 'my desire and my will, like a wheel that spins with even motion, were revolved by the Love that moves the sun and other stars.' (p. .23)

Bion (1970) writes that: 'We can say that the reality we deal with as analysts, i.e. psychic reality, is infinite and has many facets . . . ' 'O' is 'the unknown, new and as yet not evolved . . . *The language of achievement* derives from the possibility of tolerating half-doubts, half mysteries and half truths' (p. 55).

In Jungian thought the numinous transpersonal is conceived of as 'the relationship between the unconscious of the analyst and the unconscious of the patient not mediated by consciousness' (Guggenbuhl-Craig, 1971). Whereas Freud (of course) called physis 'a pleasing illusion', Jung uses the concept of 'physis' many times, but often in its split-off Platonic and neo-Platonic meanings (see Clarkson, 1996c for review).

RET and CBT
Ellis (1962) writes about the goal of RET including a *'joy of being'* (p.336). The existentialist philosopher Heidegger (1987) recognised that *being* means *physis* — an ancient Greek word for the life energy in everything and no-thing. Mingers (1995) has pointed out the identity of 'Being' with Maturana's (1981) notion of 'autopoiesis' — life creating itself[1].

---

1. *Autopoeisis* is the term coined by Maturana to describe the self-generating process of life. (Maturana, 1981) In this view, life is not caused, but creates itself — 'pulls itself up by its own bootstraps' so to speak. It is to be contrasted with the notion that there is an outside 'force' which causes life (e.g. the . . .   contd over . . .

Ellis (1962) even writes that the Zen Buddhist notion of *satori* (enlightenment) would not be incompatible with some of the goals 'a devotee *(sic)* of rational emotive living might seek for himself' (p. 336). He also suggests as a cure for the pains of being human that people acquire a good *philosophy of life* which will enable us to live successfully and happily in spite of our intrinsic biological limitations as human beings.

Padesky (1995), a senior colleague of Beck, explicitly recognises the powerful effects of ethnic, racial and religious/spiritual affiliations in the therapeutic relationship. 'Cognitive therapy is compatible with religious beliefs as long as the therapist is sensitive to and helps the client explore fears that therapy will be inconsistent with religious faith . . . [she shows the client] how to frame the questions within her religious beliefs' (p. 50).

Humanistic/existential approaches

Where it is not reduced to one (usually Indo-European) system of belief, the transpersonal in this tradition is represented by various names such as Rogers' self-actualising tendency or life energy, Perls' use of the term 'elan vital' and Berne's use of the notion of Physis. Heidegger, Merleau-Ponty, Derrida, and Irigary use the concept in its proper Heraclitean sense. Physis (or Phusis) is an ancient Greek word used to refer to life energy as it manifests in nature, in growth and healing as well as in all dimensions of creativity (Clarkson, 1996c). *Physician* or physic (as in medicine) and *physics* (as in Quantum and Chaos understandings of the world) are both derived from it.

Heidegger (1987) wrote that 'physis as logos is the poiesis of physis — the ultimate source of thought as well as of language and poetry. The human *logos*, as it shows itself in language and poetry, is merely a response to the *logos* of *physis*'(p. 61).

Mingers (1995) has pointed out how Heidegger and Heraclitus' physis anticipate the notion of *autopoiesis* in complexity science (see also Clarkson, 2000). Poetry and art are indeed major ways in which the transpersonal physis both reveals and conceals itself in life and in psychological therapy.

Transcultural perspectives

In all of history — as well the contemporary two-thirds world — there is, of course, hardly a culture which does not use traditional healing practices based on ancient appreciations of the power of shamans, medicine people and other kinds of prophet-healers to invoke the supreme powers of God (or whatever the Life-force may be called locally) to assist in healing, helping and harvesting. Sometimes it is called NTU or Umendu as in some parts of North Africa, pran (Indian), chi (Chinese) or kiruenugii (Japanese).

A review of the major texts in Psychology in the UK (Clarkson, BPS Counselling Psychology Conference paper 1999 on transcultural issues)

. . . ghost in the machine or vitalist models). It postulates 'the ghost' and 'the machine' as one co-creating *process*. The conceptual problem in understanding this is usually an unequivocal allegiance to the notion of mechanical causation to explain *all* phenomena. (Even if it, despite all attempts, fails to work!) Many other cultures do not have this problem.

showed:

(a) that race and culture is never integrated and rarely on the curriculum or in the indices,

(b) that the three major traditional approaches favoured in UK psychotherapeutic psychology neglect or exclude non-Eurocentric approaches, and

(c) that there is almost no mention *at all* of transpersonal, spiritual religious dimensions of existence. Mention of the post-positivistic sciences in any of the prescribed texts is also glaring by omission.

But people from the two-thirds world cultures are, with some exceptions, generally deeply spiritual or religious. For people from these traditions, the life-force, ancestors, the entanglement of individuals and community, of body and mind, of nature and spirit are not *ideas*; they are living *realities* (see Clarkson and Nippoda, 1998, Chapter 6).

Often a harsh interpretative reductionism is applied to explain the transpersonal away, for example, in terms of 'internalised object relations' or religious worship is defined as coming from the 'psychotic part of the personality' (Symington, 1990, p. 115). For the African-Jamaican community in this country, for example, Christianity in various forms is part of people's daily lives in a way almost impossible for other people to imagine. Yet our Eurocentric psychotherapies too often make 'God-talk beyond the pale'.

So when I hear from some colleagues how clients (especially those from oral cultures and those who do not share our Eurocentric cultural conceptions about time) 'don't keep their appointments', are 'always late', 'don't want to make a contract', 'are resistant', 'are not psychologically minded', 'want to go over time' or 'expect me to wave a magic wand', I wonder what we think we are doing? The requirement that the defeated take on the oppressor's language is as old as war. If there isn't place for God in our therapeutic psychology, there isn't place for the African experience in it either.

There was a woman who came to a traditional healer because she could not fall pregnant. She had tried everything else — including western medicine — and nothing had helped. The indigenous healer prescribed that she washed herself and go and sit in a particular tree for three days and nights. When she came down he said she would fall pregnant before her next menstruation. And so she did. *Be careful* in criticising or looking down from a lofty colonial height on such narratives and such prescriptions.

People get cured of their emotional ills in such ways too — and always have. Furthermore, the best most advanced pharmacological products lead our western-trained psychiatrists to say: 'Take these pills.' Yet the placebo rate for anti-depressant medication is between 25–35%. This means that of people whose clinical depression is 'cured' — by their own criteria — some 35 out of a 100 patients might as well have been taking sugar pills.

Encountering the inexplicable (transpersonal) in psychotherapeutic psychology

'Much of the therapeutic literature indicates an allegiance to a modernist view of the world . . . The shape and direction of the talk is dictated by models, stages and methods clearly identified in texts and professional journals and books' (McNamee, 1992, p. 190) Nowhere are the wobbly foundations of the therapist's account made known; nowhere do the therapist's personal doubts, foibles, and failings come to light (Gergen and Kaye, 1992, p. 171; see, Clarkson, 2000).

Implied in the transpersonal relationship as I see it is a *letting go* of certainties, our preferred language, our conventional skills, our received knowledge, our preconceptions. Bion (1970) points out the importance of the capacity to tolerate the suffering and frustration associated to 'not knowing' and 'not understanding' (pp. 51, 55).

However, it is quite possible that psychologist psychotherapists may delude themselves in ways which may be dangerous for them — and for their clients if they mistakenly, prematurely or naively focus on the transpersonal. This makes the paucity of literature, research and training in this area particularly problematic. There are always the twin dangers of 'spiritualising the psychological' or 'psychologising the spiritual' (see the Transpersonal chapter in Clarkson, 1995).

Some preliminary distinctions

It may be useful to consider *religion* as that aspect of human experience which can be subsumed under notions such as the organised church, membership of a sect, loyalty to a creed or a chieftain or a guru, a spiritual practice in some kind of tradition or another or even the avowed values in a person's life such as atheism, Marxism, Socialism, nationalism, vegetarianism, capitalism, pantheism, and all other such varieties of *systems* of belief.

The systems of values or beliefs may be very vague or be elaborately worked out; rigorously enforced (e.g. Sharia) or only used for special occasions (Humanistic funerals); encoded in oral history or parchments, inscriptions on monuments or in the millions of volumes in the Vatican Library.

Usually such systems (explicit or implicit) carry certain norms, laws, rules or regulations for their adherents which are followed or broken, for example, Kosher kitchens or baptism or the genital mutilation of young girls (or Freud's female analysands who had their clitorises surgically re-positioned to achieve 'mature' vaginal orgasms). Whatever one's views on various religions throughout the world and throughout the ages, human beings seem to have had need of them at all times and in all places. Without doubt they have been used to commit much evil; arguably they have also done some good along the way.

The word 'spirit' is often used as a synonym for soul or the transpersonal. Ani (1994) defines it as: 'The creative force which unites all phenomena. It is the source of all energy, motion, cause and effect. As it becomes more dense, it manifests as matter' (p. xxviii).

In response to the question, 'What is the *soul*?' Rumi (1991), the founder of Sufi Whirling Dervish mysticism answers:

> 'A joy
> when kindness comes, a weeping
> at injury, a growing consciousness.' (p. 117)

The current situation in psychology, psychotherapy and counselling

Our clients, however, come to us, whatever their current views are, with their lives already having been coloured by *normative* systems in their families, their schools, their places of worship, their culture's acceptance, rejection or modification of such systems. They are inescapably culturally situated in compliance, defiance, certainty or questioning. (And so are we.)

'Traditions associated with human intercourse of all kinds, whether in work, in gendered activity, religious ritual, and so on, are likely to be seen as unintelligible or absurd merely because these issues for them [produce] no digitally unambiguous "read-out" of their meaning' (Smail, 1987, p. 138). For example, many European psychologists inured to the positivistic scientific paradigms of the nineteenth century find the exuberance and passion of syncretistic rituals strange or indicative of serious psychological disturbance — from their own limited cultural perspective.

More than anything else, the factional division within the 'schools' of psychoanalysis and psychotherapy affect the workings and expectations of the therapy with people with religious histories, questions or yearnings.

On the other hand, if we accept that the capacity to experience the sublime, the awesome, the peak experience or oceanic dimension, and that this is a capacity that all human beings can enjoy and grow from, then we stand accused to the extent that psychology falls short of enabling people to open themselves in this way.

So, in addition to the religious or normative domain of the usual discourses, we can differentiate another 'domain of discourse' or level of experience about the transpersonal — that which is not *necessarily* connected to the normative level, but which coexists with it. This essentially cannot be expressed in language. Simply put, it goes beyond words. If it can be expressed in words, it is no longer the transpersonal of the transpersonal or the seventh domain: 'The Tao which can be described is not the Tao'.

Implications for practice, research, training and supervision

1. Learn from other disciplines

'The way to attain an integrated concept and practice of knowledge, and consequently to address many crucial issues of our age through a transdisciplinary approach, does not lie in applying ready-made, "mechanical" procedures based on automatic, stereotyped formulas and standardized recipes' (UNESCO report, 1998, p. 7).

For example, Brandtstädter (1990) and Gergen, Gloger-Tippelt and Berkowitz (1990) explored women's conceptualisations of an orderly sequence of child development in German and North American contexts. Their research led them to conclude that such a notion of child development was more the result of cultural belief systems than *the true nature of the child.*

2. Centralise the therapeutic relationship rather than adherence to 'theory' or 'manuals'

'Just as the discovery of Deinonychus [a dinosaur] dramatically changed how dinosaurs were viewed, converging empirical evidence — regarding the importance of clients and their perceptions to positive outcome — is transforming how clients are treated and therapy is conducted' (Hubble et al., 1999, p. 425). 'The customary rejection of *the common factors* is an indulgence the field can ill afford. If the professions will not come to terms with the knowledge it now possesses and continues to promote assertions rich in bombast but bereft of fact, others will surely define a reality for us. All signs indicate that the emerging reality in 'behavioural health care' is an unpleasant one for many' (Hubble et al., 1999, p. 407).

'It also demands a higher measure of flexibility on the part of the therapist and a willingness to change one's relational stance to fit with the client's perception of what is most helpful' (Bachelor and Horvath, 1999).

3. Integrate practice and research

Counsellors and psychotherapists could instead take up the position of a participant-observer (Barnes, 1983), '. . . one who recognises degrees [or levels] of subjectivity and objectivity, empathy and critical evaluation' (p. 48). To do this on a session-by-session and day-to-day basis requires careful monitoring of the client's reaction to comments, explanations, interpretations, questions and suggestions. From an African-centric perspective Ani (1994) challenges the researcher who:

> believes that by disengaging herself from the phenomenon she wishes to understand, she comes to 'know' it; it becomes an object of her knowledge. She therefore attempts to transform all phenomena in either total 'matter' or pure mathematical symbol. She despiritualizes it. But let us suppose that Plato was essentially mistaken; a good mathematician but a weak humanist (social theorist). If human intelligence is not limited to rationality as defined in terms of order and control (power), but rather is revealed in spirituality that may include but certainly transcend rational order, then the European utumawazo [urge to dominate] does not equip Europeans to deal successfully with the 'human' in themselves or with other human beings. (p. 480)

In an earlier paper (Clarkson, 1995b) I suggested that perhaps the end of the divide between supervision and academic research can begin to be made as the work of doing and reflection becomes integrated. What would be required is a reconceptualisation of the primary task of supervision from that of an expert to that of a consultant or co-researcher in every case or situation brought for disciplined reflection.

> The practice of the clinic should not be separated from rigorous and constant research borne from and bearing theory. For example, a qualitative research project such as a disciplined and methodologically informed case study is not something to be done once for a dissertation or a paper — I believe it needs to be conducted with every client, every session, for as long as a clinician/supervisor thinks and works in the profession. (Clarkson, 1995b, p. 203)

My colleagues and I have described the use of such methods (in Clarkson 1995a, especially Chapter 7; Clarkson, 1996a; Clarkson, 1998b, as well as in a forthcoming book on the Transpersonal Relationship in Psychotherapy).

4. Abandon Schoolism

Youngson and Alderman (1994), cognitive behavioural psychologists, reports substantial behavioural change *without* the theoretically required cognitive changes. It only takes one apple *not* to fall, to disprove Newton's (or Beck's) law of gravity.

> Clearly the one-approach-fits-all strategy is guaranteed to undermine alliance formation. Combining the findings on both client/extra-therapeutic and relationship factors, this conclusion follows: Therapeutic success depends on enabling and confirming the client's resources in a partnership informed by the client's goals and perceptions. (Youngson and Alderman, 1994, p. 418)

5. Value religious/spiritual diversity

A man was telling his friend in a pub about his 'near-death' experience. He said he had died and gone to heaven. His friend asked him: 'Did you get to see God?' 'Yes,' he said. His friends asked 'please tell me what he looked like.' The man said: 'She's black.'

Rawlinson (1997), a phenomenologist of religion, believes that 'opposite truths apply to the human condition. The only option to us, therefore, is to come to terms with ambivalence' (p. 17).

Since it is obvious that people choose different kinds of approaches to the transpersonal (which may all be equally effective — or not — at the final judgement), Rawlinson provides a pragmatic but *approximate* taxonomy (classification) of characteristics of different mystical traditions. Although they may overlap and interpenetrate, they operate from different 'centres of gravity' and with a different metaphorical temperature. Very roughly, for me, they correspond to the Jungian personality typology of thinking ('cool structured', e.g. Wilber), feeling ('warm structured', e.g. Kabbalah), sensation ('hot unstructured', e.g. syncretic Christianity) and intuition ('cool unstructured', e.g. Rinzai Zen Buddhism).

6. Ask the client
Many counsellors and others have asked me: 'How do you introduce the transpersonal into a counselling session?' I have always been rather surprised by this question for two reasons: (a) I do not see how any healing can take place without the transpersonal — I surely do not 'do it' myself! and (b) how can you do therapy of any kind without knowing how this unique person makes sense of their life — and inevitable death?

So at the initial consultation I almost invariably ask the client (or clients) what I have come to call *'the meaning of life question'*. The words may differ depending on whom I am speaking to and their own particular 'language', but the question is essentially very simple: 'What are your ideas about the meaning of your life?' or 'What is your religious or spiritual background?' or 'How do you make sense of what has happened to you?' No one has ever found this question strange or uncomfortable. Even if someone responds by saying: 'I think this life is all there is and we just have to make the most of it', I have been given an answer which is at least as (and perhaps more) important than their GP number or whether they are currently taking drugs or medication.

Frank and Frank (1993) write that 'ideally therapists should select for each patient the therapy that accords, or can be brought to accord, with the patient's personal characteristics and [the client's own] view of the problem' (p. xv). I grew up in South Africa where Sangoma's ('witchdoctors' or medicine-people) are consulted for human pain at least as often (if not more often than) black and white western-trained doctors.

Indeed I heard about a European-trained clinical psychologist who was at the same time a local sangoma in the village where he lived. When asked how he knew which clients wanted the clinical psychologist's services and which clients wanted the sangoma's services (narratives), he replied: 'It all depends on which door they come into my consulting hut. One door is for me as a western clinical psychologist and the other door is for me as a traditional healing medicine-man.' 'So what's different in your practice?' 'Just the stories we tell and the prescriptions I make for them — I work from where each client is.'

7. Learn philosophy
According to Wittgenstein (1922), 'Philosophy is the discipline of thinking about thinking. The object of philosophy is the logical clarification of thoughts. Philosophy is not a theory, but an activity' (p. 77).

Rigorous definition of terms and conscientious specification of domains of discourse or knowledge (epistemenological clarity) and of the different truth values which apply at different levels would be of inestimable help to clinical and supervisory practice, the courts, our profession and particularly our patients (who already suffer from enough confusions of feeling and thinking, moral values and fact, fantasy and phantasy, observation and trance induction, truth and lies).

This is not, however, the direction in which the various professional organisations look to be heading. For example the DSM, in spite of continuing to be plagued by poor reliability and validity and *having absolutely no predictive power in terms of treatment outcome* (Kirk and Kutchins, 1992; Kutchins and Kirk, 1997), is now a fixed part of most graduate training programmes and a prominent feature of the whole empirically validated treatment movement (Hubble et al., 1999).

Rudkin (2000) writes that:

> Safe uncertainty, on the other hand, is a position from which the therapist explores a multitude of possible explanations from a number of experiences. The position is not a fixed one, but is in a constant state of flux as new ideas and experiences present themselves. There are no solutions, just less distressing dilemmas due to the reframing of experiences. In this case, the therapist moves alongside or even slightly behind the client, using what skill they have to create or acknowledge new meaning . . . authoritative doubt [which] encompasses both expertise and uncertainty is the most beneficial (p. 48).

8. A different kind of training

> A fuller appreciation of the importance of the realm of meaning for understanding human beings will require a different kind of training for scholars in the human sciences . . . The object of their inquiry, the human being, exists in multiple strata of reality, which, although interrelated, are organized in different ways. (Polkinghorne, 1988, p. 183)

Never, as far as I know, does the client's opinion form a significant part of the psychologist's professional assessment of competency. It is other colleagues who examine the candidate for how well they can describe *post hoc* what they did (or do) in a particular theoretical language. If they can't, they 'fail' — no matter how many clients have been healed in the therapeutic relationship with them. (See 'Accreditation procedures in psychotherapy', Clarkson 1996b, pp. 14 and 15) Yet,

> Research results show a weak correlation between amount of training and clinical outcome, strongly suggest that admission to training and eventual credentialing be based on the ability to perform rather than the mastery of various theories or techniques. The survival of the mental health professions, in other words, will be better ensured by identifying empirically validated treaters rather than empirically validated treatments.' (Hubble et al., 1999, p. 439)

I have for some years been experimenting rather successfully with a training programme for psychologists, psychotherapists, counsellors, supervisors and organisational consultants (based on the ideas outlined in this paper) called 'Learning by Enquiry' (*Dieratao*) (For further information see Chapter 12 in Clarkson, 1998b and www.physis.co.uk)

9. A transpersonally inclusive kind of supervision
In our research on competencies in supervision (Clarkson and Angelo, 2000) we found that the transpersonal (whether called 'inexplicable', 'scientific' or 'spiritual') was not mentioned in any of the published 'lists' of competencies. Yet, further research found that this is perhaps the most personally meaningful and clinically useful aspect of the supervisees' experiences of the supervisory relationship. (See also Clarkson, 1998b, Chapter 10 and Clarkson, 1997b.)

Finally ...

There was a man hanging by his fingernails over a terrible abyss. He could not even look down, it was so frightening. So the man shouted: 'Is there anybody out there?' And God answered: 'Yes, my son.' So the man said: 'Please tell me what to do!' And God said: 'Let go my son.' After a moment's reflection on God's advice, the man shouted again: 'Is there anybody else out there?'

References

Ani, M. (1994) *Yurugu – an African-centred Critique of European Cultural Thought and Behavior.* Trenton, NJ: Africa World Press.

Bachelor, A. and Horvath, A. (1999) The Therapeutic Relationship. In: M. A. Hubble, B. L. Duncan and S. D. Miller (Eds.) *The Heart and Soul of Change.* Washington DC: American Psychological Association.

Barnes, B. (1983) Doubts and certainties in practising psychotherapy. In: D. Pilgrim (Ed.) *Psychology and Psychotherapy: Current trends and issues.* London: Routledge and Kegan Press.

Berne, E. (1966) *Principles of Group Treatment.* New York: Grove Press.

Bion, W. R. (1970) *Attention and Interpretation.* London: Karnac (ex-Tavistock).

Black, D. M. (2000) The functioning of religions from a modern psychoanalytic perspective. *Mental Health, Religion and Culture, 3,1,* 13–26

Brandtstädter, J. (1990) Development as a personal and cultural construction. In: G. S. Semin and K. J. Gergen (Eds.) *Everyday Understanding: Social and Scientific Implications.* London: Sage.

Buchanan, M. (1999) An End to Uncertainty. *New Scientist (American),* 6th March, *2176,* New York.

Capra, F. (1976) *The Tao of Physics.* London: Wildwood House.

Capra, F. (1983) *The Turning Point: Science, Society and the Rising Culture.* London: Flamingo.

Clarkson, P. (1990) A multiplicity of psychotherapeutic relationships. *British Journal of Psychotherapy, 7 (2),* 148–63

Clarkson, P. (1995a) *The Therapeutic Relationship: In Psychoanalysis, Counselling Psychology and Psychotherapy.* London: Whurr.

Clarkson, P. (1995b) Counselling psychology in Britain — the next decade. *Counselling Psychology Quarterly, 8, 3,* 197–204

Clarkson, P. (1996a) Researching the 'therapeutic relationship' in psychoanalysis, counselling psychology and psychotherapy. *Counselling Psychology Quarterly 9, 2,* 143–62

Clarkson, P. (1996b) Accreditation Procedures in Psychotherapy, *Self and Society, Vol. 23, No.6*, pp. 14–15

Clarkson, P. (1996c) The archetype of physis: The soul of nature – our nature. *Harvest: Journal for Jungian Studies, 42 (1)*, 70–93

Clarkson, P. (1997a) Beyond Schoolism summary. In UKCP's *The Psychotherapist*, Autumn, 1997, p.9

Clarkson, P. (Ed.) (1997b) *On the Sublime*. London: Whurr.

Clarkson, P. (1998a) Beyond Schoolism. *Changes, 16, 1*, 1–11

Clarkson, P. (Ed.) (1998b) *Counselling Psychology: Integrating Theory, Research and Supervised Practice*. London: Routledge.

Clarkson, P. (2000a) *Ethics: Working with Ethical and Moral Dilemmas in Psychotherapy*. London: Whurr.

Clarkson, P. and Angelo, M. (2000) In search of supervision's soul: A research report on competencies for integrative supervision in action. *Transpersonal Psychology Review, 4 (2)*, 29–34

Clarkson, P. and Nippoda, Y. (1998) Cross-cultural issues in counselling psychology practice: a qualitative study of one multicultural training organisation. In: P. Clarkson (Ed.) *Counselling Psychology: Integrating Theory, Research and Supervised Practice*. London: Routledge.

Cottone, R. R. (1988), Epistemological and ontological issues in counselling: implications of social systems theory. *Counselling Psychology Quarterly, 1, 4*, 357–65

Duncan, B. L., Hubble, M. A. and Miller, S. D. (1997) *Psychotherapy with 'impossible' cases: The efficient treatment of therapy veterans*. New York: Norton.

Ellis, A. (1962) *Reason and Emotion in Psychotherapy*. Secaucus, NJ: Citadel Press.

Farrell, B. A. (1979) Ways of talking. In: B. Babington Smith and B. A. Farrell (Eds.) *Training in Small Groups: A study method of five methods*. Oxford: Pergamon.

Foucault, M. (1974) *The Archaeology of Knowledge*. London: Tavistock Publications (Original work published 1969).

Frank, J. D. (1961) *Persuasion and Healing*. Baltimore, MD: Johns Hopkins University Press.

Frank, J. D. and Frank, J. B. (1993) *Persuasion and Healing: A comparative study of psychotherapy*. Baltimore, MD: Johns Hopkins University Press

Frankl, V. E. (1964) *Man's Search for Meaning: An introduction to logotherapy*. London: Hodder & Stoughton.

Freud, S. (1986/1907) *The Origins of Religion*. Harmondsworth: Penguin

Gergen, K. J. and Kaye, J. (1992) Beyond Narrative in the Negotiation of Therapeutic Meaning. In S. McNamee and K. J. Gergen (Eds.) *Therapy as Social Construction*. London: Sage.

Gergen, K. J., Gloger-Tippelt, G. and Berkowitz, P. (1990) The cultural construction of the developing child. In: G. S. Semin and K. J. Gergen (Eds.) *Everyday Understanding: Social and scientific implications*. London: Sage.

Guggenbuhl-Craig, A. (1971) *Power in the Helping Professions*. Dallas, TX: Spring Publications.

Heidegger, M. (1987) *An Introduction to Metaphysics* (R. Manheim, trans.). New Haven: Yale University Press (first published 1959).

Hubble, M. A., Duncan, B. L. and Miller, S. D. (1999) *The Heart and Soul of Change. What works in therapy*. Washington DC: American Psychological Association

Isham, C. J. (1995) *Lectures on Quantum Theory – Mathematical and structural foundations*. London: Imperial College Press.

Jacques, E. (1988) Death and the midlife crisis. In: E. B. Spillius (Ed.) *Melanie Klein*

Today. Vol. 2, London: Routledge.

Kirk, S. A. and Kutchins, H. (1992) *The Selling of the DSM: The rhetoric of science in psychiatry.* New York: Aldine.

Kutchins, H. and Kirk, S. A. (1997) *Making us Crazy.* New York: Free Press.

Levenson, E. A. (1991) *The Purloined Self-Interpersonal Perspectives in Psychoanalysis* (A.H. Feiner, Ed.). New York: William Alanson White Institute.

Lyotard, J-F. (1989) *The Post-modern Condition: A report on knowledge.* Manchester: Manchester University Press.

Mandelbrot, B. B. (1974) *The Fractal Geometry of Nature.* New York: Freeman.

Maturana, H. (1981) Autopoiesis. In: M. Zeleny (Ed.) *Autopoiesis: A theory of living organization.* New York: Elsevier-North Holland.

McNamee, S. (1992) Reconstructing identity: the communal construction of crisis. In: S. McNamee and K. J. Gergen (Eds.) *Therapy as Social Construction.* London: Sage.

Mental Health Foundation (1999) *The Courage to Bare our Souls.* London: The Mental Health Foundation.

Mingers, J. (1995) *Self-Producing Systems: Implications and applications of autopoiesis.* New York and London: Plenum Press.

O'Hara, M. (1991) Horizons of Reality: Demystifying Post-modernism (Book Review). *Networker, Jul/Aug,* 71–4

Padesky, C. A. with Greenberger, D. (1995) *Clinician's Guide to Mind Over Mood.* New York: Guilford Press.

Polanyi, M. (1958) *Personal Knowledge.* London: Routledge and Kegan Paul.

Polkinghorne, D. E. (1988) *Narrative Knowing and the Human Sciences.* Albany, NY: State University of New York Press.

Rawlinson, A. (1997) *The Book of Enlightened Masters: Western Teachers in Eastern Traditions.* Chicago: Open Court.

Rudkin, A. (2000) Having the courage to lack conviction. *Clinical Psychology Forum, 141,* 47–8

Rumi (1991) *One Handed Basket Weaving. Poems on the theme of work* (Versions by C. Barks). Athens, GA: Maypop.

Shapiro, D. A. (1996) Foreword. In: A. Roth and P. Fonagy *What Works for Whom? A critical review of psychotherapy research.* New York: The Guilford Press.

Shotter, J. (1992) Getting in touch: the meta-methodology of a post-modern science of mental life. In: S. Kvale, *Psychology and Post-modernism.* London: Sage.

Silverman, D. (1997) *Discourses of Counselling — HIV Counselling and Social Interaction,* London: Sage.

Smail, D. J. (1987) *Taking Care: An alternative to therapy.* London: J. M. Dent.

Sterling, S. (2000) Is anyone out there? *Clinical Psychology Forum, 141,* 3

Symington, N. (1990) *Religion and Psychoanalysis in Groups, Crowds and Culture.* London: Free Association.

UNESCO (1998) Towards integrative process and integrated knowledge. *International Symposium of Transdisciplinarity,* pp. 1–12. New York: United Nations.

Wittgenstein, L. (1922) *Tractatus Logico Philosophicus* (trans. D. F. Pears and B. F. McGuinness). London: Routledge.

Wittgenstein, L. (1967) *Zettel.* Berkeley: University of California Press.

Youngson, H. A. and Alderman, N. (1994) Fear of incontinence and its effects on a community-based rehabilitation programme after severe brain injury — successful remediation of escape behaviour using behaviour modification. *Brain Injury, 8, 1,* 23–36

Zohar, D. (1990) *The Quantum Self: A revolutionary view of human nature and consciousness rooted in the new physics.* London: Bloomsbury.

The Immanence of Transcendence in Psychotherapy

8

Arthur Still

A television news item on famines in Africa predicted that ten million people are in danger of starvation. There was more cheerful news in the paper, news of a cure for a modern illness. 'British doctors are carrying out a ground-breaking study into anhedonia' an aspect of depression which 'sucks the joy out of most things that make life worth living — food, sex, relationships and achievements'. The article, written by a sufferer, reports that brain imaging will enable us to pinpoint the source of the problem (somewhere in the hippocampus, which is smaller in this condition) and enable us 'to find appropriate psychological or pharmacological treatments'. A picture shows young people drinking wine at a pavement restaurant, with the caption: 'Dining alfresco . . . losing enjoyment in such pleasures can be devastating' (*The Guardian*, 4 April 2000).

This victim of 'anhedonia' wished to return to what she had been, and hoped for the right medicine. But for many clients (and perhaps for her) it is not so simple. They are themselves painfully aware of the contrast between their own inexplicable suffering in the midst of wealth and comfort, and the pain of those deprived of the conditions of life. This indeed is part of their suffering, and it is likely that beefing up the hippocampus will need to include forgetfulness or insensitivity when faced with the material misery of a large proportion of human beings. Unless we adopt the solution of St Thomas Aquinas who faced a similar problem in the twelfth century. The eternal bliss of heaven is necessarily perfect, but how can that be so when down below in hell countless millions are being tortured without end? Assuming the facts cannot be kept from them, the saved must gain some kind of pleasure from it, some satisfying insight, perhaps, in the divine moral plan.

Maybe a more spiritual approach is called for. As John Rowan observes, 'If we once admit we are spiritual beings, then the whole game takes another turn. Instead of patching wrecks, or even realizing potentials, we are dismantling the barriers which are keeping us away from the divine. That which separates us from our spiritual centre has to be questioned, seen through and transformed' (Rowan, 1993, p. 2).

Spirituality: the sacred and the otherworldly

Some psychotherapists equate 'spirituality' with 'religious', often seen as an intrusion to be dealt with as sensitively as possible (Spilka, 1986). But writers like Rowan extract spirituality from its common religious context, and make it central to an understanding of therapy. 'Spiritual' has an obvious etymology — pertaining to spirit. But nowadays there is more to it than that. It is part of a complex of words which includes 'sacred', 'higher', 'transcendent', 'holy', 'religion', 'timeless', 'mystical', 'otherworldly', 'immaterial', 'esoteric', 'numinous', 'divine', 'mystery', etc. Such words occur repeatedly in discussions of spirituality. Metaphors of height abound, often linked with transcendence (beyond or outside ordinary experience). There is also a sense of seriousness, of awe, of sacredness, and the words thus form two groups: the sacred (holy, mystical, numinous) and the otherworldly (transcendent, immaterial, timeless, higher). If the spirituality in question is Christianity then the sacred naturally goes with the otherworldly. To the Natural Theologians of the seventeenth century the world still had a sacred quality, not in itself but because it is the creation of God, a transcendent being. And even today a church is sacred to a Christian because it belongs to God. But when we ask whether there is something about psychotherapy that is essentially 'spiritual', it does not entail 'Christian' or even 'religious', and the separation of the sacred and the otherworldly is a key issue for this paper.

Transcendence is opposed to immanence, which means present or indwelling. The realities of both science in its theoretical concepts and Christianity in its ontology of the divine are weighted towards the transcendent. This holds even for everyday experience, since what we encounter directly through our senses is sparse and apt to be misleading, at least when described in the language of physics. Meaning is added through perception and cognition, and this scheme is a metaphysical ground on which scientific psychology has flourished. Almost from the beginning, laboratories found ways of submitting subjects to defined inputs, and limiting their responses so that they could be described as engineering 'black boxes'. The mathematics of light or sound were used to describe the inputs, so human beings became treated as part of the mechanistic world of physics — as wonderful brain machines to explain how what is actually immanent, judging from the bleak inputs of the perceptual laboratory, is so surprisingly different from the colourful and clamorous world we seem to experience. If sacredness is immanent in this world it is a delusion, or a projection of the mind, or (for believers) a divine visitation.

Prophets of doom like William Blake and Thomas Carlyle had been warning the world about the effects of this metaphysics throughout the nineteenth century, but the final knell for the sacred in human life was sounded by Max Weber in 1919, when he announced the disenchantment of the world by rational science (Weber, 1946). We may yearn for something else, for the sacred, but it is not there, and, like Freud, Weber could see no alternative but sorrowful acceptance in the face of such frustrated longing. There has been much resistance to this pessimistic view, and there were movements at the time in Germany which aimed to give an alternative, less mechanistic account of science (Harrington, 1996). At their best they led to Gestalt psychology and furthered ecological thinking in biology, at their worst they were adapted to the service of Nazism.

A different response to disenchantment has been to develop a spirituality alongside science, sometimes actually using the methods of science as a means of investigating a supernatural world. Perhaps the purest example of this is the interest in spiritualism towards the end of the nineteenth century. The spiritualist movement accepted science's domination of the physical world, but supposed in addition the existence of a transcendent spirit world, which could be contacted through special states of consciousness. A modern example of this approach within the broad field of psychological therapies is John Heron's *Sacred Science* (1992).

Heron is well known for what he calls in this book 'Person-Centred Inquiry', which he uses there to inquire into the spiritual, into a transcendent world rather than just spiritual experiences. He has no doubts about its existence: 'It is for me a truism that human beings survive the death of their physical bodies with the self-same personal identity. I find this to be so because of my encounters with people in the post-death realms in my out-of-the-body experiences, and my strong awareness of them at different times and under different sorts of conditions when I am in my body' (Heron, 1992, p. 26). Few inquirers into the spiritual have this degree of what Heron calls 'ontological robustness', and the usual approach in psychotherapy is to focus on experiences themselves, and to inquire into the conditions under which they become called spiritual. Two ways in which this has been done will be described briefly through single representative examples. Therapy itself has been described as (1) a spiritual path; or (2) as a source of experiences which are so intense and which point so clearly to transcendence that they are claimed as spiritual.

Therapy as spiritual path

For John Rowan in *The Transpersonal: Psychotherapy and counselling,* 'psychotherapy is already a spiritual exercise' (Rowan, 1993, p. 2). They share for him a metaphor of adventure, '*daring* to open up to what is inside' (my italics) and 'going further into this deeper level' (Rowan, 1993, p. 2). So spirituality is continuous with psychotherapy, rather as the summit of a mountain is continuous with the foothills, or the land across the bridge is continuous with here. 'It seems pretty clear to me now that what is at the other end is spirituality. In other words, to reach the end of the bridge means facing and exploring the numinous, the holy, the divine' (Rowan, 1993, p. 3). Thus transcendence becomes immanent. In elaborating his model he draws on Ken Wilber's charts of levels of consciousness, mapped directly onto stages of psychotherapy: mental ego, real self, soul and spirit. Like most developmental theories this is hierarchical, which Rowan is uneasy about, but justifies by appealing to Ken Wilber on evolution:

> Each higher level has capacities and characteristics not found at lower levels. This fact appears in evolution as the phenomena of creative emergence ... But failing to recognise that elemental fact — that the higher cannot be derived from the lower — results in the fallacy of reductionism. (quoted in Rowan, 1993, p. 117)

So the quest for the spiritual involves going higher (or deeper) in the sense of more complex or more organised. This is seen to be an acceptable hierarchy of actualisation rather than the domination by force 'characteristic of the human rank orderings in male-dominated societies' (Rowan, 1993, p. 118). More like increasing knowledge or higher education perhaps, since 'no one can bring someone to this level who has not reached it themselves' (Rowan, 1993, p. 119). But these are intellectual achievements and Rowan is ambivalent about the intellect: '. . . it is the intellect which does most of the contracting and avoidance which prevents movement further along the scale' (Rowan, 1993, p. 119).

There is a subtle tension in Rowan's metaphor of development. Inquiry, by whatever new paradigm, is intellectual, and it is reductive to the simplifications of prose and maps. So if the present interest in the spiritual is a reaction to the disenchantment of the world by science there is a paradox here. The spiritual heights themselves are in danger of disenchantment, like the once sacred Mount Everest being trampled on by climbers in big boots, leaving litter.

Therapy as spiritual experience

In *Person-Centred Counselling: Therapeutic and spiritual dimensions*, Brian Thorne (1991) describes times when he and a client:

> . . . attained a level of communication which could certainly be described in terms of an altered state of consciousness or as a breakthrough into the transcendental . . . My contention . . . is that therapists have a particular obligation to ensure that they prepare themseles with the utmost discipline for the task of creating a climate where both they and their clients can be fully open to the mysterious power in which they share but which is greater than they. (Thorne, 1991, p. 106)

During these times of 'heightened awareness', when the transcendent becomes immanent,

> . . . there is a sense of the therapist being responsive to the intuitive rather than to the powerful rational part of his or her being and as a result being endowed with new and often complex understanding . . . there is a powerful experience of relating at a new and deeper level . . . there is the experience of the transcendent, that is to say of two people being linked into something greater than themselves . . . in this transcendent state there

is an overpowering sense of energy, well-being and healing. (Thorne, 1991, p. 183)

Thorne quotes with enthusiasm Carl Rogers' discovery late in his life that 'Our experiences, it is clear, involve the transcendent, the indescribable, the spiritual. I am compelled to believe that I, like many others, have underestimated the importance of this mystical, spiritual dimension' (quoted in Thorne, 1991, p. 183).

Thorne concludes by redefining what is transcendent as present to others in 'shared belongingness to a transcendent order' (Thorne, 1991, p. 186).

Words and metaphors

In examining these books it is the words and metaphors (and the underlying metaphysics) that are focused on here, not the undeniable value of the practices and experiences described. Rowan and Thorne, like Heron, take transcendence as the essential mark of the spiritual. In Rowan's metaphor the transcendence of spirituality is a place, and psychotherapy can become a journey towards it, towards making it immanent. For Thorne the transcendent may become immanent during certain intense experiences of heightened awareness which occur during psychotherapy. Rowan's spiritual story is like that of a climber looking for new mountains to conquer. Thorne is different, more a contemplative than a conquistador, though a very energetic one. In their different ways they move away in their spirituality from the everyday world, away from the world that has become disenchanted by science. Metaphors of height abound, and achieving spiritual peaks is a Herculean effort which always involves letting go of the intellect as though it were so much surplus baggage.

Historically this may be inevitable. 'The intellect' is a peculiarly western construct which usurped the heights early on, in Plato and in Scholastic philosophy, and continues to play a dominant role in the supposed disenchantment of the world. As Dawkins is reported to have commented in response to the Prince of Wales's personal disenchantment with science in his first Reith Lecture: 'Far from being demeaning to human spiritual values, scientific rationalism is the crowning glory of the human spirit' (*The Guardian*, 17 May 2000). This is a shot in the battle for power between intellect (reason) and feeling — perhaps the answer is not to continue the debate and to judge between them but to give up the old metaphors altogether. This in itself has the structure of therapy, of exposing and retelling the stifling narrative of western metaphysics by which our thinking at the deepest level is controlled. The narrative has three aspects, philosophical, ethical and psychological, and each is changed in the new narrative. A place for spirituality is then uncovered.

Is re-enchantment possible?

1. Philosophy: Being-in-the-world

Instead of rejecting the intellect in the interest of spirituality, let us use it in its proper place, to examine again Weber's announcement of the disenchantment of the world. Was the disenchantment inevitable, the painful result of a process of reality testing? Ben-Chaim (1998) has recently answered this question in the negative, and I reach the same conclusion by another path, through questioning the metaphor of otherworldly transcendence.

In the usage of this paper, immanence is what is or can be experienced directly, and transcendence is what is beyond direct experience. The traditional view of immanence from both science and religion makes immanence alone too sparse to bear the weight of the sacred, except when it contains a projection of or visitation from the divine. With the decline of religious belief, these possibilities have receded. Ironically, it is due to this traditional bias that western philosophy, religion and science have been a fertile breeding ground for otherworldly transcendence and spirituality. The bias is towards the present, that which is immediately and instantaneously before the eyes (and other sense organs, but characteristically eyes) as a paradigm for direct contact with the world. This is sometimes referred to as the 'metaphysics of presence' (Fuchs, 1976). Relative to presence, virtually everything is experienced indirectly and is therefore transcendent, from chairs and tables and other people, through most scientific and psychological entities, including the unconscious, to the past and to God. One striking consequence of the metaphysics of presence is that it places a heavy burden on cognition and the intellect in accounting for human experience.

Edmund Husserl's phenomenology, especially his later work, may be seen as a concerned reaction to the disenchantment of the world by science, and he began to understand and question the metaphysics of presence. This was carried further by Martin Heidegger during the 1920s. Given the cultural background of the time, as expressed in Max Weber's paper, Heidegger's philosophy may also be seen as a response to this disenchantment, a radical attempt to rip up the philosophical tramline that had allowed a limited perspective, successful beyond the wildest conjectures in practical applications, to so drastically curtail our view of the world and of being human. Using Husserl's phenomenology, and his own deployment of hermeneutics (Still, 1999), Heidegger exposed the metaphysics of presence, and drew out the consequences of a different starting point. This irreducible beginning is Being-in-the-world, and in Heidegger's thought transcendence plays a new and different part in the structure of experience. What we experience directly is not a series of static moments, with time added to unify them, but 'ek-stasis' ('out of place'): never just 'here' but always a flow from the past, to the future, and in the present with its surrounding possibilities. Each of these (past, present and future) is unlimited, with horizons, and possibilities beyond the horizons. Thus: 'Having its ground in the horizonal unity of ecstatical temporality, the world is transcendent' (Heidegger, 1962,

p. 417). This transcendent world is presupposed in all our experience, but it is also experienced directly, so immanence and transcendence become one and the same.

2. Ethics: The Face-to-Face

Emmanuel Levinas took this further and in a different direction. Born in 1906, he was a Lithuanian Jew who studied with Heidegger, and settled in France during the 1930s, where he introduced Heidegger's work to the young generation of philosophers that included Sartre and Merleau-Ponty. Levinas's ethical philosophy was driven by the need to separate the profundity in Heidegger's philosophy from the same man's collusion with the Nazi regime in 1933.

His first major work was *Totality and Infinity* (1969; the first French edition was 1961). A totality is like a system. If something is part of a totality, it is reducible to its part of that totality. Thus reduction can be (perhaps always is) to something transcendent to experience, whether it is physiological processes,[1] or the human community. What is irreducible, on the other hand, cannot be limited in this way, and is infinite. Levinas's irreducible situation is not just Being-in-the-world, but what he calls the 'face-to-face' with the 'other', and the demand or responsibility that it brings forth. In Levinas's reading, Heidegger had characterised the basis of human community as 'along-side of', potentially allowing the ethical responsibilities to derive from the community or the culture. For Levinas, on the other hand:

> The conjuncture of the same and the other . . . is the *direct* and *full face* welcome of the other by me. This conjuncture is irreducible to totality; the 'face-to-face' position is not a modification of the 'alongside of . . .' (Levinas, 1969, p. 80).

Heidegger's 'being-alongside' (his term for our absorption in the world — including the human world and what we deal with in it) is in danger of reduction to a transcendent human community (as Thorne claims), and ethics to the morality of that community. Levinas's face-to-face is not just visual, but includes touching, and especially 'saying' (the translation of Levinas's 'Dire'). It is irreducible, since the other is not some entity beyond the horizon which can in principle be explored and reduced to a totality; nor is the other part of Being-in-the-world. Thus:

> . . . 'face-to-face' is irreducible, because the Other is 'inexhaustible' . . . just as *Dire* is not absorbed . . . in grammar, rules, and themes of language. *Dire* is that which is not thematized, which is both transcendent and immanent in language. (Werhane, 1995, p. 63)

So, for Levinas, ethics begins in the face-to-face, the 'saying' that is part of

---

1. These are transcendent because they are always inferred from instrument readings, never experienced directly.

the face-to-face, the irreducible otherness (and transcendence) and the responsibility to the other that it releases. This is more than the now familiar dialogic account of human nature that derives from Martin Buber and Bakhtin (Sampson, 1993). The ethical does not stem from one's participation in a transcendent human community, but is given directly as a demand from the face-to-face. Its immanence and its transcendence are one and the same.

3. Psychology: Direct Perception

Heidegger and Levinas are philosophers, not psychologists, and they describe ontological structures that are different from those of the metaphysics of presence. Just as the old laboratory provided a psychology fit for the metaphysics of presence, so a psychological grounding of both Heidegger's Being-in-the-world and Levinas's face-to-face can be found in James Gibson's Ecological Psychology (Still and Good, 1998). As a close colleague of the Gestalt psychologist Kurt Koffka, Gibson was a distant heir of 'Re-enchanted Science'. Like Levinas he seems to have been motivated to develop a direct perception of the world and other people to undercut the relativism that he saw as powerless against prejudice (Costall and Still, 1989).

In the perception laboratory the subject's eye is usually static, as befits the metaphysics of presence. James Gibson discovered that this leads to a misleading account of perception when the person's eyes are moving, as in landing an aeroplane, walking, talking face-to-face, gardening, inspecting an object, dancing, etc. In fact it is inadequate for most of the things we do as beings-in-the-world, except perhaps looking through a microscope or a telescope, those fitting paradigms for a classically scientific metaphysics of vision. Instead of concluding that the eye moving in the world is just a much more complicated case requiring extra massive cognitive computations, he recognised in a stroke of genius that the opposite is true. When the projected image on the retina is in motion, reflecting the flowing projection of the surrounding environment, he showed that the available and usable information is far more specific than from a static image. In vision, people do not receive information like a snapshot, and then work out its meaning, but actively pick up information that specifies meanings. It is a direct realism, since no inferential processes are involved in this unfolding of an experienced world. The relationship between transcendence and immanence is the same as for Heidegger. We perceive the world directly, so it is immanent, yet it is also transcendent, a whole that is beyond immediate experience.

The world is not a neutral world upon which we impose our projects. Instead it already points to possible actions. We perceive what Gibson called affordances. Like the face-to-face, affordances are neither objective nor subjective. An affordance 'points two ways, to the environment and to the observer' (Gibson, 1979, p. 141). If Levinas is right, the face of the other is perceived directly, and the ethical demands are part of what it affords or means for the observer.

Discussion

Through Heidegger, Levinas, and James Gibson, an alternative ontology to the metaphysics of presence has been outlined; a different philosophy, a different ethics, and a different psychology. What is immanent is given value or meaning by being one with the transcendent, but not by reduction. If the metaphysics of presence is responsible for the the disenchantment of the world, then the way is open for undoing this process, for restoring the sacred to Being-in-the-world. As a commentator on Levinas has written:

> The Name is never pronounced, but always remembered. As inspired by the Good, we are in the trace of its passage. To live this inspiration is spirituality. (Peperzak, 1995, p. 192)

Thus the sacred and the spiritual are not something to be *added* to ordinary experience. They are *presupposed* by it, but usually overlaid by other preoccupations. Psychotherapy is emblematic of this ontology, just as observing through a microscope or telescope (or accessing the world through a computer screen) is emblematic of the metaphysics of presence. It is a paradigm of the face-to-face, with all the responsibility and the possibilities afforded by it.

The paradox (a paradox in thought but not in perception) at the heart of this paper is familiar in Mahayana Buddhism; what is immanent is transcendent and what is transcendent is immanent — 'is' and not merely 'contained in'. In the Heart Sutra '. . . emptiness does not differ from form, form does not differ from emptiness' which Edward Conze glosses:

> 'Emptiness' is our word for the Beyond, for transcendental reality. That the transcendental is Beyond is self-evident. The corollary, that it is also immanent, in its opposite, and coexists with it, is taught even to children and ordinary people. But that it should be precisely identical with its exact opposite, or with that which it is not, that surely passes belief. And yet that is the message. (Conze, 1975, p. .83)

The same holding together of opposites in a single experience enables Samsara to be the same as Nirvana, your client to be seen as both an alcoholic and a Buddha, and is behind the famous Zen account of Enlightenment:

> Before I had studied Zen for 30 years, I saw mountains as mountains, and waters as waters. When I arrived at more intimate knowledge, I came to the point where I saw that mountains are not mountains, and waters are not waters. But now I have got its very substance I am at rest. For it's just that I see mountains once again as mountains, and waters once again as waters. (quoted in Watts, 1962, p. 146)

Similarly the sufferer from anhedonia quoted at the start of this essay once delighted in dining alfresco, as well as food, sex, relationships and achievements. At the start of psychotherapy (if that and not drugs is her choice) she takes no pleasure in these things — she is, I have imagined, plagued by unhappy memories, and weighed down by the suffering in the world. At the end she once again delights in dining alfresco, as well as food, sex, relationships and achievements. The difference is that she is fully aware of impermanence and the suffering in the world, not because she is constantly reminding herself (as she was at the start of therapy), but because she can see it with compassion in the face of others and feel it in herself. In one and the same experience, she is aware of the transcendent world and the immanent setting of the moment. There is no hierarchy and she is not like one of the blessed viewing the torments of the damned, since she sees no permanent difference between herself and others.

References

Ben-Chaim, M. (1998) The disenchanted world and beyond: toward an ecological perspective on science. *History of the Human Sciences, 11*, 101–27

Conze, E. (1975) *Buddhist Wisdom Books* (2nd ed). London: George Allen & Unwin.

Costall, A. and Still, A. (1989) Gibson's theory of direct perception and the problem of cultural relativism. *Journal for the Theory of Social Behaviour, 19*, 433–41

Fuchs, W.F. (1976) *Phenomenology and the Metaphysics of Presence.* North-Holland: Martinus Nijhoff.

Gibson, J.J. (1979) *The Ecological Approach to Visual Perception.* Boston: Houghton Mifflin

Harrington, A. (1996) *Re-enchanted Science: Holism in German culture from Wilhem II to Hitler.* Princeton, New Jersey: Princeton University Press.

Heidegger,M. (1962) *Being and Time.* Oxford: Basil Blackwell (the original, German version was first published in 1927).

Heron, J. (1992) *Sacred Science: Person-centred inquiry into the spiritual and the subtle.* Ross-on-Wye: PCCS Books.

Levinas, E. (1969) *Totality and Infinity.* Pittsburgh, Pennsylania: Duquesne University Press.

Peperzak, A.T. (1995) Transcendence. In Peperzak, A.T. (Ed.) *Ethics as First Philosophy: The Significance of Emmanuel Levinas.* London: Routledge.

Rowan, J. (1993) *The Transpersonal: Psychotherapy and counselling.* London: Routledge.

Sampson, E.E. (1993) *Celebrating the Other: a Dialogic Account of Human Nature.* Hemel Hempstead: Harvester Wheatsheaf.

Spilka, B. (1986) Spiritual issues: Do they belong in private practice? Yes — But! *Psychotherapy in Private Practice, 4*, 93–100

Still, A.W. (1999) Authenticity and change in psychotherapy. *Changes, 17*, 3, 188–202.

Still, A.W. and Good, J.M.M. (1998) The ontology of mutualism. *Ecological Psychology, 10*, 39–63.

Thorne, B. (1991) *Person-Centred Counselling: Therapeutic and spiritual dimensions.* London: Whurr Publishers.

Watts, A. (1962) *The Way of Zen.* Harmondsworth: Pelican Books.

Weber, M. (1946) Science as a vocation. In: H.H.Gerth and C.Wright Mills (Eds.) *From Max Weber: Essays in sociology.* Oxford: Oxford University Press.

Werhane, P.H. (1995) Levinas's ethics: a normative perspective without metaethical constraints. In: A.T.Perperzak (Ed.) *Ethics as First Philosophy: The significance of Emmanuel Levinas.* London: Routledge.

Psychosis and Spirituality: Finding a language

9

Isabel Clarke

Psychosis and spirituality both inhabit the space where reason breaks down, and mystery takes over. For me as a psychotherapist working with people with psychosis, this encounter poses questions: questions such as; 'Why is religious/spiritual preoccupation and subject matter so prominent in psychosis?' 'How come they both share a sense of portentousness and supernatural power, and where does this sense come from?' 'How is it that all civilisations but our own have honoured the sacred — are the sacred and spirituality fundamental or expendable?'

First a word about definitions. In this paper I intend to question received boundaries between concepts, and, in particular, the assumptions that lie hidden in the very language we use. However, I have to start from somewhere. I am aware that both terms, psychosis and spirituality, raise questions and resistance. What I mean by each will become clearer as the chapter progresses. For now, I would like them to be taken essentially as starting points, and in their most generally understood sense. I am taking psychosis as a widely recognised social construct (leaving aside questions of its defensibility). For me, this construct applies if one or more of the following situations occur: the individual suffers subjective distress as a result of mental events; is cut off from others by the nature of his/her experiencing, or their everyday functioning is impaired. These circumstances frequently result in psychiatric involvement, and therefore diagnosis, but this aspect is not relevant to my definition. Spirituality, I suggest, is also generally recognised by a quality of experience — about which, more later.

As my work as a clinical psychologist working with a psychiatric rehabilitation team led me deeper into empathic encounter with the experience of psychosis, the mystery deepened and the boundaries became more blurred. I already knew from long interest in the spiritual traditions, particularly the Christian contemplative tradition, that the mystical writers enjoined their disciples to beware of terrifying and deceptive experiences that sounded remarkably psychotic. They warned that such experiences were frequently encountered when pursuing the goal of unitive experience of the divine. I now learned that ecstatic experience was a reasonably frequently reported stage in a psychotic breakdown. Peter Chadwick's book *Borderline*

(Chadwick, 1992 — discussed below) was for me important corroboration of this observation.

So the questions started to coalesce, and the answer appeared to lie in a psychological conceptualisation that would combine psychosis and spirituality as a unified area of human experience. In attempting this, I am all too aware that spirituality is one of those topics that defy conceptualisation. The illusion of certainty that diagnosis gives to psychosis in some quarters has also been deconstructed (Bentall, 1990), leaving both in something of a conceptual quicksand. This is hardly surprising since all the great religious traditions have stressed the paradoxical nature of the truths they pursue; the paradox that I propose to explore in this chapter is the paradoxical relationship between spirituality and psychosis. Far from being at opposite ends of the spectrum of worthwhile human endeavour, I am going to suggest that both represent one way in which human beings can encounter reality, and the same way at that. The difference in the experience, where difference there is, and I will question whether the difference has been exaggerated, comes with the experiencer rather than the experience.

I will start by examining the ideas that William James (1902) had on this subject, as we are only now beginning to catch up with his insights. I will then consider the research evidence for overlap between psychosis and spirituality, founded in the concept of schizotypy, and the crucial role of the spread of cognitive behaviour therapy for psychosis in facilitating the encounter between psychotherapy and the experience of psychosis. As re-examination of the relationship between psychosis and spirituality entails challenging received ideas about spirituality, this is tackled next, leading on to scrutiny of the rigidity of language which has inhibited creative thinking in this field. I then introduce a possible unifying conceptualisation, based on Kelly's construct theory. I conclude the chapter by arguing that, far from being expendable or an optional extra, the spirituality of connectedness that emerges from this argument is central to all that we value, and, indeed, to our very survival.

William James (1902) in his series of lectures entitled 'Varieties of Religious Experience' succeeded in grasping at this mercurial subject matter in a way that comes over as just as incisive and fresh a century later. He made a number of important points that provide a good foundation for the argument that will follow. He cut through centuries of theological argument at a stroke by founding his definition of religion on experience, as follows: 'Religion . . . shall mean for us the feelings, acts, and experiences of individual men in their solitude, so far as they apprehend themselves to stand in relation to whatever they may consider the divine'. This definition sits well with the wider term, spirituality, employed in this book. However, it raises the issue of the suitability of individual subjective experience as the subject matter for scientific, and therefore psychological, enquiry. In James' day, following Wundt and others, this was perfectly proper, but has since been trampled underfoot by the success of behaviourism, and is only now resurfacing in the development of methods of enquiry that can deal validly with experience. Heron's *Sacred Science* is perhaps the most apposite example to the present subject (Heron, 1998).

James distinguished two contrasting attitudes to religious experience, that of the 'healthy-minded', 'once-born', and that of the 'the sick soul', whose spiritual happiness depended on becoming 'twice-born', and for whom 'the world is a double-storied mystery'. This phrase uncannily echoes one quoted by the anthropologist Natalie Tobert (Tobert, 2001); the phrase 'the double house', used by the Tukano people to describe the natural and the spirit world — an interpretation that it took the anthropologist studying these people (Reichel-Dolmatoff) a couple of years to get to the bottom of, so foreign is it to our culture. The contrast is that for the Tukano, this concept will have been accepted by all, not confined to the 'sick soul'.

For the twice-born 'there are two lives, the natural and the spiritual, and we must lose the one before we can participate in the other' (p. 163). James sees the expansion or blurring of what he terms the 'margins of consciousness' (p. 226) as a crucial entry point into this spiritual state. James lays the groundwork for a model of spirituality which also accommodates psychotic experience when he writes:

> The most important consequence of having a strongly developed ultra-marginal life of this sort is that one's ordinary fields of consciousness are liable to incursions from it of which the subject does not guess the source, and which, therefore, take for him the form of unaccountable impulses to act, or inhibitions of action, of obsessive ideas, or even of hallucinations of sight or hearing. (p. 229)

This is made more explicit in the often quoted:

> It is evident that from the point of view of their psychological mechanism, the classic mysticism and these lower mysticisms spring from the same mental level, from that great subliminal or transmarginal region of which science is beginning to admit the existence, but of which so little is really known. That region contains every kind of matter: 'seraph and snake' abide there side by side. (p. 419)

These quotations illustrate James' recognition that people vary in their constitutional susceptibility to enter into such non-ordinary states of consciousness, which is precisely what Gordon Claridge, and the other researchers in the field of schizotypy, have explored at length (Claridge 1991). This approach normalises the varied incidence of schizotypy in the population, and stresses that, as well as entailing vulnerability to psychotic breakdown, high schizotypy brings advantages such as greater creativity and availability of lateral thinking.

James was also referring obliquely, at the end of the passage quoted above, to the then new study of the unconscious, which has since developed into psychoanalysis. Among the pschoanalysts (or analytical psychologists), C. G. Jung must be acknowledged as the one to have delved into the realm of the seraphs and the snakes, and to have brought many treasures to the surface (e.g. see Jung 1963). However, his pioneering work has not led to the widespread practice of psychotherapy among people with psychosis. Such work, and its impact on our notion of spirituality, has had to wait until more recent times.

The overlap between psychosis and spirituality has recently been recognised and researched. Mike Jackson tackled the subject with both a broad survey study, that compared the subset of a normal population who reported 'spiritual' experiences with a diagnosed sample, and found much overlap, as well as including a fascinating qualitative study in his PhD thesis (Jackson, 1991). His work has since become more widely available through published papers and chapters (e.g. Jackson, 1997; 2001). Emmanuelle Peters has similarly compared people involved in New Religious Movements with a clinical sample, finding differences in mood and adjustment, but not in quality of beliefs (Peters et al., 1999; Peters, 2001).

Recognising this overlap between spirituality and psychosis, and its relationship with universal human experience, must have implications for the psychotherapist working with people with psychosis. Preoccupation with the spiritual is a characteristic of psychotic thinking. Voices that people hear are frequently attributed to God, the Devil, or other supernatural entities. 'Delusions', particularly grandiose delusions of identity, often involve religious figures, and the characteristic psychotic discourse is suffused with the supernatural, or a sense of spiritual importance. Immediately the therapist is challenged. Usually it is manifestly in the client's interest to gain a stronger footing in the real world, but who is the therapist to pronounce on deep metaphysical matters? How do you prove who is right and who is wrong in such an area of discourse? Alternatively, the therapist might hold a definition of spirituality which precludes psychosis, so that the client is, by this definition, presenting a 'false' spirituality. Again, who is to say?

I consider these issues to be very important, both so that psychotherapists do justice to the rich variety of experience that our psychotic clients present us with, without dismissive or reductionist reactions, and so that we are not sentimental about psychosis. We need to honour the experience, but also help people through the real distress and dysfunction that can accompany psychosis if we are to be any use as therapists. However, taking these issues seriously leads us into uncharted territory. Despite the insights of pioneers such as James, Laing and Grof, there has been reluctance bordering on defensiveness to consider psychosis and spirituality together. As I argue below, the very language we have at our disposal steers us away from such identification. I hope to show that tackling this issue head-on leads to new insights into both psychosis and spirituality, and to a better grasp of at least the borderland of the great mystery at the heart of both.

Talking therapy for psychosis

The arguments that follow were developed through listening to the experiences of people with psychosis, and striving towards shared meaning-making with them. This shared enterprise alerted me to other writers and researchers who were shedding further light on this area of discourse, such as those I have already mentioned (Chadwick, 1992; Jackson, 1997; Claridge, 1993). These authors, along with others, collaborated with me in an edited volume (Clarke, 2001), whose aim was to shed light on this area.

The timing of this enterprise owes much to the increased availability of talking therapy to people with psychosis through the NHS, which I would attribute to developments in cognitive behaviour therapy for psychosis. When I started working in the NHS, 12 years ago, there was little talking therapy available to people in hospital with chronic psychosis, outside one or two major centres — which certainly did not include Southampton where I was employed. Slow progress or exacerbation of symptoms appear to have blunted enthusiasm for earlier initiatives. The cautious adaptation and application of CBT approaches to psychotic problems from the late 1980s onwards has yielded more positive results, probably because the explicit and collaborative nature of the approach allowed for greater groundedness and safety in the therapeutic alliance than the earlier initiatives. The result of this is that this particular talking therapy is now very widely available to people with psychosis, whether of recent onset, or with more chronic difficulties (e.g., see Chadwick et al., 1996; Kingdon and Turkington, 1994).

CBT for psychosis entails a paradigm shift in thinking by challenging the medical model (Bentall, 1990; Boyle, 1989). The medical model stresses the distinctness of psychotic from normal experience, through the Present State Examination and the whole apparatus of diagnosis, and sees it as purely pathological. The new psychological understandings stress the continuum with normal cognitive processes, and the comprehensibility of psychotic concerns in the context of the individual's life (e.g. Chadwick, Birchwood and Trower, 1996). I fully embrace this view, and indeed it shapes my clinical practice. However, I wish to take the argument a stage further and emphasise the essential discontinuity between psychotic experience (and spiritual experience involving altered consciousness) and everyday experience, but without reverting to the medical model. I deliberately use the word 'everyday' rather than 'normal'.

I see psychosis and spirituality as two aspects, or points on a continuum, of the common human experience. I am interested in the way in which they have been so separated by the modes of conceptualisation current in our society. This is reflected in the language we use. My contribution to this debate will therefore be an examination of these modes of conceptualisation and an attempt to develop a means of discourse that is common between the two.

Spiritual experience and altered consciousness

There is a growing recognition that the dominance of the materialist scientific world view over the last three or so centuries has seriously stunted and distorted our understanding of the spiritual and religious dimension of life (e.g. Sheldrake, 1990; Zohar, 1990). It has been demanded of religion that it fits into the scientific scheme. This has resulted in 'the God of the gaps' phenomenon, and the loss of the appreciation that there are two ways of encountering reality (or two 'realities'). This appreciation has been fundamental to every human society from the most primitive until the present age.

I am here referring to a huge debate which is well beyond the scope of this article, but would direct the reader to anthropological research such as that of Felicitatas Goodman (1988) which elaborates the role of altered states of consciousness, or trance, in religious ceremony in most societies — surviving in pale shadow in modern church services in the form of incense and repetitive chanting — and to the marginalisation of spiritual/mystical experience in a lot of contemporary religion. Neil Douglas-Klotz traces this marginalisation to the way in which the essentially mystical middle-eastern religious traditions of Christianity and Islam have been subjected to the concretising influence of Graeco-Roman culture. He writes:

> Due to this [limited language concerning these states] western culture developed a massive split between the 'inner' psychic and 'outer' normative consciousness, as well as splits between cosmology and psychology, body and soul, and humanity and the natural environment. (Douglas-Klotz, 2001)

These splits have led westerners to seek in oriental traditions something that was once integral to our own, and has, I believe, led to a spiritual hunger in modern society that is fed by consciousness-altering drugs.

I am therefore starting my argument from the premise that 'spiritual experience', entered into deliberately as through meditation, mystical practice, etc. takes the experiencer into a different relationship to everything, and that, in a less controlled fashion, this is the same space that is stumbled upon in psychosis.

The nature of psychotic experience

One factor that disguises the overlap between psychotic and mystical experience is the underreporting of the frequent (but not invariable) ecstatic experience at the start of the psychosis. Peter Chadwick (1992) has written eloquently of this from his own experience. Even where it is recognised, and along with it the spiritual dimension of psychosis, as by Grof, Laing, etc., the language used distances this insight from the generality of psychotic experience.

I suggest that psychosis, revolution and similar social movements, and profound spiritual experience which is often described as mysticism, follow a common process which encompasses euphoria, bewilderment and horror in a sequence that is actual for some of the time and potential at others. By this I mean that, in mysticism, euphoria is an obvious feature; horror a potential that is less generally recognised and thankfully not so often realised (perhaps more often in the fake mysticism of hallucinogenic experience). In psychosis the euphoria stage, which is often, but not invariably, present, is not usually talked about. It is mentioned as a possible part of an individual's prodromal signature in connection with identifying early signs of relapse in Birchwood and Tarrier (1992), but not in its own right. It sometimes features in clinical histories as a time of well-being before breakdown. The bewilderment in psychosis is also a feature of the early onset phase when the world is experienced as confusing, and this is the time when delusion formation takes place, as noted by Chadwick, Birchwood and Trower (1996) in their discussion of 'predelusional puzzlement'. In revolution, both the euphoria and the horror stages are usually accessible.

Developing a language of comparison

There is a problem about trying to draw objective and generally accepted conclusions about spiritual, psychotic and revolutionary group experiences, because they are in their nature individual, subjective and difficult to communicate. The language available to discuss these subjects is inadequate and harbours assumptions that hinder comparison. Psychoanalysts talk of the emergence of un- or sub-conscious contents into consciousness (according to school). For the transpersonal psychologists it is called the 'transpersonal realm'; Grof (e.g. 1990) speaks of 'non-ordinary states of consciousness'. Religious writers have a different set of terms: nirvana; higher states; the divine, etc. Metaphors of height exclude psychosis; metaphors of depth, such as subconscious, denigrate the religious experience.

In addition to the problem of the spatial metaphors, frequent and contradictory use of the term 'reality' sows confusion. Some religious writers and transpersonal psychotherapists claim a superior grade of reality for the spiritual. This contrasts spiritual with psychotic experience, which, as everyone knows, is about losing touch with reality. Mike Jackson (1997) discusses these confusions in the introduction to his thesis on the subject, and invented his own term, 'p-s experiences', to facilitate comparison across the spectrum. I see, as an essential precondition to exploration of this topic, the development of a clear psychological understanding of this area of human experience which embraces both the spiritual, the psychotic and the transpersonal so that group phenomena are included. What follows is an attempt to do this, using Kelly's personal construct theory as a basis.

Two sorts of experience

I start from the recognition of two possible modes in which a human being can encounter their environment. The most normally accessible of these two modes can be described as ordinary consciousness. The other mode is a less focused state which renders both psychotic and spiritual experience possible, as well as being the source of creativity and personal growth. Starting from problem-focused conscious thought, it is possible to envisage a continuum towards more automatic modes of operation. An example of the latter is the experience of reverie, of letting the mind wander as opposed to focused thought. Such a state of reverie is easily accessible to all but the most stressed. Most people attain it naturally, whether by listening to music, lying in the bath or on a sunny beach. In this state the elusive solution will drift into the mind of the person who has been straining fruitlessly for weeks. Travelling further along this progression from focused to less focused thought, the next distinction is more difficult, as this is where, I would argue, the real discontinuity is encountered.

This is the experience of trying to still and centre the mind, whether in wordless prayer, in meditation, or by participating fully in a relaxation exercise or guided fantasy. A state of reverie is a necessary starting point, but on its own merely leads to daydreaming and unfocused thoughts. The internal dialogue becomes muted but does not disappear. Switching into a prayer/meditation mode requires a special sort of 'attention' which is recognised in Buddhist practice. I find the writings of Simone Weill, an unconventional mystic in the Christian tradition, particularly helpful in elucidating this area. Weill writes of it thus in *Gravity and Grace* (1952) 'Absolutely unmixed attention is prayer'. The fact that this is difficult, without considerable practice, and does not appear to come naturally, is my starting point.

A personal construct understanding of the two sorts of experience

Kelly's idea of Personal Constructs captures the dichotomy well. (See *Inquiring Man* by Bannister and Fransella (1971) for a good introduction.) Kelly saw the human being encountering the world as a scientist, making hypotheses and predictions based on past experience and any other information that lay to hand. These predictions, or constructs, would be recycled and come to constitute the individual's unique model of the world, both shaping perceptions and actions, and being constantly modified by feedback born of experience.

Successful living requires a sufficient range of constructs to be able to deal with most situations encountered with relative ease, but with enough flexibility to be able to assimilate the novel situation. When encountering a new situation, the person needs to loosen their construct system sufficiently to accommodate the new material, thereby expanding the system. It is important that this should be followed by a consolidation phase where the constructs are tightened again, or the person will be unable to make valid predictions. Thus, Kelly's conceptualisation contains within it a natural rhythm of expansion and tightening of constructs, very like breathing. According to this analogy, expansion of the system is compared to breathing out, and consolidation, to breathing in. A well functioning construct system is adaptive as it helps the individual to operate successfully in the world.

Viewed like this it is not surprising that leaving the construct system behind does not come naturally, as it entails moving away from the safety net of construction that the individual has created to operate effectively in the world. It means moving into the unknown. More challengingly, according to this model, as my understanding of myself is essentially a construction, I lose touch with this when I pass beyond the horizon, along with other constructs, and thereby lose the means of making predictions. Laing (1967) writes about this: 'The "ego" is the instrument for living in *this* world. If the "ego" is broken up, or destroyed . . . then the person may be exposed to other worlds, "real" in different ways from the more familiar territory of dreams, imagination, perception or phantasy.' William James (1902) puts it thus: 'an immense elation and freedom, as the outlines of the confining selfhood melt down'.

These ideas are developed further in my chapter in Clarke, 2001.

The advantages of this model

What are the advantages of this construct theory model of the contrast between everyday and spiritual/psychotic/transpersonal reality? The only justification for introducing a new mode of conceptualisation is that it explains a wider range of observable phenomena, and I hope to show that this is the case.

The process I have been describing has two stages; the euphoria of encountering unmediated reality, and then the loss of bearings because of having drifted out of reach of the construct system, which people rely on to make sense of their environment. The often cited timelessness of the mystical experience shows that time is one of the parameters lost in this transition. In the case of a mystical experience attained through spiritual practice (or, as often happens, occurring spontaneously, but within a spiritual context that gives it meaning for the experiencer), managing the transition back to construed reality after the experience generally (but not invariably) occurs naturally and after a short space of time. Where the same state is achieved by taking a drug, the return again normally (but not invariably) occurs when the drug wears off.

In psychosis (and drug or spiritual experiences that go wrong, or shade into psychosis), the orderly return does not happen. The individuals find themselves stranded beyond the reach of their construct system, trying to operate in the world. Not surprisingly this is extraordinarily difficult. The familiar boundaries between people, events, time and space are not accessible as before. Telepathy seems normal. Other people can read, and worse, interfere with, the individual's thoughts. Coincidences abound — everything is connected and everything is disconnected. Everything is possible and nothing is possible. Where this new reality might be exhilarating for a short while, the sustained experience is terrifying. The desperate sufferer tries to make sense of the unfamiliar environment, clutching at whatever connections come to hand. In this way delusions, which usually have their origin in the early stage of the breakdown, are born. In another dissolution of normal boundaries, internal concerns are experienced as external communication, and the person hears voices. Normal thought is disrupted — or, as the psychiatrist would say, disordered.

This model does not deny a physical aspect through some disruption of brain functioning for these phenomena. In the case of drug taking, there is a simple physical cause, and indeed some ascetic practices such as fasting can create a physical precondition for mystical states in the context of spiritual practice. It offers a complementary psychological understanding of the experience of the person suffering from psychosis as one who is trying to make sense of the world, as all human beings do, but with their usual bearings removed. It is in the tradition of the normalising exposition of psychotic symptoms in cognitive therapy for psychosis.

Indeed, emphasising the overlap with spiritual experience brings psychosis in from the cold region of the utterly alien and incomprehensible where it is traditionally relegated. Our society's particular illiteracy in the area of spiritual experience contributes to the even greater isolation of the person with psychosis. In *Recovery from Schizophrenia* Richard Warner (1985) notes that in societies where experience of the spiritual/psychotic realm is valued, people diagnosed with schizophrenia have a far better prognosis than in modern western society.

This conceptualisation might finally have the advantage of bringing spirituality into a clearer focus in the scheme of things. It postulates that the spiritual mode of experiencing is available to all, but more easily accessible to some than others, according to variable schizotypy. Whereas construed thinking has many obvious advantages in terms of precision and predictive power, it inevitably jettisons some of the data. The spiritual mode of apprehension takes in the whole picture — in all its wonder and terror. It holds the key to the added ingredient in the beauty of art, and of perfection in nature; to the excitement of grasping at truth, and the 'madness' of falling in love. Without this dimension and colouring, life would be dull. Our ancestors recognised and honoured the sacred. They respected its resources of power and 'spirit', and cultivated the relationship with the divine and the beyond. They also sought to construe it in dogma and belief systems, which then collide with our scientific rationalism. Perhaps we need more than ever to grasp the paradoxical nature of the spiritual; to recognise that in this mode of experiencing, two contradictory things can be simultaneously true, so that we can cope with this collision, and reconnect with sacred. Without it, we lose our sense of connectedness with and responsibility to the whole. Our current danger is that, without this sense of connectedness and responsibility, we are destroying the material basis for our life through the recklessness and carelessness of our relationship with the earth. Paradoxically again, I suggest that we need to reconnect with the spiritual in order to safeguard the material, as our future is bound up with both. Psychosis means being lost in this mode of experiencing — but perhaps the rest of us could do to be less divorced from it, and have the humility to respect the experience of those, wherever they are on the schizotypal spectrum, who inhabit more easily this 'other' wavelength.

References

Bannister, D. and Fransella, F. (1971) *Inquiring Man.* Harmondsworth: Penguin

Bentall, R.P. (1990) *Reconstructing Schizophrenia.* Routledge: London.

Birchwood, M. and Tarrier, N. (Eds.), (1992) *Innovations in the Psychological Management of Schizophrenia.* Chichester: Wiley.

Boyle, M. (1989) *Schizophrenia – a Scientific Delusion?* Routledge: London.

Chadwick, P., Paul, Birchwood, M. and Trower, P. (1996) *Cognitive Therapy for Delusions, Voices and Paranoia.* Chichester: Wiley.

Chadwick, P. (1992) *Borderline. A Study of Paranoia and Delusional Thinking.* Routledge: London.

Claridge, G. A. (1997) *Schizotypy: Implications for illness and health.* Oxford: Oxford University Press.

Clarke, I. (Ed.) (2001) *Psychosis and Spirituality: Exploring the new frontier.* London: Whurr.

Douglas-Klotz, N. (2001) Missing Stories: Psychosis, spirituality and the development of Western religious hermeneutics. In: Clarke, I. (Ed.) (2001) *Psychosis and Spirituality: exploring the new frontier.* London: Whurr.

Goodman, F.D. (1988) *Ecstasy, Ritual and Alternate Reality.* Indiana University Press: Bloomington and Indianapolis.

Grof, S. (1990) *The Holotropic Mind.* Harper Collins: San Francisco.

Heron, J. (1998) *Sacred Science. Person-centred inquiry into the spiritual and the subtle.* Ross on Wye: PCCS Books.

Jackson, M. C. (1997) *A Study of the Relationship between Psychosis and Spiritual Experience.* Unpublished Thesis. Oxford University: Oxford.

Jackson, M. C. (2001) Spiritual and Psychotic experience: A case study comparison. In: Clarke, I (Ed.) (2001) *Psychosis and Spirituality: Exploring the new frontier.* London: Whurr.

James, W. (1902) *The Varieties of Religious Experience.* New York. Longmans. (Edition from which pages are referenced: New York. The Modern Library.)

Jung, C. G. (1963) *Memories, Dreams and Reflections.* London: Routledge.

Kingdon, D. G. and Turkington, D. (1994) *Cognitive Behavioural Therapy of Schizophrenia.* New York: Guildford Press & London: Psychology Press.

Laing, R.D. (1967) *The Politics of Experience.* Harmondsworth: Penguin.

Peters, E. R., Day, S., McKenna, J., Orbach, G. (1999) The incidence of delusional ideation in religious and psychotic populations. *British Journal of Clinical Psychology, 38,* 83–96

Peters, E. R. (2001) Are Delusions on a Continuum: the case of religious and delusional beliefs. In: Clarke, I. (Ed.) (2001) *Psychosis and Spirituality: exploring the new frontier.* London: Whurr.

Sheldrake, R. (1990) *The Rebirth of Nature.* Century: London.

Tobert, N. (2001). Polarities of Consciousness. In: Clarke, I. (Ed.) (2001) *Psychosis and Spirituality: exploring the new frontier.* London: Whurr.

Warner, R. (1985) *Recovery from Schizophrenia.* Routledge: London.

Weill, S. (1952) *Gravity and Grace.* Routledge: London.

Zohar, D. (1990) *The Quantum Self.* Bloomsbury: London.

Culturally and Religiously Sensitive Help: From a Jewish perspective

10

Kate Miriam Loewenthal with M. Brooke Rogers

In this chapter, I (KML) shall say something about why cultural and religious issues are important for those offering psychological help. I shall not dwell on all the reasons, but will focus on one general issue: that of understanding and feeling understood. Finally — and in the largest part of this chapter — I would like to describe some experiences of those working to provide culture-sensitive services.

My perspective

This section tells you something about who I am and where I am coming from. I read recently that it was a good idea to do this before writing up qualitative research, but I can't see why it can't be done before writing about any kind of research, or indeed any kind of psychology, qualitative research or otherwise.

I am an orthodox Jew, strictly orthodox, and a common corollary of that is having a very large number of children. As the years go by, we have an increasingly large number of grandchildren. I am also an academic psychologist. I started off my academic career in the 1960s by doing a thesis on the relations between thinking and speaking, and particularly the question of whether the outcome of thinking was affected by talking about it. When I began teaching, I felt that I stood with a foot in social psychology, and a foot in cognitive psychology, and for many years I taught both. But I got softer and softer, or perhaps it was harder to find people to teach social psychology, so I began to teach more and more social psychology, and less and less cognitive psychology. Then my boss, the late Brian Foss, met a philosophy professor from Kings College (London), the late Hywel Lewis. Lewis was looking for a psychologist to teach the psychology of religion, and I think I was the only psychologist that Brian knew who didn't think religion was a meaningless word. So I began teaching the psychology of religion, which got me interested in personality theory, including psychodynamic theory, and psychometrics, as well as doing the kind of research in which the researcher collects accounts of people's experiences. I am still a bit confused about what personality is, and about what is being measured in psychometrics, but in spite of this (or, more likely, because of this) I began teaching personality, and psychometrics. Meanwhile the number of my children grew, and I began wondering about Brown and Harris's (1978) report that women with several young children to care for, were more vulnerable to depression. The anthropologist Jeanette Kupferman (1979) thought that strictly orthodox Jewish women might be more cheerful in their lifestyle full of boundaries and rules, large families notwithstanding. I wondered who was right. Tirril Harris was very encouraging about the idea of doing a replay of the Brown and Harris Camberwell and Hebridean studies among orthodox Jews, and I was happy to get some funding for this work. This led me deeper and deeper into issues relating to religion and mental health. As the younger children grew older, I began to write and publish more and more on different aspects of religion and mental health.

Cultural and religious issues in mental health

Why are cultural and religious issues important in mental health? Ideally I would like to start with some nice-sounding suggestions about spirituality, and the importance of profound religious feelings and spiritual awareness for psychological balance and adjustment. I would not want to deny the importance of these feelings and states of awareness, and I have personally been involved in work which generally supports the importance of these, empirically (e.g. Loewenthal and Cinnirella, 1999; Loewenthal, Macleod et al., 2000). However, the generally positive relations between religion and better mental health mask a range of very complex effects, not all of them positive (e.g. Schumaker, 1992; Loewenthal, 1995; Bhugra, 1996; Pargament, 1997; Koenig, 1998). In particular, I should like to focus on a very big issue which can be illustrated with a series of vignettes:

> A dying Hindu in a British hospital manages to get out of bed and lies on the ground. Harassed nurses rush to replace the patient in the correct place — bed. The dying victim becomes deeply depressed or agitated. The efforts being made by the Hindu to die properly are being thwarted by the uncomprehending medical staff. A 'good death' involves lying on the ground. (Firth, 1997)

> 'It [speaking in tongues] is comforting, and you feel it helps. When my child was very ill in hospital, I sat by him and spoke [in tongues] for hours, but very quietly, so that the nurses would not notice and think I was odd.' (Christian man, quoted in Loewenthal, 2000)

> Louisa, a cult victim rescued by her family, was suffering from 'religious monomania'. Louisa in (enforced) confinement (in a psychiatric institution) was depressed, but '. . . walked up and down singing what she termed praises, making use of no intelligible words'. The Commissioners in Lunacy declared that '. . . her extraordinary and irrational opinions on

religion . . . were irreconcilable . . . with soundness of mind', but that apart from her religious opinions, she was competent, calm and rational (Schwieso, 1996). (It is interesting that there were cults, cult victims, and deprogramming attempts in the mid-nineteenth century.)

Two controlled studies suggested that otherwise identical cases are likely to be seen as suffering from more serious levels of psychological disturbance, if the people described are said to be religiously active. (Gartner *et al.*, 1990; Yossifova and Loewenthal, 1999)

I am labouring the point. Years ago, a fellow orthodox Jew warned me: 'You have to be careful of psychiatrists and psychologists and social workers. They can say that the kids are disturbed because they *shockel* [sway backwards and forwards as they are encouraged to do, when they study sacred texts]. Social workers can say the mothers are neglecting the children because they see a *sheitel* [wig, worn by a married woman for reasons of modesty]. They think the mother is spending her money and time on nonsense like wigs instead of looking after her family properly.' If you are Jewish you might be misjudged as neurotic or dysfunctional, simply on the basis of some normative piece of religious observance, and you don't want this to happen.

To stop this happening, you *might* think about changing or hiding your religious practices. But suppose that changing or hiding would mean a loss of spirituality, a feeling that you had severed yourself from your spiritual roots, and were denying your essential identity and purpose. In Judaism, religious commandments are called *mitzvot*, and the Hebrew word has an ambiguity (through a similar Aramaic word). It also means binding, being close. So it would painful to change or hide those practices and beliefs which give spiritual satisfaction, feeling close to G-d, even if this means misjudgement by others. What else might one do? One might try to set up a liaison system with the medical and psychological and social services. This has been done, although noone seems to have much evidence on the results. And one might set up culture-sensitive support services, using provision from within the community, drawing on outside expertise where possible (Bhui and Olajide, 1999). This has also been done, although, again, noone seems to have much evidence on the results. Culture-sensitive support is politically correct, but how does it function and does it work?

In the rest of this chapter I would like to describe some themes emerging from an interview study on culture-sensitive support groups serving the strictly orthodox Jewish community. What is this community?

The strictly orthodox Jewish community in the UK

The Jewish community in the UK is tiny, estimated at less than one-third of a million. One way of categorizing the differences in lifestyle within the community, is by level of religious orthodoxy. An unknown number are not affiliated to any synagogue, but it has been suggested that this unknown number might be quite small, because synagogue affiliation gives burial rights, and it is thought that most Jews want to ensure a religiously correct burial. Of those who *are* affiliated, about 15% are affiliated to a strictly orthodox group, 15% non-orthodox, and the remainder are affiliated to a centrist orthodox synagogue (Shmool and Cohen, 1990). The strictly orthodox will adhere closely to the religious laws regulating the observance of the Sabbath and holidays — for example not using motorized transport, or using electrical appliances. Dietary laws, for example, the strict separation of meat and dairy products in the kitchen, and in eating: marriage laws; monogamous sex only, and no intercourse during and after wife's menstrual period: education; the study of sacred texts and religious law, and a host of other religious guidelines regulating behaviour, from using the lavatory, to the heights of religious ecstasy, from the cradle to the grave, all mean that almost all strictly orthodox Jews find it impossible or very inconvenient to live outside one of the few enclaves in the UK. There are several such enclaves, all offering kosher butchers and grocers, a host of synagogues, prayer and study houses, schools, ritual baths, and many other services essential to the maintenance of Judaism in this form. Communities are quite close-knit, with many family and neighbourhood ties, as well as connections by marriage to strictly orthodox communities in other parts of the world. Women may have very few dealings outside the community. Outside the workplace, the same is usually true for men. One striking feature which dominates the economic, social and emotional life of the community is the value placed on large families. Contraception is normally prohibited, and the married state is strongly encouraged — men and women are regarded as spiritually incomplete, literally 'half-souls' unless and until they have found their soul-mate. The result is an average current family size of five (Loewenthal and Goldblatt, 1993). Families with ten or more children are commonplace. This can have striking effects, both beneficial and harmful, on the emotional wellbeing of the parents (Loewenthal, et al. 1997a; 1997b), and of the children. Many of these effects remain to be studied.

There are several strictly orthodox enclaves in the UK: Manchester, North and North-West London, and Gateshead are the largest, and their streets are peopled with men in dark suits or caftans, black or fur hats, often bearded, and often escorting a quota of young children to school, synagogue, shops or the park. There are modestly dressed women, the younger ones usually pushing a pushchair and surrounded by a bevy of young children. There are distinctive shops, for example selling kosher meat or Jewish books. There may be signs of the festivals: for example in the autumn, leafy booths (*sukkot*) in yards and gardens and on balconies, in the winter, eight-branched candlesticks (*Chanukias*) in windows, and sometimes in public places. A typical house will have a respectable room lined with gold-lettered *seforim* (Jewish books), with a large table used for Sabbath and festive meals, used during the week for (religious) study. There is usually a large kitchen with two sinks (one for meat food, one for dairy food) and space for the family to eat and for children to play. Strictly orthodox families seldom or never eat away from home: most restaurants are not *kosher*, and those that are kosher are beyond the means of the normal strictly orthodox family. There might be an occasional visit to a relative or friends, but not too often — to entertain a family with, say, eight-plus young children is not a simple undertaking. So, without remission, the mother has a major catering operation, several meals a day, sometimes eaten in shifts, for averages of around seven people, often ten or fifteen or more. Her work is never done, and she has to keep it going no matter how ill or exhausted she may feel. The unremitting demands do not go away just because she has given birth, or has flu, or has to help or visit an elderly parent who is suddenly taken ill. The floor may be cluttered with play objects and playing children. The bedrooms will be crowded, with sleeping accommodation and cupboard space for four or more children in each. The washing machine whirrs incessantly, and there are daily massive piles of laundry to be folded and put away. Children get bored, upset, start arguing, need help with homework, start doing something constructive but with dangerous or messy or destructive consequences. The telephone and the doorbell add to the multiple demands, and life is one unremitting attempt to do many things simultaneously, to prioritise, to assert that it is simply not possible to respond to all demands, to keep a measure of cool, to keep speaking pleasantly, to monitor and influence the spiritual, moral, intellectual, social and practical skills development of each child. To care for the welfare and well-being of each member of the family, including her own. To try to stop the house falling down or becoming irretrievably cluttered. To stop hoping that she will ever get a night's sleep. To try to feed and clothe, house and educate eight or ten or fifteen people on an income more appropriate for a family of three or four. All this is religiously and socially encouraged. Each child is valued. But, like mountaineering, the costs and risks are high.

I have written this last description from the woman's perspective because it is my own. I have included it because it now seems to be important, in understanding a central issue for most of the support groups I am examining. As I write, I wonder how I coped when there were ten children at home, including several of preschool age, and over 20 years of being pregnant, nursing, or both. I wonder how I cope now, when most of them are married but keep closely in touch, and often come to stay with excited gangs of lively grandchildren. I hope it is apparent that coping is difficult, and that any extra demand could tip a very precarious balance. I am quite sure that the social and managerial skills required for bringing up and coping with a large family are completely different from those involved in dealing with an average-sized family. And it isn't just coping with the physical chores: it is bringing up children and adolescents and young adults to the religious practices and the spiritual and moral values inherent in strictly orthodox Judaism.

Culture-sensitive support groups: how do they work and how are they perceived?

I am conducting a study of culture-sensitive support groups serving the strictly orthodox Jewish community in North London. Here live about

15,000 Jews, in an ethnically and religiously diverse area falling within the London boroughs of Hackney and Haringey. To qualify as a listed community member you have to belong to one of numerous synagogues affiliated to the Union of Orthodox Hebrew Congregations. This involves being *Shomer Shabbos* (Sabbath observant) and adhering to the dress codes, and norms with regard to lifestyle, kosher diet, education of children, prayer, marriage, and other matters.

Communal charitable organisations have a long history in Judaism. These might provide meals for the sick, help for needy brides, support for families where the breadwinner has died or is disabled. More recently, particularly over the last decade, the community has seen a growth of organisations offering a less material kind of support; counselling, telephone helplines, and support groups. Many of the organisations offering practical services and information are saying that there is a need for situation-specific counselling and support, which they are now beginning to provide.

While writing this chapter, I scanned the four weekly publications widely available in the community: two newspapers, and two magazines full of fascination for the social anthropologist, carrying nothing but advertisements for goods and services for the community. Each carried one or two advertisements for a charitable or support group. Advertising, however, is expensive, and the existing services cannot afford to advertise on a regular basis. They rely on a directory issued approximately yearly by one of the newspapers serving the community, and on listings in the *Shomrei Shabbos* telephone directories, listing the telephone numbers of community members, schools, synagogues and other religious institutions, businesses, and support services. Finally, there is word of mouth.

The current *Shomrei Shabbos* directory lists several dozen support services, charitable organisations and social groups.

I selected eight groups offering either general counselling and support services, or situation-specific counselling and support. I am interviewing a key informant from each of the groups, to discover their accounts of each group's history and activities, problems and plans. I am also interviewing 24 randomly-selected members of the community being served by these groups, to learn how much is known about these groups, perhaps to hear some direct and indirect reports of experiences with these groups, and to learn whether community members would use their services.

What follows is an account of some of the emerging themes. I have confined the quotations to material about three of the groups:

- *Chai:* the word *Chai* means 'Life', and the group is a cancer support group offering information, a helpline, counselling, alternative therapies, financial help for specific services, screening, and other services, in a culture-sensitive environment;
- *Ezer LeYoldos:* the term means 'help for women who have given birth', and the group offers support to women who have given birth, in the form of meals, help with other children, and help with housework. Recently the group has expanded its activities to include counselling, courses in parenting skills, befriending, advocacy, and links with a

culture-sensitive childbirth preparation and labour support group;
- *Chizuk*: the term means encouragement and support. This group offers support to orthodox Jews suffering from mental illness, and their carers. It organises care packages, support groups and drop-ins, hospital visiting and other services and activities, including some counselling.

From the service providers

A sense of urgency, and of dedication in the face of difficulties

Almost all the groups were founded by women, typically initially one woman, often getting together a nucleus of two or three, with a sense of mission. Almost every group is an outcome of a critical experience, or a series of experiences. These gave birth to a feeling that the Jewish person is not comfortable, not fully understood, and not well enough supported, when she or he passes through this critical experience and receives support from someone outside the community, no matter how professional or well-intentioned:

(Chai) *My mother suffered from a rare form of cancer. At the time I was a young woman with young children. I was the person most actively involved with my mother's care. At that time there was very little information available (for the public, for patients, and for their families). Doctors did not want to talk. That was not the climate of the time. Feelings were not considered. Doctors were focused on the disease only. It was very hard to get information, and it was also very difficult to get appropriate practical support. I felt it would have been helpful for my mother to speak to someone who had experienced cancer, and who had survived, so that she could see that there could be light at the end of the tunnel. It was hard to find former cancer patients to come and speak to her, because many (former cancer patients) wanted to put it behind them. I remember her lying ill in bed, and saying, please G-d, when I get through this I will make it my business to go and speak to people. Jewish people ... have feelings and problems to which other people could not relate.*

(Ezer LeYoldos) *It began when a niece of (the founder's, AZ) asked her for help: the niece was expecting her ninth baby, and she needed help. AZ realised that friends and family are often overloaded and cannot provide all the help that is really needed at such a time. So AZ started a group of ladies to send in freshly prepared meals for the family for two weeks after the birth of the baby, and to send in cleaning help, and make childcare arrangements during the mother's confinement, or when a mother is ill.*

Each of these informants has a similar sequence of events:

Critical experience >> realising that Jewish support would be helpful >> thinks about setting up a support group >> talks to others who are supportive >> starts work on setting up the group.

This did not happen in a political and social vacuum. Very few such organisations were around ten years ago. In the early 1990s it became possible and desirable for culture-sensitive support groups to develop. The reasons for this are beyond the scope of this chapter to consider. Through the 1990s, terms like *politically correct, ethnic minority, culture-sensitive, empowerment* spread into the lexicon, empowering those who wished to develop culture-sensitive support for ethnic minorities, endowing them with the politically correct kitemark. As well as social approval, there were occasional financial tit-bits: local authority funding, lottery grants, charity funding, and gifts from private donors. Never enough, but enough to make the coordinators feel that their venture is justified. But the struggle to make ends meet is a thankless one.

Need for a culture-sensitive service

These, and all other informants, reflected concerns about feeling comfortable, feeling understood. The myriad specific ways in which potential misunderstandings might occur were potently expressed by the coordinators of the support groups. Every single group is dealing with a huge load of culture-specific, spiritually-related values, assumptions, experiences, fears and other feelings.

(Chai) *People remote from Judaism come in and feel more comfortable. It is now accepted that each group needs its own specific care. For example, Jewish patients before Rosh Hashanah [New Year] or other Yomim Tovim [festivals], may have feelings and problems to which other people could not relate. Every ethnic or religious minority group needs its own support system. Going back to roots gives a feeling of stability and comfort. People walk in here and feel at home. We cater for people across the religious spectrum but our standards are such that the strictly orthodox would feel comfortable, for example the strictest kashrus [dietary laws], tznius [laws relating to modesty, usually applied specifically to modesty in dress]. The patients don't have to wander around not properly dressed. There is a dress code for all staff in the centre so that they won't offend anyone.*

These concerns about dress are not 'just' about being prudish, old-fashioned, up-tight. This informant is telling us of one of the many practical ways in which a culturally and religiously-sensitive support group helps clients to feel comfortable. Clients may not even be aware of the efforts that have been made. But these efforts enable clients to escape the discomforts of acting as an awkward patient, of being judged as difficult and prudish, when asked to wear religiously unacceptable hospital gowns which (for example) don't close properly, or don't cover the arms. The orthodox Jew genuinely feels positive spiritual value in modest dress, in treating the body with respect, in dealing with body as a means of expressing holiness. But it is difficult to communicate this in the context of the pressured hospital environment.

Ezer LeYoldos deals with the problems of mothers with large families trying to recover from childbirth, or to weather an illness that might be trivial if she could take it easy for a day or so. But she can never take it easy. I have first-hand experience of the problems, and time and time again I, my friends, my daughters, and countless others, have felt that the statutory service workers — nurses, doctors, midwives, health visitors, social workers, and other experts on child care — have totally failed to grasp the quality and enormity of the tasks faced by mothers of large families. At the same time, I have found it very hard to communicate *why we do it*. It is as if the 'outsider' is saying: 'If it is so hard, why do it? If you want to do it, you must see a purpose in it, and that somehow makes it easy.' The believing Jew (and believers of other religious traditions) feels that each soul that is brought into the world into a human body is precious; each has spiritually significant tasks to accomplish; the parents are privileged to be the means of enabling this. *But it is still difficult.*

It is difficult to communicate with someone who is not familiar with the spiritual values and assumptions that underlie child-bearing and child-rearing. Each child is precious, a spiritual gem. Outsiders might think the system is crazy. Just learn to use contraceptives, limit your family to a level that you can cope with. They do not understand. They might think I am crazy. Or bigoted. Or narrow-minded. Or ignorant. Or oppressed. Even if they said nothing, I might think that they were thinking those things. They could not really listen. *I would not feel comfortable or understood.*

(Ezer LeYoldos) *From the cultural point of view, patterns of crises among orthodox Jewish children and families differ from patterns in wider society. Most crises involve childbirth or illness, i.e. when the mother of a large family is not available. Illness is a crisis which does not affect just one or two people, when a parent is affected. We are holding up many people, by providing support during illness or at the time of childbirth. We try to catch crises before they become irreversible. It is a huge investment to hold a family together, in order to build stable citizens.*

Every single one of these support organisations deals with myriads of interlocking behaviours, values and assumptions that, it is felt, could not be readily explained to outsiders. If we tried to explain our feelings and our problems, they would not understand. Or we feel they would not understand.

Confidentiality
'We live in a goldfish bowl,' said one participant. Perhaps an aquarium, where the dwellers in each glass bowl can watch the goings-on in the other bowls. There is stigma associated with every one of the issues which the support groups have been set up to deal with: cancer, coping, or failing to cope, with family demands, stress, mental illness, loneliness . . . several authors have described the orthodox Jewish woman's wish to see herself as the perfect *baalabusta* (mistress of the household), always cheerful, warmly welcoming and hospitable, immaculate home, well-behaved children, all healthy and doing well in their spiritual and moral and interpersonal development, who manages to run the home and support the family, while enabling the husband to engage in prayer and religious study (Goshen-Gottstein, 1987; Loewenthal, 1998). It can be hard to admit to deviations from this ideal, this picture of perfection. It can take some courage to seek help.

(Chai) *The strictly orthodox are very worried about confidentiality. Some clients will only give their first names. They may not feel comfortable in our support*

groups (because they are seen and can be recognised by other people).
(Chizuk) *One problem is stigma, and the related problem of confidentiality. In a small closed community like this, these are difficult issues. There is a lack of suitable venues. It is important that clients do not have to go buildings where it is obvious why they are going.*

The issue of confidentiality may be the biggest problem faced by culture-sensitive support groups. My colleagues and I have certainly heard strong concerns about this issue from other minority groups (Cinnirella and Loewenthal, 1999; Loewenthal and Cinnirella, 1999). How *can* you provide support and understanding from within the community, if your clients are afraid that 'everyone' will get to know that they are depressed, or have cancer, or are not coping? Maybe a therapist who may not comprehend whole areas of experience is a fair price to pay for comfortable anonymity. The support groups are making extraordinary efforts to ensure confidentiality, but the concerns and fears remain, permanent items on the agenda.

From the community

The community informants had been randomly selected from community listings, and most of them had not had first-hand experience of using support groups, and some groups were not known to every informant. But most people interviewed in the community were aware of most of the groups' main functions, and some had heard of others' experiences, and some had first-hand experiences. The themes that emerged mirrored and reflected those emerging from the interviews with the people running the groups. The inspiration and dedication expressed by the coordinators is reflected in admiration and praise from the community (though this is sometimes qualified). The coordinators' perception that people will feel more comfortable and better understood in a culture-sensitive service is reflected in the community participants' views that people would and do feel more comfortable in these groups. And the coordinators' concerns with stigma and confidentiality are reflected in the concerns and fears expressed by the community participants.

Admiration for the work done by the groups
(Chai) *They provide good information.*
(Chai) *It is for cancer support. It does wonderful things.*
(Ezer LeYoldos) *It is marvellous. My daughter wants to put her name down to help.*
(Ezer LeYoldos) *I only heard about it recently. I heard that they will pay for help after the mother has given birth, and help with babysitting, and so on. I was very impressed. I would certainly want to use them.*
(Chizuk) *I have heard people say that it is helpful . . . Builds confidence.*
(Chizuk) *It is a pop-in place for people with problems . . . a very good thing.*

'Good', 'wonderful', 'marvellous', 'helpful', 'very impressed', 'a very good thing' — these are reassuring things for the hard-working coordinators to hear. There are concerns, as we shall see, but there is a fundamental positive appreciation.

Feel safe, understood

(Chai) *Jewish people would feel more secure and more supported with other Jewish people. They have very specific problems which would not be understood by non-Jews.*

(Chizuk) *I believe that anyone can walk in and you cannot tell who is a volunteer and who has mental health problems. That is much better than private meetings with psychiatrists.*

(Chizuk) *If you have a problem you can phone them up and they will recommend the right people, the right doctors (who will understand the needs of orthodox Jewish people).*

The community understands why these groups are there, and what their fundamental advantage is. But there is a 'but'…

Concerns about confidentiality and stigma

(Ezer LeYoldos) *I would only consider using it if it was government funded and available for everyone . . . otherwise it should be reserved for those in real need.*

(Ezer Leyoldos) *I wonder what type of families need this? Is it just those who can't cope? I might feel ashamed to ask for such help.*

(Ezer LeYoldos) *My daughter works for them, but she never discusses the families that she goes to help, as it is confidential.*

(Chizuk) *Do they still meet in Stamford Hill Library? I only know about them from reading advertisements, and Boruch Hashem (thank G-d) have had no need for anything like this. I would think that many people would prefer something more confidential than an open meeting.*

These members of the community do indicate general admiration for the work of the groups. At the same time there is the cleft stick, the inherent conflict between the safety and understanding offered by community-led support, and the threat and fear that the client and her family may become known and stigmatized precisely because she is using a community-led service.

Conclusion

In this conclusion I would like to recapitulate on the emerging themes, and reflect on two issues that are latent in the material, the first to do with gender, and the second to do with spirituality.

In describing themes, I have not picked up on every single theme that emerged from these interviews. This is largely because of my wish to try to tell a story that is not overburdened with too many intricacies and subplots. There were other themes, for example to do with funding and fund-raising, professionalism, and the role of the rabbinate.

The themes that have emerged clearly at this point do relate to each other, and are reflected in the accounts of the groups' coordinators, and in the knowledge and experiences and views of the community informants. These are the sense of a real need for a culture-sensitive service, in which people will feel comfortable and understood. This is appreciated by the community. At the same time, there is a down-side, and this is part and parcel of providing a service in a community in which managing to be a perfect wife and mother of many children is religiously-valued and spiritually-fulfilling. Failure is stigmatizing, and thus confidentiality is a huge issue. This leads to an intrinsic paradox, a contradiction which both the service providers and the community have sensed and are struggling to come to terms with. On the one hand, it is comfortable to be supported by other orthodox Jews, who can understand one's feeling and experiences, but on the other hand, one does not want the community to know about one's difficulties. All the groups have developed and are developing strategies for dealing with this issue of confidentiality. The issue has quite different dimensions from those normally seen in professional practice. Some of the solutions involve contortions which are quite clearly appropriate, but which might never appear in a standard professional code-of-practice manual. For example one voluntarily-staffed helpline will never try to raise funds for its rental and training expenses by approaching likely donors within the community — in case these donors might have used, or might think of using the helpline, and be concerned that they might be recognised.

Finally, two latent issues. The first is *gender*. Even though I have lived in this community for most of my adult life, well over 30 years, and although I thought I understood the profound ways in which gender and gender-related roles are seen as routes to spiritual fulfilment, I was still startled by the minor and peripheral roles played by men in these support groups, both as providers and as users. My first 'explanation' is that this was a conclusion caused by my culture-sensitive approach to doing research in this community. In this community, it would not be considered very appropriate for a woman to ask to interview a man, and in previous research I have found that gender-matching of researchers and research participants is most comfortable and yields the best results. So I recruited community participants by writing to the female head of household, mentioning in the letter, however, that I would be happy to interview any one adult member of the household. In the follow-up telephone call, I have suggested that I interview a male household member, where this seems appropriate, where the woman approached has not been able or willing. This resulted in only one male participant. Similarly, the support groups, with only one exception, have been developed by women. The focus is often on women and their specific needs, though I have not discovered whether the majority of callers to the several helplines available are women. In running the groups, men are called upon to play very specific roles — funding committees are often seen as men's work, and so too is the provision of rabbinic advice and approval. These roles are seen as essential, but peripheral to the main business of providing practical and psychological support. Where groups have been set up to provide for needs that exist among men as well as women, the men are often seen as more difficult to provide for. It may be that there is a whole other world of masculine support, but there is little trace of them. The support groups that I accessed through the community directory were generally run by women, and either focused on women's needs, or where the needs were ungendered, men were often seen as less interested, or more difficult to provide for.

The second latent issue is *spirituality*. When I first thought about writing this chapter, I had thought about considering spiritual and religious issues that genuinely do come in therapy. I have written about some of these elsewhere (e.g. Loewenthal, 1995; 2000). But there was no sign of such issues emerging explicitly in the interviews and discussion I have had about these support groups. Nevertheless, as I have tried to indicate in this chapter, these issues are latent. Having provided a service in which the providers and clients share religious and spiritual values, the need for these to come into explicit focus is eliminated. Having children is a spiritual activity, having faith that G-d will provide the means to support them is a fundamental belief, loving one's fellow and providing for his or her needs is a fundamental value. And one that seems to underlie the provision of the groups that I have described in this chapter.

Acknowledgements

Most of the work described here was enabled by a Research Fellowship from the Leverhulme Trust. This has provided a wonderful opportunity for an aging researcher to go back to actually recruiting and doing all the interviews in a project. Thank you Leverhulme Trust. And thank you to Brooke Rogers, who undertook many of my teaching duties, as well as support work on this project, which enabled me to conduct the interviewing, analysis and writing. I would also like to thank my husband and family for their patience and support, and also my colleagues at Royal Holloway, including Rosemary Westley for her perennial willingness to provide financial and other information, advice and help. The Rabbinate of the Union of Orthodox Hebrew Congregations, particularly Dayan A. D. Dunner, have enabled the project to go ahead by offering time, advice and approval. Finally, thanks to the coordinators of the groups, and to the members of the community, who gave their time to describe their experiences of these important expressions of human goodness.

References

Bhugra, D. (Ed.) (1996) *Psychiatry and Religion: Context, Consensus, and Controversies.* London: Routledge.

Brown, G., and Harris, T.O. (1978) *The Social Origins of Depression.* London: Tavistock.

Cinnirella, M., and Loewenthal, K.M. (1999) Beliefs about the causes and cures of mental illness among different cultural-religious groups in Great Britain.

British Journal of Medical Psychology, 72, 505–24

Firth, S. (1997) *Dying, Death and Bereavement in a British Hindu Community.* Leuven: Peeters.

Gartner, J., Hermatz, M., Hohmann, A., and Larson, D. (1990) The effect of patient and clinician ideology on clinical judgment: a study of ideological countertransference. Special issue: Psychotherapy and religion. *Psychotherapy, 27,* 98–106

Goshen-Gottstein, E. (1987) Mental health implications of living in an ultra-orthodox Jewish subculture. *Israel Journal of Psychiatry, 24,* 145–66

Koenig, H.G. (1998) (Ed.) *Handbook of Religion and Mental Health.* New York: Academic Press.

Kupferman, J. (1979) *The MsTaken Body.* London: Paladin.

Loewenthal, K.M. (1995) *Mental Health and Religion.* London: Chapman and Hall.

Loewenthal, K.M. (1998) Haredi women, Haredi men, stress and distress. *Israel Journal of Psychiatry, 35,* 217–24

Loewenthal, K.M. (2000) *The Psychology of Religion: A Short Introduction.* Oxford: Oneworld/Penguin.

Loewenthal, K.M., Goldblatt, V., Gorton, T., Lubitsh, G., Bicknell, H., Fellowes, D., and Sowden, A. (1997a) The costs and benefits of boundary maintenance: Stress, religion and culture among Jews in Britain. *Social Psychiatry and Psychiatric Epidemiology, 32,* 200–7

Loewenthal, K.M., Goldblatt, V., Gorton, T. Lubitsh, G., Bicknell, H., Fellowes, D., and Sowden, A. (1997b) The social circumstances of anxiety among Anglo-Jews. *Journal of Affective Disorders, 46,* 87–94

Loewenthal, K.M., and Cinnirella, M. (1999) Beliefs about the efficacy of religious, medical and psychotherapeutic interventions for depression and schizophrenia among different cultural-religious groups in Great Britain. *Transcultural Psychiatry, 36,* 491–504

Loewenthal, K.M., and Goldblatt, V. (1993) Family size and depressive symptoms in orthodox Jewish women. *Journal of Psychiatric Research, 27,* 3–10.

Loewenthal, K.M., MacLeod, A.K., Goldblatt, V., Lubitsh, G., and Valentine, J.D. (2000) Comfort and Joy: Religion, cognition and mood in individuals under stress. *Cognition and Emotion, 14,* 355–74

Pargament, K.I. (1997) *The Psychology of Religion and Coping: Theory, research and practice.* New York: Guilford Press.

Schumaker, J. (Ed.) (1992) *Religion and Mental Health.* Oxford: Oxford University Press.

Schwieso, J.J. (1996) 'Religious fanaticism' and wrongful confinement in Victorian England: The affair of Louisa Nottidge. *The Social History of Medicine, 9,* 158–74

Shmool, M. and Cohen, F. (1990) *British Synagogue Membership in 1990.* London: Research Unit of the Board of Deputies of British Jews.

Yossifova, M. and Loewenthal, K.M. (1999) Religion and the judgement of obsessionality. *Mental Health, Religion and Culture, 2,* 145–52

Clinician in the Church: Veritable angel or tolerated guest?

11

Michael Len

There are anomalous and uniquely unconventional aspects in the professional life of a qualified clinician if clients are employees of a Christian church organisation or members of a monastically based religious order. Such discordant workday nuances are more exaggerated than those experienced by a secular in-house specialist who is valued, consulted and respected for expertise and experience, e.g. a mental health nurse specialist in a clinic or a psychiatric social worker in a hospital. Nor is the provision of ethical, professional and well-regarded therapeutic services made easier if the clinician were a clergywoman in the town or a fully vowed 'religious' in the convent. Unfortunately and surprisingly, these are observations backed by personal experience, research and anecdotal evidence.

The role of a clinical consultant in the church setting, whether or not ordained in a parish or resident within the cloisters, is fraught with ambiguity and unpredictability. At best, a trained and even talented psychology-affiliated professional is a tolerated guest − seated at the low end of the table − and rarely deemed an angel in disguise. And therein lies the paradox; such a specialist is very much needed by those whose careers are church-based. So often that which is confrontational and disruptive among church staff could be ameliorated by the competencies by virtue of formal training in one of the clinical professions.

Yet it is the exceptional church body which enthuses about a professional in its ranks. Even Fr Damien, the psychiatrist-priest in *The Exorcist*, revealed that he had been sent for training only after joining his order, leading one to question whether he would have been admitted were he already a clinician. Why isn't the welcome mat out for a person who is competent and conversant in psychosocial evaluations, counselling techniques, problem solving, crisis intervention, and treatment planning − who wishes to do good, in the manner of the 'good book', and not necessarily do well, as in the area of the bank book? This chapter will address that issue and view the life of the professional 'serving' church members as well as some noteworthy aspects of the counsellor's role while simultaneously a full-fledged member of the church hierarchy.

Are we 'secular priests'?

It would be accurate to use that cliché to describe therapists. For convenience I will use the following terms in synonymous fashion: professional, consultant, clinician, mental health specialist, counsellor, therapist, social worker, psychotherapist, psychologist — to indicate an individual trained to deal with matters pertaining to behaviour, emotions and relationships. My use of the titles priest, minister, clergy, religious, vowed, chaplain and cleric will likewise be used synonymously for persons employed by Christian religious bodies and spiritual residential organisations, whether or not they are financially remunerated.

Therapists are indeed as closely involved with their clients as parish priests and chaplains are with congregants. 'Psychotherapy can in part be likened to a confession; a more searching and more intimate confession than usual' (de Berker, 1996). Aspects such as explicit rather than implied rules of confidentiality, informed consent, fee-for-service, and secular premises may even make for more and fuller 'confessions' than would the church arena where clerics are known to the entire family and are a familiar presence at social events.

However, the church and the cloister give no credence to these facts. In the world of religion, what matters are the espousing of vows — being 'vowed', or consecrated, and becoming a religious, i.e. a nun or monk — or the ordination process for ministers-priests, i.e. official recognition by a denominational governing body as a precursor to assuming leadership in the name of that denomination. Any qualification in a secular profession is of secondary import.

Sometimes having a clinical career can even be a hindrance when answering 'the call' and seeking to be ordained or vowed:

> *James was a qualified psychotherapist who contracted for professional supervision from me. Exploration of his background revealed that he had been refused entry into an ordination programme by his minister, a decision seconded by the minister's boss, a bishop. Some of the reasons were: 'You knew I was having trouble with [my wife] yet you never asked me how I was [coping].' James replied that he did not want to appear to be currying favour, especially while seeking ordination. He feared any overture would lead to discussion — this minister being extremely verbose — which might later be misinterpreted as intrusive, interfering and controlling. His mindset as a professional included the essentials of ethics, confidentiality, proper referral, etc. The bishop, meanwhile, cryptically advised the minister that ordination might negatively affect James' functioning as a psychotherapist. This comment and the minister's: 'You don't act like other psychotherapists', bewildered James. Neither man had any training in the field of therapy, which might have led to those suppositions. Interestingly, the minister was like no other James knew either, for he abandoned his wife of 30 years and married a congregant with whom he 'had been doing marriage counselling' and who had two young children. The bishop later resigned over issues involving diocesan financial misjudgement.*

This example illustrates a significant difference between the two roles in practice and policy vis-à-vis social fraternisation, sexual liaisons, and sexual impropriety. These actions by a clinician are universally deemed unethical and even subject to legal prosecution and forfeiture of credentials (Len and Fischer, 1978). The church meanwhile acts on a case-by-case basis when incidents of a sexual nature are brought to its attention, even if the occurrence occurred in a counselling setting or involved minors. So it can be said that the clergy and the vowed have it all ways — functioning as therapists, even with impunity should they not necessarily have been trained to do so; not being bound by principles of counselling ethics and conflicts-of-interest; and not necessarily being liable to disciplinary action should they transcend professional rules of conduct.

Returning to the matter of refusing James' entry into the church's power-holding, decision-making offices: it could be assumed that a simple jurisdictional attitude enters, e.g. 'you already have a trade, why are you trying to take the living of someone who wants her first career?' And the deliberate avoidance of credence given psychological counselling could result from the innocuous phenomenon of having a 'healthy suspicion of worldly occupations'.

More disreputably, however, it might be the case that the already vowed or ordained incumbent feels she has everything under control, thank you; that she has a 'direct line to God'; and that collegiality, consultation, peer review, supervision, and second opinions are unnecessary.

This officious attitude is more prevalent when the clergy, monks, and nuns themselves do counselling and spiritual advising. They may even realise they have none or not as much of the requisite training in therapy as has the professional. Hospitals in the United Kingdom, for example, hire for clinical chaplaincy primarily those in the ordained ministry, and rarely require other relevant training. Yet this is a pivotal position, involving close interaction with patients, their families and even staff members in distress or in great emotional need. This is not the case in New Zealand, Canada, America and even some non-western countries, where Clinical Pastoral Education qualifications are required — CPE being a closely supervised, highly structured course of months of didactic and experiential learning in mental health counselling, human dynamics and relationship, rules of confidentiality, communication skills, etc.

Interestingly, this again highlights a major difference: the training for entry into most clinical professions does not include — and in fact codes of ethics may explicitly preclude — any in-depth advising on a client's spirituality, beliefs, and religious preferences. It would be the unusual practitioner who dialogues in these areas with someone who presents for, say, family counselling. Yet even without clinical pastoral education of any kind most clergy would not hesitate to engage a congregant in 'secular' counselling, i.e. on an issue not related to spiritual matters. To be fair, the role of eclectic advisor had been a major part of a minister's job before the advent of highly trained and qualified professionals and specialists. But in this day of collegiality and specialisation, it seems a disservice to clients to maintain a territorial attitude which in effect says: 'as I am in direct contact with God, according to the organised church, I am therefore entitled to deal with all matters brought to me . . . I can handle it all; why should I refer out? And we certainly do not need in our ranks any of those other professionals'.

Are professionals necessary or valued?

Many professionals believe that they 'are first and foremost people, and only secondly theorists and technicians . . . need to draw from the richness of a wide range of disciplines and life experience, the arts, literature, philosophy, religion, the sciences, etc. for their work . . . [and need to] honour the parts of oneself that cannot be categorised, and recognise that which cannot be caught in any net of concepts or procedures' (Psychology and Psychotherapy Association, 2001). Such a practitioner who combines psychology, ethics in practice and clinical skills with a respect for the spiritual, the mystical, and the intuitive is a hybrid commodity seemingly suitable for inclusion in the religious-spiritual world. Open-minded and mature, inclusive and non-rejecting, non-judgemental — these are values integral to human growth and development as well as aligned with the acceptance of a supreme being, a higher power, and a divinity.

Nonetheless such talent and qualities are often overlooked and minimised by the clerical and cloistered world. Even after achieving ordination or vowed status the clinician's other profession and skills may be played down, and she herself occasionally ridiculed, as superfluous to dealing with the presenting problems of clergy colleagues or worshippers.

The following vignette illustrates this point:

> *Irene was granted temporary dispensation from living as a member of her cloister — she felt she needed a respite. She kept a foot in both camps — visiting the convent while maintaining employment with a counselling service. She confided that even her residential time with the sisters had never been comfortable due to the manner in which they viewed her 'touchy-feely' profession — as they described it. Nor had relations improved by living out. Of course, her no-confidence vote and move out of the house, however temporary, exacerbated matters. They became more disparaging, referring to her in manner, tone and explicitly as 'that woman'. She was making greater financial contribution to the order even though living elsewhere, and some members continued to seek her counselling services — these factors may have increased the jealousy on the part of the critics. So she was in a no-win situation.*
>
> *Irene was also castigated for seeking counselling herself when she realised that being a religious was not a panacea for her. She still had sexual identity problems, she still encouraged romantic liaisons with both genders and then sabotaged their success and she still remained indecisive about a return to 'a life in the habit'. She was amused, however, that she was viewed in bad light when she had intimate knowledge of the many psychological problems and internecine relationships existing in-house, e.g.*
>
> *1. the doubters, who now questioned the sincerity and fervour of their*

previous 'call' to the cloister; 2. the emotionally-devastated who, when given new assignments, grieved the loss of their previous high status and power; 3. the work-shy, mentioned in 'The Bell' (Murdoch, 1962), who present a sense of superiority and eminence elevated above manual labour, or, more pathologically, hypochondriasis and even a fear of being afflicted with chronic fatigue syndrome; 4. those blatantly suffering extreme mood disorders; 5. the closet alcoholics; 6. the snoopers who will not 'keep custody of their own eyes', prying into others' movements, liaisons, conversations, and even private quarters and correspondence; and 7. the tittle-tattle who runs to the house superior with gossip and the fruits of snooping forays.

Despite, or because of, such a roster of personalities, a counsellor in the cloister is often made to feel less than welcome — when obviously quite the reverse would be desirable. This is stark evidence that those who require therapeutic attention are often the most fearful or envious of those who can provide it.

Ethical and other professional concerns

There would be requests for special consideration should the cleric be allowed to practise professionally. These include time off to attend supervisory, peer support and continuing education sessions; permission for clients to use her secular title, Doctor, Sister (in the case of a nurse-practitioner) or Professor; extra funds for journal subscriptions, professional dues, liability insurance, and even fashionable clothing. If these demands become too unwieldy for the hierarchy, it can result in an ultimatum: 'choose . . . it's either us or your counselling job!'

A different scenario arises when congregations become very generous and tolerant of their leader's outside activities. Then it proves difficult to distinguish between the 'day-job' and the 'extras'.

Revd Dr John was one of my Masters of Social Work internship supervisors. He was working in a substance detoxification unit, having been released by the Catholic Church after his marriage. During our training relationship John acquired ordination in another denomination and was given a parish. We were colleagues for two decades, he even referring parishioners to me. He was a most energetic cleric cum counsellor — some of his interests and avocations: leadership in Alcoholics Anonymous; advising in several spiritual retreat movements; association in more than one private practice accredited in marriage-family-child therapy; office-holding in several professional groups; patrolling as a police chaplain; university-level research in the 'Twelve Step' Minnesota Model regime; acquisition of his doctorate; pastoral counselling lectures to ordination candidates; and perhaps more, of which I or even his worshippers were not aware. He boasted to me: 'They [my congregation] let me do whatever I want . . . It's easy [parish work] . . .' meaning he had so much discretionary time for mental health endeavours however loosely-connected with or entirely separate from church purview.

Come the questions: was he — and those like him who are salaried as full-time ministers but engaged in many outside interests — fleeing the parishioners and running toward the extra-curricular clientele, i.e. a twist on the traditional 'flight from the client' phenomenon? Was his busy schedule in any way doing disservice to his primary 'clientele' — his parishioners? How would his parochial outlook, ethics and ethos inform the counselling of his secular clients? Was John really signalling that he had lost his 'calling' for ministry, and that he was subconsciously easing toward a wholly secular life (unbeknownst to the group looking to and paying him to be primarily their minister)?

We hear more about and from the clergy and vowed who are bishops and cardinals, media commentators, best-selling authors, human potential gurus, chaplains to royalty, or even choir leaders. However, the vast majority who were attracted to church service were carers and pastors by nature. They even married partners with similar personalities. Perhaps some overestimate their capabilities and become too involved with their flock although they do not possess the proper qualifications and ethical grounding.

> *Sam and Jane had one of the larger, more prosperous churches in the city. They mixed with the fashionable, trendy set that could indulge in self-examination and human potential movements. Sam welcomed parishioners who sought counselling — and even touted his availability — although he had no clinical qualifications. Jane felt unfulfilled despite a part-time job in occupational therapy and entered into social work study at the university. She became inappropriately involved with their female counsellor when undergoing family therapy — a necessity as they had come to the point of living separately. Jane became the housemate of the former wife of Sam's ministerial predecessor. She began keeping company with the counsellor, even relating that she was receiving massage from her. She also made herself available as a counsellor to parishioners and suffered a reputation of befriending the wives of disputing couples in the congregation, i.e. 'taking sides'.*

Examples like this illustrate that clergy and their partners have more visibility, higher ascribed status, and a captive audience on whom to practise their brand of 'therapy'. Aside from any questionable aspects regarding their appropriateness for counselling others, i.e. even when they reconciled and when Jane finished her training, there would be thorny issues peculiar to their situation. Three which come to mind are that of confidentiality vis-à-vis clients they are both acquainted with; how they would cope with not being chosen over the other to help a mutual acquaintance, i.e. popularity issues; and jurisdictional or referral priorities, e.g. 'because she is with me in the choir, he is in the study group, etc. I should be her/his counsellor'.

Clinicians are needed

The film *JFK* depicted one of the principal plotters of the American President's assassination as a homosexual wronged by the church. 'All I wanted in the world was to be a Catholic priest, live in a monastery . . . pray to God. They defrocked me. All I had was this . . .', he laments. The audience is left with the impression that had he been allowed to continue his sincere calling he would not have led such a subsequently troubled life.

The experience of mental health clinician-clerics attempting to practise their profession resembles the ostracism suffered as well by gays and lesbians in churches: '[We] count among our many friends certain ministers, lay readers and preachers, choristers, organists and church members . . . all of them homosexual . . . Many have been eased or pushed out of the Church'. (Hopper, 1997).

It would have been reasonable to assume that church organisations discharged their unwanted members in a humane manner. The former monk in *JFK* suggests that he did not have a satisfactory closure to that episode in his life. And there is evidence noting that religious groups can be most unsympathetic and callous in such dealings. 'Unfortunately, religious houses have a very nasty habit of making those who leave them feel like criminals in the condemned cell. They treat them like pariahs . . . The day of departure arrived and he [was made to feel] as if he were suffering from the plague . . .' (Walker, 1981). 'Some of those who have left have experienced rather negative, uncaring and even vindictive attitudes . . . and made to feel a "traitor to the cause" . . . Excuses were made for not giving more help. No thanks were given for perhaps many decades of loyal service . . . "You have let us down . . . get on with it then . . . but don't expect us to support your 'irregular' lifestyle!"' (McCann, 1996). There is justification even on simple humanitarian grounds for a counselling professional to conduct exit interviewing, aftercare and referral to outside mental health resources. Even basic supportive counsel — everyday fare for professional social workers — would seem the least that could be offered, especially as it has been shown (Church, 1996) that the devastating effects of redundancy closely resemble the trauma suffered by terminally ill patients.

Counsellors can also be extremely useful in assisting those who entered the church or cloister as a means to escape from personal problems, found this was the wrong choice and are indecisive about remaining. Others who looked to religion simply as a practical means of earning a living and became disillusioned need counselling and guidance. It calls to mind a conversation held during a train journey with the proverbial English clergyman in the compartment; to paraphrase him: 'My son just graduated from university . . . he has no great desire to enter any other field . . . Why not be like the old man, and so he applied to the diocesan director of ordinands — why not!' And one can but smile at the comedy film *Kind Hearts and Coronets* with Sir Alec Guiness playing different members of the same family. Upon his appearance as the simple, doddering clergyman, the narrator chimes in with the explanation that it was typical for families of that period to send the child with least potential into the church.

Whatever the rationale for having sought religious employment, one would expect that the manner of separation from an organisation, which touts itself as kindly and charitable, should reflect those same qualities. And it would seem most efficient and ideal if a counsellor-cleric were available to serve those making the change. This versatile professional role would be well qualified for dealing not only with their emotional problems about spiritual guilt and separation, loss of identity and self-esteem, etc. but with practical matters regarding future stages in the ex-member's life.

It is much publicised today that serious ramifications occur when maladjusted personalities seek religious life. Priest and specialist consultant S. Rossetti (1995) writes: 'Sometimes people speculate that men with a sexual attraction to children might be drawn to the priesthood because of its requirement for celibacy. I suspect it is just as likely that some paedophiles are drawn to the priesthood because of the power the priest can wield [over the victim].' At times even the formal policies and procedures make for facile admission of those who can repress undesirable traits. Priest and former head of the Psychology Department at University College, Dublin, Professor E. F. O'Doherty (1971) confessed that the church was 'not particularly careful about [pathological] factors in the past . . . that if we apply categories of psychopathology to the discerning of vocations we shall lose a great many excellent vocations . . . [and that] there were saints who seem to have been neurotic but this does not mean that we should not try to discover neurotic and psychotic personalities . . . and decide that on psychological grounds they should not be incorporated into religious life.' He adds that 'with many young sisters entering religious life . . . the demands of the day and the prescribed exercises, and . . . the requirements of study during these years [mean that] there is not a single unfilled interval during the day when she can turn in and look at herself . . . The sexual problem subsides for awhile and she can coast along without recognising the problem.'

The presence of psychotherapists themselves in religious life would be of tremendous value as readily available sounding boards and learned advisors to those who struggle with their unique lives. Even those who are well-suited and prepared for their vocation find 'emotional starvation in various forms [imposed] upon them . . . they are lonely . . . they are always in demand; their time is not their own. Where can their own needs be satisfied?' (de Berker, 1996).

It might be appropriate to mention Jung's finding (1933), from an international survey: '. . . all the relatives of clergymen who answered my questionnaire pronounced themselves against the clergy' were they to find themselves in spiritual distress and had the choice of consulting a physician or a clergyman. An appropriate first step in confronting this embarrassing conviction would be the reduction of negative opinions about mental health clinicians and an increase of their numbers in church service. The gatekeepers and power brokers in the denominations and residential communities must lead this strategy. If a kinder view of the disciplines results from collegiality with their practitioners, church personnel might be more amenable to in-service training and continuing education in these fields.

Towards community

A clinician who has been ordained or undertaken vows can be of great benefit to the church and the cloistered community. It has been shown that even individuals trying to live by cooperation, tolerance, and a shared belief in a higher power would gain from the mediating influence of a specialist in human relations and mental health counselling.

Professionals are utilised at present: '... the mother superior ... will have to seek a second opinion, in borderline cases, from a psychiatrist, who must be a Roman Catholic' (Follain, 1999). But are they under-utilised, and is there added value when the specialist is in the ranks and actually living the same life? Some organisations recognise and even require this, e.g. many schools appoint as counsellors those who are or have been teachers; many police forces prefer to hire as legal advisors those individuals who had been sworn officers before or while undergoing legal training — higher regard is given to the expertise of those who have been or still are on the front lines.

It has to be said that their additional qualification is not always well regarded and their presence not always favoured even though they had been or are members of the in-group — exactly one of the points of this chapter. I am reminded of a black humour example of this while I served as civilian psychologist to members of the armed forces. My colleague flight-surgeon, i.e. a medical doctor, Naval Academy officer-graduate, flying with aircrews to assess their work first-hand, mentioned that he was made to endure his commanding officer barking out at a squadron-wide briefing: 'My flight-surgeon tells me you're all showing signs of stress — which may even affect your flying. Well, you've got exactly ten seconds to get rid of that so-called stress and get your air planes and your asses in the air!'

It would be more efficient in the first instance to welcome and accept those professionals who are as qualified as other candidates applying for the ministry and the cloisters. Their membership would allay suspicion and devaluation of these professions and the mental health field itself. The effort by the in-group to 'understand, work through, and obtain a more secure sense of self and more satisfactory relationships' (Kiesler and Van Denberg, 1993) would be made easier with the influence of those who possess and utilise sound interpersonal skills. Such qualities are part and parcel of clinical training but not necessarily included in theological and ministerial training. Whether an ordinand or novice is introduced to them and becomes competent in them is more a matter of chance than of certainty.

The rewards for including a seasoned counsellor into membership are several: morale would be enhanced if carers themselves are cared for; worshippers and pastoral clients would be served by emotionally healthier personnel, which itself brings secondary gains such as greater church participation and even increased financial contributions; and mechanisms can be put in place to deal with controversies and stressful events earlier rather than later, i.e. team-building groups, announced office hours, and peer counselling.

Therefore it is seems advantageous to work through admittedly bothersome professional concerns, some of which are detailed above, and create a hospitable environment for psychology, psychotherapy and counselling to exist alongside churchmanship and theology. By first being a caring place for its own carers, the church and the spiritual community would then have integrity in their calling as charities offering solace and healing to the needy. And its own survival is enhanced, for according to Bettelheim (1974): 'I am convinced communal life can flourish only if it exists for an aim outside itself. Community is viable if it is the outgrowth of a deep involvement in a purpose which is other than, or above that of [only] being a community.'

References

Bettelheim, B. (1974) *Home for the Heart*. London: Thames and Hudson.

Church, G.J. (1996) Disconnected. How ATT is planning to put 40,000 members of its workforce out of service. *Time, 147* (3), 44–5

de Berker, P. (1996) A priest alone. *The Tablet, 250*, 540

Follain, J. (1999) Nuns put faith in their shrink. *Sunday Times*, 15 August 1999.

Hopper, G.S.E. (1997) *Reluctant Journey. A pilgrimage of faith from homophobia to Christian love*. Leeds, UK: G.S.E. Hopper.

Jung, C.G. (1933) *Modern Man in Search of a Soul*. London: Routledge and Kegan Paul Ltd.

Kiesler, D.J. and Van Denberg, T.F. (1993) Therapeutic impact disclosure: a last taboo in psychoanalytic theory and practice. *Clinical Psychology and Psychotherapy, 1* (1), 3–13

Len, M.W.H. and Fischer, J. (1978) Clinicians' attitudes toward and use of four body contact or sexual techniques with clients. *Journal of Sex Research, 14* (1), 40–9

McCann, J.G. (1996) How does an ex-priest live? *The Tablet, 250*, 782

Murdoch, I. (1962) *The Bell*. Harmondsworth: Penguin.

O'Doherty, E.F. (1971) *Consecration and Vows. Psychological aspects*. Dublin: Gill and MacMillan Ltd.

Psychology and Psychotherapy Association. (2001) About the PPA. *Journal of Critical Psychology, Counselling and Psychotherapy, 1* (1), i

Rossetti, S. (1995) Child sexual abuse: a conversion of perspective. *The Tablet, 249*, 74–6

Walker, L.M. (1981) *Brothers of Habit. Life in a monastery*. London: Robert Hale Ltd.

Working with Survivors of Torture and Extreme Experiences 12

Kate Maguire

> *You talk when you cease to be at peace with your thoughts;*
> *And when you can no longer dwell in the solitude of your heart you*
> *live in your lips, and sound is a diversion and a pastime.*
> *And in much of your talking, thinking is half murdered.*
> **For thought is a bird of space that in a cage of words can indeed**
> **unfold its wings but cannot fly.**
> *. . . And there are those who talk, and without knowledge or forethought*
> *reveal a truth which they themselves do not understand.*
> *And there are those who have the truth within them, but they tell it not*
> *in words.*
> *In the bosom of such as these the spirit dwells in rhythmic silence.*
> Kahlil Gibran, The Prophet p. 76

People often ask me why I chose to be a psychotherapist who works with survivors of torture and extreme experiences. I think it has to do with the experience of so much pain in the world, a need to understand its meaning in our existence, to comprehend why we inflict it on each other individually and collectively and how to help each other survive it. Then they might ask how I can work in this field and not be affected. But I am affected, and sometimes I struggle to find the words to explain how. I think of many of the people I work with who have a distrust of words, seeing words as having paradoxical powers: building trust and betraying it, enlightening and contaminating, liberating and imprisoning, judging and accepting. So much depends on the listener. I hope I can find the right words so that you can hear the way I hear, and experience the way I experience, my encounters with these people who have given me more than I have given them, who have helped me to enter a place of pain where 'we see through a glass darkly but then face to face. The knowledge I have is imperfect; but then shall I know as fully as I am known' (I Corinthians 13: 12).

I am

I was born and brought up in a deprived area of Glasgow, one of seven children living in a tenement block. Violent things happened around us but our own immediate family surroundings were of love and safety. I remember crying a lot, not really knowing why. I remember sometimes feeling like a stranger, trying to understand this place I had arrived in, not knowing the language.

My earliest dark memory was not the suicide by hanging of our neighbour downstairs, or hearing a woman neighbour being battered to death by her husband with an iron; it was seeing a photograph in one of my father's war books before I had achieved reading age. It was of a very thin man, lying on the ground with his head raised slightly, looking at something burning in a little fire beside him. I was fascinated by this picture although I had no idea what it was about. But when I learned to read, the full horror of what I learned would not leave me and it remains with me today. It has informed my choices and my work. The caption was: *Inmate of concentration camp watches his own stomach being burned.* I did not want that to ever happen to me, to any of my family, to my friends. I did not want that to happen to anyone at all. I needed to know how that could happen, how to make it stop and how to help the man in the picture.

You are

I went to university, too young at 17, at the end of the 'sixties and I studied Psychology thinking this would best help me with my task, help me not to be afraid. I combined it with Social Anthropology because I loved the name and the mysteries it promised to unfold. Psychology turned out to be of an uncompromising behavioural school spent in laboratories doing experiments on animals and being taught that there was no spirit in the sky or in the machine. It was the Anthropology which was to teach me far more about human behaviour, about humankind's relationship to the world, about the non-judgemental acceptance of the 'other', about the art of language which could communicate complex concepts and experiences in simple images and word combinations, but most importantly about the existence of and deep respect for the spiritual not as a separate entity but as an integral part of the community of life. This was a language that spoke to me in a way that psychology never could. It spoke to me of the spirit of humanity and I feel it is still the anthropologist in me which informs my psychotherapy and helps me towards that deep humanity that many survivors have struggled to convey.

> Anthropology will never succeed in being a dispassionate science like astronomy that springs from the contemplation of things at a distance. It is the outcome of a historical process that has made the larger part of mankind subservient to the rest. During this process, millions of innocent human beings have had their resources plundered and their institutions and beliefs destroyed while they themselves were ruthlessly killed, thrown

into bondage, and contaminated by diseases they were unable to resist Anthropology is daughter to this era of violence. Its capacity to assess objectively the facts pertaining to the human condition appropriately reflects, on the epistemological level, a state of affairs in which one part of mankind treated the other as an object. (Levi-Strauss, 1978, p. 54)

In the darkness

My intense fear of pain and torture drew me to seek it out in an area of great historical and contemporary pain, the Middle East, where I started research into refugee camps and the dynamics of power. But within two years Lebanon's long civil war had begun. This was to be a period of great personal pain for me and a violent connection to the pain of others. The photograph in my father's book became part of my own experience and reality, only this time I often knew both the victim and the perpetrator and came to know the victim and the perpetrator in myself. My friends were kidnapped and murdered, bodies were scattered in the streets, car bombs went off regularly killing and maiming people and I was held in prison myself. I felt a darkness being touched in me, a cynicism, which was becoming increasingly seductive. Brian Keenan, the former hostage in Lebanon, had his kind of darkness too:

> *I know that nightmares have their source*
> *Like the abstract has some social sense*
> *Time fluxes in the dark*
> *Night stalking mind, closer than blood.*
> *Dreams, words, things felt − not said,*
> *Spaces on every side:*
> *Bat's wings beat like heart*
> *Or drum*
> *Translating silence to insanity*
> (Keenan, 1992, p. 297)

But Lebanon's geographical beauty, this crossroads of many cultures was also the birth place of Kahlil Gibran and his words tried to speak to me through the intellectual din of the growing meaninglessness.

> Your pain is the breaking of the shell that encloses your understanding. Even as the stone of the fruit must break, that its heart may stand in the sun, so must you know pain. (Kahlil Gibran, 1986, p. 61)

I found myself becoming split between my very rational side, analysing political systems to try to understand what it is about them that makes ordinary people torture and kill, and the other part of me that identified so much with the victims and wanted to help them. For a long time I saw it as one thing or the other, as if trying to do both was impossible: a kind of mutual betrayal, fearing my rationality could rob me of my value of experiencing and that my experiencing could divorce me from my rationality, spiralling me down into some form of personal anarchy and chaos. I struggled with an overwhelming sense of powerlessness, a powerlessness that is present in every survivor and aid worker I have treated as a therapist. Even if I did know how the systems worked how could I change them? If I did give my life over to helping the victims I would just be patching things up till the next time. I would not be able to stop what was happening to them. There had to be something I was missing. In such dark moments I remembered my father's answer to many of our frustrations as children. Don't try and do everything, just do what you can, as best you can, and everything will become clear.

Of being human

So it was there that my awareness of the paradoxes of life which had started with the photograph came into too sharp a focus. For to be human is to be elementally schizoid: being both an individual and a member of groups; part of nature and exiled from it; having the capacity to create and destroy; being rational and emotional; a perpetrator of abuse and a victim; being body and mind; physical and not physical. We struggle to reconcile these splits, and search primarily for the meaning of each individual life more than of the collective life. In the end, no matter which way we choose to live life or which way life lives us, we know that our deepest need and longing is for non-transient love, a belongingness, an assurance of identity that can be located and expressed in both individuals and communities, things which seem to be increasingly elusive and illusory. We struggle to understand the unfair selection criteria of suffering, loneliness, loss and pain: why me, why not him or her? The rapid advances in technology and genetics have pulled the traditional carpet from under our feet and we feel ourselves precariously balanced, pulled in several directions as we try to keep a hold on who we are and why we are here. For some it is towards the boundaried, orthodox havens of more fundamental religious beliefs. For others it is towards a humanism with no illusion or mystery or towards a sort of freestyle gnostic individual quest for a personalised holy grail. Sadly for many it is towards depression. In this precarious moment we are perhaps now more sharply aware than ever before that something is missing, that the science *gesellschaft* collective is about to consume the uniqueness of the individual and its *gemeinschaft* communities, that the collective's discoveries will steal our own individual mystery — and if there is no mystery are we then nothing? We are looking for more than a reason to live. We are looking for the spirit of life.

So I chose to help the man in the picture and he helped me to see more clearly.

Bound in the pain

As psychotherapists we are faced today with existential issues deeper and more acute than ever before. It is no wonder that we are called New Age priests. But we do not have the answers. We are supposed to help individuals to find the answers in themselves, but what if the community frame for identity and support needed to reach those answers has been ripped away and we are left floating in an anonymous macrocosm that alienates us from self and from each other, and that macrocosm is enclosed in a huge juggernaut that is driving forward along a motorway too fast to read the signposts? Then think how much more severe that experience of alienation is for individuals who have been tortured, who have experienced the full impact of the worst that a human being is capable of inflicting on another, when the mask of illusion and trust is ripped away.

The demolition

> There comes a moment (moment in a structural sense) where the pain moves away from the aggression to the physical body of the subject towards the more destructive experience of dereliction. This moment occurs after a time of imprisonment and torture which varies according to the individual and the context of the situation. It can be a few hours, a few days, a few months.
>
> Starting with the intensity of the physical pain, sensory deprivation, obscurity, blindfolding, the breaking of all affective and effective links of the personal world which was loved, the subject finally arrives at the constant presence of the painful body, hurting, broken, totally at the mercy of the torturer; all other perceptions of the world, which are not centred on the present experiences, cease to exist. We call this moment: **the demolition**. (Vinar, 1989)

Then we wonder how this human being manages in some extraordinary way not only to hold on to some sense of his or her individual uniqueness but to nourish a deep and painful compassion for humanity. Like Naomi

> There were times when her struggle with sadness and fear almost overwhelmed her. But she fought this fight well . . . a strong and courageous mother who persevered and gave to her children when there was little left inside her. She gave with her heart, although her heart had been broken. She gave with her soul, although her soul had been robbed. (J. Samson (2000, p. xi) about his mother, Naomi, a holocaust survivor.)

Why? How? What defines us at any moment as this individual? Firstly, perhaps, the uniqueness of our genetic make-up, the uniqueness of our experiences and environmental conditions and the unique way in which these intra-act and inter-act with the outside world. Secondly, the something more than the sum of the parts. Some call this the soul.

And the spirit

The majority of our encounters with self are with the individual part, few are with the soul. It is the encounters with the soul — with the indefinable part, the part beyond reason that may constitute the dwelling place of spirituality, though we have first to gently understand that it is often submerged — that one can feel silly or ashamed of speaking about. Spirituality has its own language, a metaphoric one that bridges the rational and the emotional; that in one sentence can speak volumes. It is universally understood yet unique to each individual. It can be silent and it can have words and images. Spirituality is not a hermit but wishes to communicate with all who can hear. It is collective but it guards the preciousness of individuality. It does not heal the splits but arises when the splits have been reconciled through balance or are transcended even for a moment. It has no discrimination and its potential is in everyone. When we try to define it rationally in psychotherapy with such terms as transpersonal, in a sense it seems diminished as if *it can indeed unfold its wings but cannot fly*.

To define spirituality rationally for me is not possible. I have tramped around both my internal and external worlds looking for it. I know what it is not, I do not know what it is; but I experience it when I encounter it and experience when it is not there. I know that it is not religion but that some aspects of religion can lead to an experience of it. I know that music can awaken it, and poetry and nature. I know that reason has its own beauty of logic but for me it is not spiritual. Traditionally we have associated spirituality with a higher plane, a mysticism, a deep knowledge emerging out of strict religious practice and initiation, but in my life and in my work I have experienced it most in pain and suffering.

Of compassion

I once heard a priest give a talk in which he said Jesus suffered more than any man in this world and I wanted to say that he had not, that that was not the idea at all, that I had seen so many people whose torture challenges belief, defies imagination. I have heard many of those people say that God had abandoned them, that they do not believe in God any more and no longer in humankind but I have read their poetry and they have gone beyond our earthbound, projected, imperfect God to a place we have not been invited to where, in their horrific experience of the most debased of human behaviour, they have truly come to understand the greatness of its potential for the antithesis. We appreciate and mourn most that which we have been most deprived of. There, their humanity is at its deepest and so their pain and anger of humankind's denial of its greatest gift is even more unbearable. Perhaps that was the message of the manner of Jesus Christ's death which transcends the debates as to whether he was the son of God, or a very enlightened man. He followed the path he did out of a deep compassion for his fellow human beings struggling in their existential pain with a map without compass points and in his pain he showed them that the way was through love of humanity as mythical Prometheus had done centuries before when, moved by the wretchedness of humankind suffering in the cold and darkness, he stole fire from the gods for them and for this was brutally punished.

I often think of L., one of the gentlest and most compassionate people I have ever met. L. had attempted suicide four times before he was referred to me. He was in his twenties. He had been captured when he was 12 by the Khmer Rouge and held in one of their camps for several months where he was starved and brutally tortured. At four he had seen his father blown up in front of him in the fields by a land-mine. When he first came to see me he came through the door as a 12-year-old, charming, smiling, deferential. He had been trained as a Cambodian classical dancer and his special expertise was in the role of the Monkey. He found it very difficult to speak of his time in the camp and concentrated on his current problems which he dealt with much like a 12-year-old would. He was separated from his wife and children. He was plagued with flashbacks night and day which stopped him sleeping, making him increasingly ill and physically and mentally disoriented. I worked with him through the character of the Monkey. When the thoughts came at night he would dance the dance of the Monkey and in the day he took on the strength and cunning of the Monkey. The Monkey protected him from the intrusive thoughts. At last he was able to get some sleep and regain some of his physical and mental health. One day he came to see me and he was no longer 12. He was clear and calm. He asked if I would take care of his diaries for his children until they were older. He then thanked me for being like his Buddhist teacher when he was young and for seeing him as someone tortured by pain and not as mentally ill. He said he also spoke sometimes to the Christ person on the cross because he would know about his kind of suffering. He called me a few days later at the clinic. He had been denied joint custody of his children. He said he was going to fly now. In our language together this meant he was going to die. I have selected this extract in his memory.

> We have been to a place you have not been. I want to take you there but I would stop you going there with my life because the road to there is terrible. It is hard to come back . . . because it is so painful and pain has separated us from you. Part of us is already dead to this world . . . I want to swallow my children, both of them, to keep them inside of me and carry them everywhere I go . . . so they both won't lose the love they want to have and no one will come and torture them.
>
> The beautiful dream has gone, the hope has become meaningless. Love has more pain, the world has become too small to walk . . . One day I will find a space to stand on in this wide world and things will change for me, if there is someone who can see me as a person, then I would ask her to be my friend, a good friend only because I have no more love to give to anyone. (From the unpublished diaries of L. He committed suicide in 1997.)

Building bridges

Some struggle back from that place to help us. They try to build bridges of understanding. Some remain silently in that place, in this world but no longer of it. Others destroy or are destroyed by the rage of their experience. A bridge has two sides. There needs to be people who listen, who want to understand, who are not afraid to hear. The decision to hear requires deep consideration and reflection because once these things are heard they cannot be taken away and they come to have an influence on the listener at times obvious, at times imperceptible. They bind you forever.

> Whoever among us through personal experience learned what pain and anxiety really are must help to ensure that those who out there, are in bodily need, obtain the help which came to him. He belongs no more to himself alone. (Albert Schweitzer, 1949)

There is a shortage of listeners. The pain and demands of our everyday lives leave little space to hear the extraordinary pain of others who have been subjected to extreme experiences as direct recipients or as witnesses. When a child cuts its knee we can provide a bandage and make the child and ourselves feel good that we have done something, we have made a difference. But when we are faced with what has happened to people outside the realms of our normal experience, we feel we can do nothing about it, that if we did it would be a meaningless, useless gesture, a drop in the ocean. We fear being overwhelmed and held in that distressing powerlessness that they have been held in. So we deny it, avoid it, forget it and in doing that we are cutting off the potential to grow in spirit through the shared experience of human pain to reach our humanity.

> *only the never endingness of unlimiting*
> *my knowing; not looking, I see*
> *and not knowing, I am more than I am*
> *when I go through the door of experience*
> *that awaits the instant of my own unlocking*
> (Cresswell, 2000)

Bruno Bettleheim in *The Informed Heart* struggled with trying to convey the horror of the concentration camps without traumatising the listener, trying to reconcile the rational and the emotional, trying to understand from the experiences of the camps what is it in the human psyche that can make it capable of such grotesque conscience-free inhumanity, what it is that makes ordinary people capable of such acts of torture and how a person survives all that. How does one account for over 30,000 individuals 'disappeared' in Argentina's torture prisons as recently as the 1970s? What of the killing fields of millions at the hands of Pol Pot in Cambodia? The crimes against humanity of Pinochet's dictatorship in Chile? What of Iran and Iraq, once seats of great civilisations? Of Burma and Indonesia? Of the limb-hacking in Sierra Leone?

The list is distressingly longer than this. What of the weapons not only of mass destruction but of mass torture, from atom bomb to land-mines to thermobaric warfare, developed during Vietnam and most recently deployed in Chechnya, 'in which oxygen is sucked out of the air causing victims' lungs to collapse and eyeballs to be wrenched from their sockets? Victims are crushed to death in excruciating pain' (*The Times,* Jan. 2001). We can psychologize it, account for it, explain it in rational terms, but for Bettleheim reason was not enough and like many extremely traumatised people who have tried to convey something of those experiences, his writing cannot help but be spiritual because in trying to reconcile the splits he transcends reason into a deep humanity which for me is the dwelling place of the spiritual:

> The daring heart must invade reason with its own living warmth, even if the symmetry of reason must give way to admit love and the pulsation of life. No longer can we be satisfied with a life where the heart has its reasons, which reason cannot know. Our hearts must know the world of reason, and reason must be guided by an informed heart. (Bettleheim, 1991, p. xii)

To have written this, in all that pain, he must have had such hope left in humankind.

Many of the survivors I have worked with feel relentless, numbing, hopelessness and often cannot convey what has happened to them in ordinary words and when they use ordinary words as they must with immigration, housing and social services over and over again to secure safe haven for themselves and their families, they do so with a detachment of self from their experiences. One refugee called it 'prostituting my pain so that my family will be safe'. In my early work with survivors of torture and witnesses of violent events, I came to realise that all of them without exception had developed their own private, sometimes secretive, ways of trying to make meaning of what had happened to them and those ways were mostly through poetry and imagery which is also an integral part of my way of communicating. I often work transculturally and a linguistically simple metaphor for a complex concept can overcome linguistic and cultural barriers and take us to that culture between where we can encounter and share the universal givens of pain, suffering, loss, identity, belonging, happiness, safety. The cultural specifics are the cultural expressions of these universals. It is metaphor that can transcend the barriers of the specifics to reach the universals and it is through metaphors, complex and simple, that I have encountered the spiritual in the midst of deepest pain and through these metaphors I have been able to meet these people in that place of silent rhythm where words beautiful, awful and few fly freely and we can hear there, across time, the pain, the struggle and the spirit of many. Metaphors are metamorphic. They are verbal, they are images, they are dreams. They are objects and colours and smells. Aristotle said they were a natural human ability. They help the individual to live with his or her experiences, to own them; they help to communicate pain which is one of the most difficult things to do; they help the listener to listen without being traumatised; they prevent the listener from stealing the experiences for themselves, being the voyeur; they convey so much in such few words; they are bounded by form but boundless in interpretation; they can bring beauty out of horrific pain; they are empowering when torture is the most disempowering of any human experience; they banish shame. And if you leave reason and rationalising outside the room, they will be the bridge between your souls. They are disarmingly spiritual.

The following is a summarised version of some sessions taken from my work with someone who was brutally tortured over many months. A. is a highly educated man who had a serious post-trauma breakdown. The torture he had endured was among the worst I had heard. I had been seeing him for over a year when this happened. He had been obsessed since the breakdown a few years previously with a belief that he was being constantly followed by a menacing figure whom he could not see and whom he felt wanted to do terrible harm to him. At night the figure would be in his room holding a bloodied knife but A. could never see his face. It was haunting him.

> — You know the man who hides behind secret doors and in cupboards whenever I am inside and who keeps following me whenever I am alone outside, and whenever I turn round he is not there? Remember you told me that I should try to make friends with him because he is a hurt part of me, a part of me that is really angry but which I hide? Well I had a terrible dream a few days ago and I can't stop thinking about it. (A. was in some distress relating this dream.) He was driving a car and I was sitting next to him. He was driving very fast and I wanted him to slow down but I couldn't speak. He just went faster and faster. He ran over my mother and then my father and then my children. Then he got out of the car and walked away. How can I make friends with him?
>
> — Before he was always hiding or behind you and you couldn't see him. So you didn't know what he was going to do. You were very afraid of him. But in the dream he is not behind you or hiding anymore. He is beside you. You can see him clearly now and you can see what he is going to do. You didn't run away from him so you are not as afraid of him as before. You know that you can stop him running over your family.
>
> — How?
>
> — I think he is sitting beside you because he wants you to talk to him. Perhaps he is as lonely as you, perhaps he too is tired of being alone and he is trying to get your attention.

The next week A. came back. He had had the dream again only this time he had found his voice and screamed at the driver to stop and he did. Now the figure had stopped following behind him and hiding in secret places. Then he said he hoped the next time he had the dream he would be driving the car himself and he would drive it carefully.

And then for the first time in all those months of pain he smiled.

Protecting the light

My training in counselling, psychotherapy and counselling psychology taught me many things but it did not teach me to work with this client group or to work the way I do. The practical and useful cognitive behavioural approach to trauma is an important component of treatment but in my opinion it is only a component as the rational is a part and not the whole of a human being. For me psychotherapy is not just in material reality but in the space between. It is not just practical but spaciously spiritual. It is not only clinical but humanitarian. As a supervisor and the director of a large counselling and psychotherapy service and former head of a specialist trauma unit in the NHS psychiatric services, I have to think about the profession often, what it is preparing its candidates for and what the underlying dynamics and objectives are of the whole professional process. I interview many applicants for placements and I have been struck by the changing tone and approach. It would require another chapter to share my observations with you but I sometimes feel that the profession is manifesting tensions and divisions similar to those which arose after the death of Christ between the orthodox and the gnostics. We didn't know very much about the gnostics till recently because orthodoxy was quite successful at wiping gnosticism out but new information has come to light. The early struggle between the orthodox and the gnostics was about how one arrived at a knowledge of God: by an individual interpretation of God through knowledge of self (gnostic), or a formulated knowledge by an elite community that everyone else had to obediently follow (catholic/orthodox). The gnostic debate is an interesting one for the profession of psychotherapy. The argument of the orthodox was that there were so many individual interpretations of the teachings of Jesus Christ among the gnostics that there was chaos. There could be no rules of community or guidance, nothing could be measured or followed, there was an assumption that only the enlightened could reach God whereas the orthodox could help people not at that stage yet, bring them into the community, give them a sense of belonging, make decisions for them, give their lives meaning. Gnosticism, because of its individualism, would be difficult to protect from charlatans, corrupters, mad people who could damage others. It would be difficult to monitor. It would get out of hand and dissipate. These indeed were the dangers but the gnostics also argued like good qualitative, congruent therapists that the individual needed to experience God for himself, in his own time, in his own language; that reaching God was an individual journey and that meaning could not always be expressed in concrete terms; that difference was creative and dynamic; that orthodoxy had the potential to destroy the spirit and gnosticism to release it. One had to look for the symbols, the underlying message, not just the literal words. In the New Testament, Jesus comes across as an excellent teacher. In *The Gnostic Gospels* (Pagels, 1990), he also comes across as a skilled therapist:

If you bring forth what is within you, what you bring forth will save you.

> If you do not bring forth what is within you, what you do not bring forth will destroy you. (p. 135)

and

> Christ loved Mary Magdalen more than all his disciples . . . The rest of the disciples were offended and asked Jesus, Why do you love her more than us. And he answered them, Why do I not love you as I love her? (p. 84)

Gnosticism has another parallel with psychotherapy — gnostic sources state that Jesus as teacher and guide acknowledged the need for guidance but only as a provisional measure. The purpose of accepting authority is to learn to outgrow it. When one becomes mature one no longer needs any external authority. Gnosis is 'a subjective, immediate experience concerned above all with the internal significance of events'. (Pagels, p. 139) Pagels also notes:

> Many gnostics then would have agreed with Ludwig Feuerbach the nineteenth-century psychologist that theology is really anthropology — the study of humanity. For gnostics, exploring the psyche became explicitly what it is implicitly for many people today: a religious quest.
> Some who sought their own interior direction like the radical gnostics rejected religious institutions, others like the Valentinians believed that the church was more an instrument for self-discovery than an ark of salvation (Pagels, 1990).

The Valentinian gnostics were probably the first integratives. They believed in the individual and the community. They believed in the individual road to God/enlightenment, but also that humans were born into a community and their relationship to the community was essential but had to be on terms of equality rather than in terms of power, of the few ruling the many. The orthodox were concrete and so in the end won the day and orthodox, paternal Christianity as a paradigm has ruled supreme for 2000 years affecting culture, social mores, perceptions of sexuality, politics, wars and organisational structures.

Drawing parallels with psychotherapy and spirituality, both the profession of psychotherapy and the individual practice of it, I feel I am proposing a Valentinian approach. The structure that was set up to guard the knowledge of the spirit, as a lamp protects the lit candle, can become so involved in the fabric of its function that it suffocates the very light it was so intent on protecting. On the other hand there are many candles that are lit quickly, energetically, enthusiastically which without protection can set other things dangerously on fire, burn out or be blown out by stronger forces. The psychotherapy profession needs to be both dynamic and boundaried at the same time, it needs to hold the art of human understanding as well as the science. That is its treasure. The increasing professionalisation of psychotherapy, its need to tailor to the demands and restraints of the market place, can result in its preoccupation with ever more qualifications, with assessments of the skilled practitioner being more about the qualifications, the orthodoxy, than about the insightful being, the gnostic part of the individual. Such practices can fuel the anxiety and drive of the candidates to earn money as soon as possible to get something back for the years of investment, with few jobs available. In this climate, less and less mid- to long-term therapy is being done and the client can be reverted to being the patient. On the other hand, without boundaries of good and ethical practice, first-year students can be setting up in private practice with little supervision or support. In both these scenarios the spirit of psychotherapy can be lost.

Of our humanity

The essence of the practice of psychotherapy is not to focus entirely on the individual and not to encourage the individual to focus entirely on self. It is to help the individual to achieve a sense of belonging which comes with responsibility without losing the sense of self. That is the context of existence because through that integration comes a deepening of our humanity and in the deepest experience of humanity we find the spiritual.

> *Slowly, slowly, the mist clears*
> *From the shrouded glass*
> *To reveal a splendour*
> *Of naked reaching branches*
> *Across a sunset flaming sky*
>
> *And at the sun's bright setting*
> *Their sad voices come*
> *Through still and silent air*
> *Their faces rise*
> *Out of the blood light*
> *And their hands like branches*
> *All reach out to me*
>
> *For this splendour was theirs*
> *And this glory their eyes saw*
> *And like them I do not want*
> *To kill or die.*
>
> *So in the going down of this sun*
> *I grieve*
> *And in this evening remember*
> *And with remembering resolve*
> *Against all the odds — to love*
>
> *To save this sunset for the ones to come*
> *To sanctify this dying to the ones now gone*

('Again Remembrance' from *Less Than Complete* by Philip Padfield, British hostage executed in Beirut 1986. Private Publication 1992)

I am not convinced that being open to or being able to experience the spiritual can be taught, as theories and approaches are in psychotherapy. I feel that spirituality is something shared, that it cannot exist in a human being in isolation devoid of thoughts of and feelings for others. That sharing for me is not only with people in the present but with the peoples of the past and those yet to come. I go into the past to help me link to those to come. I am seeking knowledge and awareness of the history of humanity's struggle through the ages for the meaning of life, a struggle that has cost millions of lives and the devastation of cultures and civilisations. Every war and every culture is not only a collective but it is the pain, suffering and sacrifice of millions of individuals. The ancients consistently believed that God/gods and man do not always speak the same language because there are concepts that the gods know which humankind is too young to fully comprehend. The gulf is too great. The language of the gods is often the language of metaphors and images and the skill is in how to interpret them. In torture and extreme pain the individual is taken to another realm of experience which cannot be described in ordinary language because the concepts cannot yet be shared. The separation is a gulf in which the individual and the therapist seek a way to connect that which has so brutally been disconnected and humankind, if it listens, will be spiritually renewed and humbled by the terrible journey back to us made for our benefit. The pain of those experiences being relived so that we will learn something about our value, the potential for our godliness as well as our destruction, can sometimes become too much to bear and the messenger eventually takes his or her life as Primo Levi and several others have done.

> If I had not lived the Auschwitz experience, I probably would never have written anything . . . I had been a mediocre student in Italian and had had bad grades in history . . . I was helped too by my interest, which has never flagged, in the human spirit and by the will not only to survive (which was common to many) but to survive with the precise purpose of recounting the things we had witnessed and endured . . . I was also helped by the determination, which I stubbornly preserved, to recognise always, even in the darkest days, in my companions and in myself, men, not things, and thus to avoid that total humiliation and demoralisation which led so many to spiritual shipwreck. (Primo Levi, 2000, Auschwitz survivor, *If This Is A Man*, p. 397)

Perhaps what we as therapists do, working in this area, can seem like a drop, a little area of mutual healing, in an ocean of pain and inhumanity. But a beautiful Sikh client who had suffered so badly in prison that she could not speak for months, when she found her voice, told me that she had despaired of ever finding anyone with whom she could share her terrible pain without shame. She felt the light of the world had gone out and she was in the darkness alone where her only hope was in the words her guru used to say before he was killed. Strangely, they were the same words I had heard years before at a lecture in London given by an Indian guru. 'We are moving into a time of great darkness. Light in light is invisible. It can lose its sense of purpose but light in darkness gives great light and hope to those lost in the darkness.'

For all who have suffered, for all in pain, for all hostages to freedom, we need to ensure there will always be people at the other side of the bridge or our spirituality may be in danger of being no more than an electric bulb when it has the potential to be the gentle, enduring flame that gives all life meaning.

> The weary traveller sometimes had dreams in the darkness in which he had lived for what seemed like an eternity on his battered boat, cast adrift, with no compass and a map which had been given to him by the previous owners which only seemed to take him round in circles. And what he dreamt of was light. He knew light existed because he could see the stars and the moon but even in the full moon he was always in shadow. And he knew the stars might have a message for him but he did not know how to read them. (Kate Maguire, 2000, *EACS Practitioner's Handbook*)

References

Bettleheim, B. (1991) *The Informed Heart.* Harmondsworth: Penguin.

Cresswell, E. (2000) *Journey out of Apartheid.* Private Publication.

Gibran, Kahlil (1996) *The Prophet.* London: Wordsworth's Classics.

Keenan, B. (1992) *An Evil Cradling.* London: Vintage.

Levi, P. (2000) *If This is a Man & The Truce.* London: Abacus.

Maguire, K. (2000) *The EACS Practitioner's Handbook.* London: EACS.

Levi-Strauss, C. (1978) *The Scope of Anthropology in Structural Anthropology 2.* London: Peregrine Books.

Padfield, P. (1992) *Less Than Complete.* Private Publication.

Pagels, E. (1990) *The Gnostic Gospels.* Harmondsworth: Penguin.

Samson, N. (2000) *Hide.* Bison. Lincoln: University of Nebraska Press.

Schweitzer, A. (1949) *Out of my Life and Thought: An Autobiography.* New York: Henry Holt.

Vinar, M. (1989) Pedro or the Demolition. A Psychoanalytic Look at Torture. *British Journal of Psychotherapy.* 5 (3) 359

Tara Rokpa Therapy

13

Edie Irwin and Lorna Hensey

As humans we have various kinds of awareness available to us at any given moment. We are focused on personal needs, feelings, perceptions. At the same time we have access to a larger awareness that allows us, if only briefly, to step out of the narrow focus of our attention and take a larger perspective on our daily living, experiencing some freedom from its entanglements. This awareness helps us begin to see that what we are is always wider and deeper than all the personal issues we carry around with us. Tara Rokpa Therapy is concerned with these different levels of awareness. It encourages us to work towards fulfilling our human potential. We come to know ourselves very thoroughly, facing who we really are. We are given the tools by which we can begin to work more skilfully with the seemingly unattractive parts of ourselves, those parts which we might normally keep hidden behind masks and make-up, thus finding a more open and wholesome way of being in the world. We are also given the means to access this larger awareness, free of personal needs, meanings, interpretations; this assists in our attempts to understand and work with the larger life issues such as impermanence, death, and the pain inherent in engaging with our own suffering and the suffering of others. The development of understanding and compassion both towards ourselves and others is the foundation of this approach.

Tara Rokpa Therapy draws on two main sources of inspiration: the philosophy, psychology and meditation practice of Buddhism, and western psychotherapeutic understanding. It has been developed, over the past 20 years, by Dr Akong Tulku Rinpoche, co-founder and director of Samye Ling Tibetan Centre and Monastery in Dumfriesshire in Scotland. This work was undertaken together with a small group of psychotherapists trained in Tara Rokpa methods as well as in a number of other western therapeutic approaches: psychiatry, psychology, family therapy, art therapy, constructivist/humanistic/psychoanalytic therapies, and massage.

Origins and development

The origins of Tara Rokpa Therapy go back to Akong Rinpoche's first experiences of leaving his homeland in 1959, at the age of 20. Akong Rinpoche is a Tibetan Lama and is also trained as a doctor in Tibetan medicine. Before he left Tibet he had responsibility for a number of monasteries and was known for his interest in healing as well as for preparing people to go into long and profound meditation retreats. He was unusual in that he fostered the deeper spiritual development of nuns in retreat as well as monks. Forced to leave Tibet by the Chinese invasion, he escaped along with another distinguished Tibetan teacher, Chogyam Trungpa Rinpoche, and a large group of Tibetans, both lay people and monks. Their journey was very difficult and involved much hardship. The majority of those travelling did not survive the journey. Those who did resorted to eating the leather from their shoes in the weeks before they reached their destination. Akong Rinpoche was very aware that it was only by applying the wisdom of his Buddhist training and realisation that he was able to endure such arduous conditions.

His training was also invaluable in helping him face the challenges he later encountered as a refugee in both India and the West. These experiences proved to be very difficult, coming suddenly into contact with unfamiliar societies, new customs, and different languages. When he came to live in England in 1963 it was hard for him to get work as he spoke very little English. His training as a doctor was unrecognised in the context of western medicine. He eventually got work as a hospital porter in Oxford where he lived for four years. He subsequently came to live in Scotland in 1967.

Initially Akong Rinpoche kept a low profile and did not involve himself in giving meditation instruction. This was usually done by his friend and colleague, Chogyam Trungpa Rinpoche, who was exceptionally gifted in his ability to learn English and transmit Buddhist teachings authentically and vividly in his adopted language and culture. Gradually, however, people interested in Tibetan meditation and culture, particularly those in need of healing, gravitated towards Akong Rinpoche, seeking his advice and asking him to teach meditation. This was especially so following Trungpa Rinpoche's departure for North America. Over time, through observation and direct involvement with would-be western meditators, he realised that while people were asking for meditation instruction it seemed that in general they were searching for something else. He wasn't quite sure what they were looking for, but he was aware that many people found it hard to follow the meditation instructions which he had given. They did not have the stability of mind to really undertake what was being asked of them. He saw that what people often wanted was help in facing the difficulties they encountered in their everyday lives, in particular with regard to their emotional and physical well-being. A large percentage of the people coming to see him expressed dissatisfactions within themselves, their families, and their relationships, and what they really wanted was help to find a way to stop the endless cycle of suffering which seemed to be recurring in different areas of their lives. They also wanted to find ways of dealing with the inevitable stresses and strains of modern-day living. This is when the notion of therapy began to emerge in his work.

Having appreciated the value of his own training in helping him face the suffering which he had experienced, he began to develop exercises which he hoped would help people overcome their difficulties, or, if this wasn't possible, to help them reach a level of maturity which would enable them to accept and face up to them. While the exercises were founded on his deep understanding of his spiritual tradition and also his knowledge of Tibetan medicine, he wanted to make them accessible to westerners, including those who would never choose to approach Buddhist meditation practices. When people came to him for help, he would, where appropriate, introduce them to the use of these methods. During this time Edie Irwin, who became involved with Tara Rokpa Therapy in 1979 and was the first western psychotherapist to become involved in teaching it, became a major instrument in its development. Her training prior to meeting Akong Rinpoche had been equally focused on Buddhist meditation and western therapy. This would prove to be the case with each of the therapists who subsequently pioneered the Tara Rokpa methods. Throughout the 1980s, alongside Akong Rinpoche, she began presenting these methods in Europe (in England, Ireland, Scotland, Wales, Belgium, France, Germany, Holland, Italy, Spain, Sweden and Switzerland) and in Canada, America, and Southern Africa, and despite the cultural variations it became obvious that wherever she presented it this material had a very wide application. People working with it from all backgrounds and cultures found something of true value in it. From the experience of presenting this work, Tara Rokpa Therapy began to take shape.

The integration of eastern and western approaches

At this stage in its history there was some interchange between the labels 'meditation' and 'therapy' for the exercises that were being developed. It was really at the discretion of the presenter and the recipient as to which label they felt best defined the nature of the work undertaken in using these methods. However, as the therapy evolved, professionals in the field of medicine and psychotherapy, who had engaged with the process and appreciated the value of it in their own lives, began to interact with Akong Rinpoche's ideas about therapy, with the hope that they might be able to integrate his approach into their own disciplines. While wishing to preserve the richness of the tradition from which it grew, they knew that if it was to be called therapy, in the western sense of the word, all the exercises would need to be reshaped to fit the western therapeutic contexts for which they were destined and to make them acceptable to colleagues in a number of disciplines. Akong Rinpoche was keen for this integration to happen.

An incredibly creative process then began, bringing together both eastern and western understanding of the mind. Four other western psychotherapists, Dorothy Gunne (a psychologist, psychotherapist and family therapist from Ireland), Carol Sagar (an art therapist from the UK), Brion Sweeney (a psychiatrist and psychotherapist from Ireland) and Trish Swift (a Clinical Social Worker and psychotherapist from Zimbabwe), together with Edie Irwin and Akong Rinpoche, worked over many years to achieve this integration. One of the main considerations was that Tara Rokpa Therapy take account of the ethical requirements of their various professional backgrounds in its development. Akong Rinpoche encouraged them to meet existing ethical standards and then to go beyond that in the fulfilment of any Buddhist ethical requirements. Confidentiality, discussed below, is a good example of this.

There has, at various points, been concern that the Buddhist content of the therapy might make it suspect in the climate of cult scandals, forcible 'deprogramming' and such. The notion that undue influence might be exerted towards the taking up of a particular religious view within the therapeutic context was flagged early on. One of the most interesting tasks has been to maintain alertness regarding this issue without the watering down of what is most valuable in the practices and insights coming from the Buddhist direction. Akong Rinpoche has continually endeavoured to find a language and a form which is true to the therapeutic intention but also fully acceptable to non-Buddhist participants.

There are now a small number of psychiatric and psychological and medical settings which have incorporated Tara Rokpa Therapy methods into their work with clients. In addition, there are many professionals, in various contexts, who have engaged with the therapy for themselves and subsequently integrated it into their working practices. Increasingly Buddhist teachers of various schools are also interested in Tara Rokpa Therapy as a model for working with the psychological difficulties that arise in teaching meditation to western beginners.

Who might benefit from Tara Rokpa Therapy ?

There are three main groups who are known to derive benefit:
1. Those who have made an attempt at spiritual practice but for some reason have come upon obstacles or blocks which make them feel less able to pursue their daily lives or their meditative practice.
2. Those who know that they need help to deal with the intolerable nature of their mental and emotional experiences, but are wary of any approach inclined to put specific labels or interpretations onto their difficulties. They only feel able to work in a process where their spiritual wholeness is respected.
3. Those who come because they have a nagging feeling that something isn't quite right about their lives or who are looking for something other than the pursuit of happiness on offer in the materialistic world.

Tara Rokpa Therapy explicitly incorporates a spiritual approach while also supporting a psychological investigation which addresses more personal emotional needs and problems. The notion of spiritual wholeness is fundamental to the Tara Rokpa Therapy approach and informs all of the methods used. Like many of the humanistic therapies, there is a belief that, given the right conditions, the human being will move in a direction which allows his or her basic potential to unfold.

From the Buddhist perspective there is a fundamental goodness intrinsic in all human beings, manifesting itself as openness, intelligence and warmth. This viewpoint has its philosophical and psychological foundations in such concepts as the awakened mind or the unconditioned mind. The process of Tara Rokpa Therapy is one of uncovering this inner potential which has been clouded over by layers of patterning, layers of conditioning. In this approach the focus shifts from an attempt to rid ourselves of our neuroses to one of becoming aware of, accepting, and attempting to let go of our identification with them. Problems are seen in a broader perspective which presumes that basic health and sanity are potentially there for everyone.

The structure of the therapy

Tara Rokpa Therapy now offers a six-year therapy programme. The experience gained from one year is the basis for practising the next. Each phase of the therapy is clearly defined and participants can choose to withdraw from the process having completed any number of phases.

The work is introduced in stages by Tara Rokpa therapists in a series of weekend workshops. Participants meet each other in between the workshops in small groups to practise the methods together. The primary focus of the work is, however, on individual process — individual awareness evolving over time with the least intrusion from outside, be that from individuals engaged in the same stage of the therapy or therapists supporting the work. The parameters of the therapy workshops and small groups are in keeping with this ethos.

The approach could be described as reflective. Individuals within the group are not especially encouraged to talk about themselves or their private feelings. Where problems occur it is recommended that they use the structure of the methods provided to work through the difficulties encountered. This allows participants to engage in the work with a greater sense of personal space and freedom without feeling concern that what is happening for them is going to be impinged upon by another. There is a sense that, by being together and sharing the activities of the group, support at another level occurs. Where participants do feel the need to speak about a specific problem then this happens quite naturally over time between group members as they come to know and trust each other, but within the safety of the ethos that has already been established. There is also the possibility of speaking with a therapist both during weekend workshops and between them if this becomes necessary. Naturally some participants grapple with this way of working, especially if their automatic response is to want to talk about what is happening for them or perhaps to talk about what is happening for someone else in the group. There is a certain amount of discipline required, but generally they come to a place of comfort with this more reflective approach as the group develops over time and they begin to experience the benefits for themselves.

Of course while this is the general emphasis followed in working with these methods, it is recognised that some people may need more intensive one-to-one support during different phases of the work. This need can emerge unexpectedly, especially but not exclusively in the first years of the therapy, or it may be acknowledged as a need by individual participants at the outset of the process. In this case we try to make available the opportunity of working with a therapist trained in Tara Rokpa methods. Where this is not possible a therapist who is both familiar and sympathetic to this approach is recommended. Sometimes neither of these options are feasible; participants are then encouraged to use the resources at hand to seek individual therapy for themselves.

The ethos described is also reflected in the role of the Tara Rokpa therapists supporting the work, in particular with the insistence on the importance of confidentiality in this approach. For Akong Rinpoche, as spiritual adviser, confidentiality is absolute: a guarantee of utmost respect for individuals. He has emphasised the importance of being able to contain confidences with no leaks as the one indispensable quality of a good therapist. He has encouraged therapists to keep their standards, both when working together and in other therapeutic contexts where the interpretation of confidentiality might be a little looser. Therapists attempt to work to the spirit of this approach while being prepared to acknowledge rare and exceptional circumstances when they arise. So in matters of life or death, where the life of the client or anyone else is threatened, therapists are enjoined to speak as necessary. A more common exception is personal supervision, where a therapist or trainee needs to consult with his or her supervisor on a regular basis regarding development of work with individual clients and groups. Even in supervision first names only are used, and every effort is made to disclose only material which is relevant to the therapist's understanding, and not to speak about the details of someone's personal history where there is no clear therapeutic intent. The commitment to the maintenance of confidentiality on the part of supervising therapists is taken all the more seriously as the confidences of many individuals may be gathered in a single session. This is one of the areas where a broader view, cultivated through meditation-based exercises, helps to find a perspective where this holding of confidences is not felt to be an intolerable burden or even such a special one.

The programme outline

Pre-therapy foundation: Beginning to Relax
Beginning to Relax is offered as a stand-alone course by Tara Rokpa therapists and trainees and is based on the book *Healing Relaxation* by Edie Irwin (1999). The material used is derived from early collaboration with Akong Rinpoche and includes specific relaxation/visualisation exercises and suggestions on how to get started with the practice of simple massage and self-massage as well as other simple physical exercises. In addition there are suggestions about the use of art materials. Since all of these components together form

the underlying basis of all the following stages of Tara Rokpa Therapy, those who take well to them are somewhat informed by their own experience when it comes to the possibility of undertaking Back to Beginnings.

Therapy Years One and Two: Back to Beginnings
Back to Beginnings is a process of reviewing one's whole life in depth, seeing the present implications of past experiences through a very thorough investigation of one's life story. It involves two years of sifting and making sense of one's experiences from the present back until the age of one, then forward again to the present, and then back again to the age of one week. The purpose is to become aware of the origins of our habitual tendencies, patterns of behaviour, ways of perceiving the world. We develop choices around those origins which are no longer appropriate to our adult life and which get in the way of us fulfilling our potential and living in an open way, especially with others. It is also a process of self-healing as we are given an opportunity to approach the more painful times in our life, to gradually come to an acceptance of these, and to integrate them into our life stories. In addition the nature of memory and its non-solidity is contemplated in this approach. No one ever remembers the story the same way each time. The picture is constantly changing depending upon outer circumstances and inner experiences at the time of remembering.

The method draws upon the creative as well as the self-reflective abilities of each participant. Recollecting chronologically, writing, and working with art materials are the main therapeutic tools used to facilitate the remembering of the life story. Relaxations/visualisations are also key components, bringing a sense of inner strength and tranquillity, the means by which a broader perspective can be developed. This initiates the cultivation of a greater tolerance and understanding than the narrowly held personal view generally allows. There is also the practice of simple massage in the context of group support.

Working with the five elements
During the two years of Back to Beginnings we spend five months investigating the elements earth, water, fire, air and space. This work is based on the premise that human beings are a microcosm of the whole universe, so that what makes up the individual is no different than what makes up the world out there. From the Tibetan point of view, everything we could ever come into contact with is seen as being a combination of these elements. In this work we explore the qualities of each element, how it manifests externally in the universe and how we relate to each one physically and psychologically within ourselves. We are also concerned with the balance and harmony of the elements which helps to stabilise our physical and emotional well-being.

Just as with the use of the art materials, working with the elements gives us another language through which we can begin to understand our lived experience. This language, which can be used very precisely to describe various psychophysical states, is natural and non-judgemental in that all of us are expressions of all five elements all of the time. It describes states of dynamic balance/imbalance rather than disease states or diagnostic categories. For example, someone who recognizes herself as an 'airhead' may realise that 'earthing' behaviours such as adequate sleep and gardening help her to 'keep her feet on the ground'. An acknowledged 'hothead' may find a stroll to the water cooler and a few conscious sips save him from regrettable exchanges with his boss.

Clarifying blame

This part of the work is perhaps one of the most challenging aspects of Back to Beginnings, but it is also one of the exercises which brings most benefit. We use 'clarifying blame' whenever we come upon a memory which evokes anger, blame, resentment. There are two aspects to this exercise. Firstly we fully express in private the feelings of anger/blame that we feel towards the person or people in question. It is important not to censor whatever it is we happen to be feeling but to allow a complete picture to emerge. Then, having taken a break of at least one night, we take the very brave step of putting ourselves into the shoes of those we were angry with, trying to the best of our ability to see the situation from their point of view, as they would have seen it at the time. The aim here is really to broaden our understanding of their circumstances and of how they were, emotionally and physically, within themselves. If we can go deep enough into understanding the perspective of the other, then it becomes possible to allow a reconciliation, and a letting go of the burden of resentment. This exercise may need to be done again and again before a true reconciliation can be felt. Of course we might also feel anger/blame towards ourselves. In this case we use the same procedure in an attempt to develop more understanding of ourselves and how we were at the time of a specific event. This can help greatly to release the double bind of guilt and resentment that is commonly felt.

The work of 'clarifying blame' is one of those unpredictable stages during which someone may seek individual therapy in order to deal with a particularly difficult situation that comes to light.

Birth retreat

At the end of Back to Beginnings there is an optional retreat in which we explore in depth the phase of life from conception through to birth. The perspective taken for this exploration is birth as a metaphor for changing our motivation and intention to now make full use of our human lives. While the purpose of Back to Beginnings is to come to grips very thoroughly with the past, this retreat is an opportunity to symbolically leave the past behind and to dedicate oneself to looking for answers in the present.

Therapy year three: Taming the Tiger

The emphasis in Taming the Tiger is on opening to a more compassionate understanding of oneself and others and at the same time deepening one's understanding of one's own mind and its role in creating day-to-day experience. The process of exploring the non-solidity of all conditioned phenomena is also developed here. This work is achieved through a series of visualisation exercises, which are all contained in Dr Akong Rinpoche's book *Taming the Tiger* (1994).

The image of a tiger is quite a powerful one and is very appropriate to the work we set out to do. Essentially we are hoping to take responsibility for taming the untamed part of our minds, the most difficult and unattractive parts of ourselves, which, if examined closely, are seen to be the cause of suffering both to ourselves and others. However, once we embark on this work, our approach to this untamed tiger is very significant. You can't beat a tiger into submission. The tiger trainer has to win the confidence of the tiger to gain its cooperation. There is a lot of skill involved. The trainer spends a lot of time watching the tiger's inclinations. Our approach is gentle also. We become observers of ourselves, gradually coming to know and understand the way our mind works so that we no longer need to act compulsively out of these more difficult places.

Compassion, from the Buddhist perspective, presupposes the element of wisdom. It is by developing a greater sense of inner peace that one has the ground for wise compassion. In Taming the Tiger we are also concerned with developing this sense of peace and are given exercises which help us make a connection with the awakened or unconditioned mind.

Therapy year four: the Six Lights / Six Realms practice
During the fourth year of therapy we investigate the origins, attributes and consequences of dwelling in the six emotional states of pride and arrogance, jealousy and envy, desire and busyness, stupidity and ignorance, greed and craving, anger and hatred. In exploring each state we investigate what it feels like to be in it and how each one arises within us and combines with or leads to the others. We then explore various antidotes, mainly through practising awareness and visualisation. The final stage is learning to transform the energy of these more negative mind states into an immediately accessible recognition of the positive hidden within them. A continuous colour journal is recommended as one works with this stage of the therapy.

Therapy years five and six
From this point, the therapy is concerned with the deepening of love and compassion for everyone, including oneself, and the gradual development of an attitude in which one has a strong wish to take suffering from others. This wish is free of fear, due to a deep enough acquaintance with the principles of intrinsic purity, compassion and awakeness which comprise the essence of mind. This principle begins to be uncovered in Back to Beginnings and Taming the Tiger but as the therapy develops it becomes more clearly the basis of all positive development in one's life.

It is hoped that enough wisdom has been gained to see that without profound appreciation, love and compassion for oneself, there will be something false and embittering about taking on the suffering of the Universe. For most of us, further repair work on inner relationships between different aspects within the self is needed to fully engage with this aspiration. The structure of the Compassion phase allows for this repair work to happen.

We also explore a deeper quality of awareness through sitting meditation practices. By now the actual practices are determined by individual choice and there are several different options as to how to proceed. Of course there can be times of great doubt and despair, running away and confusion, but on the whole from this stage there tends to be a confidence that one has found a way of working which has true value.

Tara Rokpa Psychotherapy Training

A four-year professional training in this work has now been developed. This training meets the standards required within the British and Irish Councils of Psychotherapy for accreditation purposes, in terms of theoretical/academic work and personal therapy as well as supervised practice in individual client work. In addition, trainees are expected to fulfil the six-year therapy programme for themselves as well as learn how to facilitate both groups and workshops in these methods.

To date, Tara Rokpa Therapy Training is in the process of bringing a second group of trainees to graduation. It is hoped that a third training will begin sometime after 2002. Completing the phases Back to Beginnings and Taming the Tiger are a requisite for acceptance onto this training.

In summary

Tara Rokpa Therapy is a distinct system of psychotherapy in which our psychological development is not separated from our spiritual development but is seen as an integral part of it. Combining both eastern and western understandings of the human mind, it remains true to its Buddhist roots while also drawing upon psychotherapeutic approaches and methodologies which are more readily accessible to us in the West. We are given the means to develop a healthy sense of self, expanding our sense of who we are by integrating the parts of ourselves that we fear and compartmentalise. At the same time we are given the means to access a larger awareness, which is free of personal needs, meanings, interpretations, entanglements, and which frees us from fixating or holding onto our own version of reality.

From the Buddhist perspective it is only from the space of this larger awareness, where we are not caught up in our own version of reality, that we can really see and hear and feel who others really are. This becomes the basis for the development of understanding and wise compassion, the foundation of this approach. Tara Rokpa Therapy is accessible yet profound. It requires a comparatively small monetary investment, yet a major investment of personal effort and honesty. It is designed to help us face ourselves and our world with spaciousness and humour, free of panic in these times of unprecedented change. Learning to take ourselves both more and less seriously, freeing us to care more genuinely for the benefit of all beings.

References

Akong Tulku Rinpoche (1994) *Taming the Tiger*. Rider: London.
Irwin, E. (1999) *Healing Relaxation*. Rider: London.

A Client-Centred Approach to Religious and Spiritual Experiences

14

Barbara Temaner Brodley

This chapter will address the practice of Client-Centred (alternatively 'Person-Centred') therapy when the client chooses to focus his or her attention on concerns, feelings, experiences or goals that may be perceived generally as spiritual or religious or that the client represents as spiritual or religious.

Client-Centred therapy can be summarized as an approach that involves the therapist in relationship with a client, with the therapist experiencing congruence — feeling integrated and genuine in the relationship, and the therapist also experiencing unconditional positive regard and empathic understanding toward the client. The therapist's behavior in interactions is shaped by a non-directive attitude that is intended to protect the client's self-determination, autonomy and sense of self in the relationship (Brodley, 1997). The theory also asserts that the therapist's attitudes must be perceived by the client to some extent in order to have a therapeutic impact (Rogers, 1957; 1959).

There are two main ways spirituality or religious beliefs have fitted into Client-Centred therapy since early in its practice. First, there is no limit imposed by the theory to the kinds of experiences or concerns that clients may discuss (Rogers, 1957; 1959). Consequently, the client's spiritual or religious experiences and issues may be the focus of all or part of a Client-Centred therapy experience. It is a matter of the client's choice or inclination.

Second, various forms of religious counselling or spiritual counselling may apply some of the principles of the person-centred approach (Rogers, 1980) to those endeavors. Religious counsellors from many denominations have been attracted to Rogers' therapy since the late 1940s. Students from the University of Chicago Theological Seminary, some preparing for the ministry, attended courses in Client-Centred therapy at the counselling centre that Rogers founded at the university. Religious persons' interests in Client-Centred therapy have probably been primarily because of Rogers' principle of unconditional positive regard or acceptance — which can be viewed as a kind of non-possessive love. This prominent attitude in the therapy has resonated with the values of many spiritual and religious people.

Religious or spiritual counsellors, however, are assumed by their clients to share the religious or spiritual beliefs of their clients and to be informed as to the values or ideas that are intrinsic to the belief system. The counsellor's help may include religious or spiritual advice or guidance. The Client-Centred therapist, in contrast, is not meant to be a guide to any particular beliefs or values and rarely gives advice of any kind. Client-Centred theory of relationships and the general 'person-centred approach' derived from the therapy, however, may be applied to any endeavour having as at least part of its purpose to foster the development of the persons involved (Rogers, 1987; Brodley, 1988; Natiello, 1988; Pörtner, 1988; Raskin, 1988). Thus the approach may influence the form and goals of spiritual or religious counselling. Respect and trust of clients, acceptance of clients and empathic understanding interactions with clients may be an important part of pastoral or spiritual counselling.

Insofar as such counsellors advise clients or have goals for their clients, however, their endeavors are not Client-Centred counselling or therapy. This is because Client-Centred therapists *have no specific goals for their clients*. Their general goal is to be of help to the client — to have a therapeutic influence. Client-Centred therapists' goals, however, are basically for themselves. They aim to experience and to communicate in relationship with clients the therapeutic conditions of congruence, unconditional positive regard and empathic understanding as best they can with the individual client (Rogers in Baldwin, 1987). They wish in this way to have a constant therapeutic presence and impact. Client-Centred clients are the source of any specific therapeutic or personal goals and the primary source of the path to reaching their goals in the therapy situation. The client, consequently, may have spiritual or religious goals.

Client-Centred therapists as well as clients, of course, may personally have religious or spiritual beliefs. Or therapists may be agnostic, atheist, or secular humanist, or they may have some combination of beliefs. Their belief systems and personal religious backgrounds may in some instances give them information or a history of experiences that assist them in empathic understanding of a particular client. An assumption of Client-Centred theory, however, is that the therapist need not personally share the beliefs or experiences of his or her client in order to empathically understand the client or to unconditionally accept the client. The theory also encourages therapists to put aside their own belief systems in order to fully engage empathically, with acceptance and non-directivity, with their clients.

Illustrations of the spiritual in Client-Centred practice

Excerpts from several different clients who have expressed religious or spiritual concerns or experiences will be used to illustrate the manner in which such experiences are treated in Client-Centred therapy sessions.

Illustration I
The client has been discussing her sexual relationship with a younger man. She is often angry and distant from her husband, who causes her emotional

pain when he expresses violent angry reactions. She has rejected her formal religious background and engages in spiritual practices with a specialized spiritual guide in addition to seeing the therapist for her depression and issues concerning her family.

> *Client*: I love F (boyfriend) and it's very hard to get through days when we don't meet or at least talk on the phone. I have to be very careful that J (husband) doesn't catch on to what I'm doing. He is always suspicious, but he doesn't know anything is going on. (Pause) I don't feel guilty about what I am doing as far as he is concerned. But I do know I'm going to go to hell when I die.
>
> *Therapist*: (Surprised) You believe you are literally going to hell when you die? Because of your affair?
>
> *Client*: Yes, I believe in hell and heaven — that they exist somewhere. Somehow I got convinced about it during my Catholic schooling as a kid. When I die I'll go into a place full of fire and I'll be painfully burned for eternity. I totally believe it. But it doesn't stop me. (Pause.) Otherwise, I'm trying to be a good person. I think I am a good person, except for cheating on J. But that will send me to hell.
>
> *Therapist*: In many ways you try to be a good person and you feel you are good. But at the same time, your passion and attachment to F is something you can't resist. That's even though you're convinced, you know for certain, you are going to be condemned to suffer in hell for your infidelity to J.
>
> *Client*: Exactly. It's strange because when I think of J finding out or when I think of hell I feel afraid, but when I'm with F the feelings of happiness and pleasure I feel with him just put the fears out of my mind.
>
> *Therapist*: You don't really feel guilty about your relationship with F. It's just the consequences of discovery — if J found out, and what you'll suffer after you die, those things make you afraid. You feel scared when you think of those things. But when you're with F it feels so good, the fears disappear.
>
> *Client*: Right.

The therapist is surprised that this client believes in damnation and does not respond empathically at that moment. Instead she asks a question. Subsequently, she regains her empathic attention and tries to follow the client's explication closely and accurately.

Illustration II

This client has suffered from undiagnosed pain for several years and had been referred to the therapist by his physician. The segment occurs in the fifth session.

> *Client*: I couldn't sleep much as usual, but I realized I've been too isolated because of this pain. I think I'll start looking for a church group that I might like. Some years ago I was going to several different churches, kind of doing the rounds, and I think I felt better then.
>
> *Therapist*: Church seemed to ease the pain, so going back to a church group

could give you some community and maybe some people to interact with. You realize you are lonely.

Client: Yeah. I am lonely. (Pause.) I remember the feeling I can get in some churches. Sort of connected and real peaceful. I think it took away my tensions, and they make the pain worse. I think talking to people distracts me from myself and gives me something besides my pain to think about.

Therapist: You remember how connected and much more peaceful you felt sometimes in church; plus the social life of church gives you things to think about. It might help you again.

Client: Yeah, I don't know why I let that go before. It makes a lot of sense and I sure have the time.

Therapist: It's a mystery why you didn't keep going when you think about how good it was for you. It feels like such a good idea.

Client: Yeah, I'll go back to one of those churches from before. I think I had an argument with one of the people in a bible class and that put me off for a few weeks and then I drifted off and lost track of how good it had been before that.

Therapist: A run-in with someone kept you away and then somehow you lost track of how much you got out of it.

Client: Yes. But this time, if something like that happens I won't let it throw me off so much.

In this second illustration, the therapist empathically, and with an attitude of acceptance, follows the client as he explores his recollections and new decision.

Illustration III

This client has been discussing the spiritual investigations she has undertaken with a mind-reader, a shaman, and a spiritual reader.

Client: Each one gives me a different perspective on myself. I don't know what they *really* mean, but they mean a lot to *me*.

Therapist: They each give you something important personally, even though you don't know how much you believe in them.

Client: Right. I don't know. But I get feelings and I get insights I didn't have before. Especially from the shaman. He found me my guardian animal when he did his trance, and ever since then I have a feeling of being safe. More safe than ever before.

Therapist: The animal is keeping you safe, protecting you and that's a new feeling.

Client: Yes. And my spiritual reader helps guide me through some of the hard spots at work. She encourages me and tells me to speak up when I feel they're unfair. It works.

Therapist: Your spiritual guides are making a real difference, really helping you feel better.

Client: Oh yes. It's amazing.

The therapist has no personal belief in the client's spiritual helpers, but genuinely follows the client's thoughts and feelings about the experiences.

Illustration IV

This is a client hospitalized with the diagnosis of schizophrenic disorder, paranoid type. He has recently been violent on the ward, hitting an aid and smashing a chair.

Client: At first they were so nice. They'd talk to me like my mama and make jokes and make me laugh and I didn't feel so lonely.

Therapist: Uhm, hm.

Client: Then they were real spiritual, telling me about God and Jesus and making me feel real good. One time Mary was whispering to me to love Jesus and pray, and I prayed real hard.

Therapist: The voices helped you; they helped you feel better. And they brought you closer to your religion and spiritual feelings.

Client: Yeah. (Pause.)

Therapist: The experience of Mary talking to you was very special and got you praying more than before.

Client: Yeah! But then it got different. I was prayin' hard to be good but that ol' angel came, the bad one, and he told me I was dirty and stupid and bad and he told me people was going to punish me, so I had to watch out. I hadda protect myself.

Therapist: You were working hard at your prayers but then the voice changed and you began to feel afraid you were going to be hurt — that someone was aiming to hurt you.

Client: Yeah! I been really scared.

The therapist does not make any point to distinguish between the client's hallucinatory experiences and report of his feelings. She attempts to empathically understand the client's perceptions as they are for the client.

Illustration V

This client is preparing to take some college courses possibly including an introduction to counselling. He is at the same time trying to come off pain medication for an injury and is feeling confused. He experiences some paranoid-type of thoughts and a preoccupation with the suffering in the world. He is anxious and depressed and not sure he is ready to concentrate on school.

Client: I've taken psych courses years ago, but that stuff would probably not be relevant now. (Pause.) I guess the best way I see that people actually change is the kind of stuff you do.

Therapist: Seems my approach works best.

Client: Yeah, and I do think I am just beginning to see the line you walk and that it takes a tremendous amount of practice.

Therapist: You're catching on to it and how much it has taken me to learn it.

Client: Yeah. (Pause.) Somehow over the last six months or so it feels to me like I have been through one heck of a time warp . . .

Therapist: Time's been wacky . . .

Client: . . . a mini battle of sorts . . .

Therapist: A lot of struggle.

Client: Yeah and I do think somehow people's consciousness will, for stuff to be good, is in a collective ball out there someplace hovering around. (Pause.)

Therapist: There's a place in space where people's thoughts are all tangled together and continuing to exist outside of them.

Client: Yeah.

Therapist: And it does some good.

Client: Uhm, hm. It's like you have to think, 'what happens to all these feelings of anguish, pain, love, hope, and so forth that people have on their own? Where does it all go?' All this stuff seems too strong to me to just drop into the dirt.

Therapist: There's so much pain and other emotions that people have all over the world, it doesn't feel right to think it's going nowhere. You can't dismiss it, or ignore especially all that suffering; somehow it needs attention.

Client: Yeah, I keep feeling I have to do something about it, but I don't know how. (Pause.) I think I am off the track. Anyhow I'm going to look around for more classes and get back to you about it.

The client is struggling with strong emotions and thoughts that haunt him but he is trying to push on to some important practical goals. The therapist follows the client empathically and tries to understand the personal meaning of his thoughts of transcendent events.

Illustration VI

The following segment is from a session with a client who had previously been in therapy with the same therapist and who, in the process of discussing her emotional and spiritual experiences, had decided to renew her original religious involvement. She has returned, having become a Roman Catholic nun. She is living in a cloistered nunnery.

Client: Some of the older nuns are very difficult and set in their ways, but at the same time, I can learn a lot from some of them.

Therapist: It's not always easy.

Client: No. Sister C was on my case for trying to introduce some classical music to the choir. The stuff they'd been singing was getting boring. At first she acted very righteously, but eventually she started explaining how the music was fitting into the sacrament, you know, the sequence of experiences, and I saw how I could better select material. It turned out she was open to more than I thought.

Therapist: You worked it out with her and discovered she wasn't just rigidly resisting your ideas.

Client: Yeah, that has happened a lot. Though some of them are awfully stuck in what they're used to. There haven't been many new sisters coming in, much less new ideas brought in over the years.

Therapist: Uhm, hm.

Client: I do have some doubts about whether this is the right vocation for me. The kids have finally accepted it. At first they were blown over. But now they come to some Friday dinners and chat-up the old sisters, and the sisters like them. But I haven't adjusted yet to the cloistered life. I have lost a lot of freedom while gaining my closeness to God. And I guess the fact that the others are almost all 20 years older than I am, or more, means I don't feel a sense of sharing concerns, mental outlook beyond the church, or even about it, sometimes. I don't know.

Therapist: You feel uncertain sometimes and maybe it's the vocation that isn't right for you. Or it just may be not being used to the life, or maybe your companions are too much from different generations.

Client: Uhm, hm. I feel I've overcome a lot of obstacles. You can't imagine how much resistance I got from everyone. But I felt so sure! I'm not sure now what's involved here. (Pause.) The sense of security is fantastic. I'm very grateful for that. But I'm not used to the lack of freedom. Satisfying as the routines are, and they really are satisfying. (Pause.) I do feel isolated mentally or intellectually, outside of the devotions and prayer and our rituals.

Therapist: So much of what you have found feels good to you but the loss of freedom and a deprivation of intimacy about personal stuff besides religion is hard for you. You don't know what it adds up to.

Client: Right. It's complicated and very mixed.

The therapist tries to understand the client, following as the client shifts her points and covers some of the complexity of her situation.

Discussion

The benefits of Client-Centred therapy are many. In the writer's experience with clients presenting spiritual or religious issues, I have detected no difference in the beneficial effects of my therapy between them and clients who have not presented spiritual or religious issues. There are many studies showing the benefits of Rogers' Client-Centred necessary and sufficient conditions for therapeutic change (Patterson, 1984). Studies focusing on the personality characteristics of Client-Centred clients have shown statistically significant changes due to the approach. There is evidence of change away from characteristics labeled as borderline psychotic, severely neurotic, and severe discomfort, in the direction of milder problems or the characteristics of an essentially well-functioning person. In those studies, clients also came to be seen by others as better adjusted, more of a separate individual, with his or her own standards and values, more responsible and less guilty. When behavior changes were assessed by the clients themselves, and by friends, there were descriptions of a significant improvement in maturity of behavior (Rogers, 1954).

Another study, of change variables using a psychoanalytic perspective on the TAT, comparing pre-therapy to post-therapy has shown statistically significant differences indicating improvement. There are positive changes in the areas of self-concept, in work, in intellectual activity, functional intelligence, energy level, defense level, threat level, sexual activities, social life, community connection, as well as improvement in relationships with significant others (parents, siblings, children, mate), superiors, subordinates, peers and in level of life-adjustment (Grummon and St. John, 1954).

Another study employing 149 clients and altogether 80 Client-Centred therapists showed improvement of clients when the therapists provided relatively high levels of Rogers' therapeutic conditions. The measures used before and after therapy tapped general insecurity, social difficulties, psychosomatic complaints and neurotic disturbances (Rudolph, Langer and Tausch, 1980).

I have witnessed evidence of all the research-reported kinds of change with my clients. In my experience, the effects of therapy with spiritual or religious clients in respect to those issues tend to be revealed in the clients' greater clarity about their feelings and greater peace of mind relating to spirituality and religion. I estimate that far more of my clients (over a 45-year span of time) have moved closer to their preferred religious or spiritual orientations than have moved away from them. In Illustration V I, I indicate there was a change towards religious involvement, the client having become a nun in part through realizations experienced during her earlier therapy with me. This is striking to me, and supports my view that I am practising consistently with Client-Centred theory, because I am an atheist and have no spiritual orientation whatsoever. I think my clients' developments toward spirituality and religious faith and participation in many instances reveal my value-neutrality in regard to those issues and that my clients have been facilitated in the growth directions towards which *they* were inclined.

Conclusion

The segments of Client-Centred interactions with six different clients have illustrated the way Client-Centred therapists typically work with clients regardless of the topics the clients are pursuing at the time. In the illustrations, several kinds of experiences that may be viewed, by the clients themselves or by others, as spiritual or religious are empathically followed by the therapist. The illustrations do not, of course, prove the efficacy of the method with spiritually or religiously concerned clients. The writer hopes, nevertheless, that the reader gains a sense from them of how clients' spiritual and religious feelings are acceptingly addressed with empathic understanding in Client-Centred work.

References

Baldwin, M. (1987) Interview with Carl Rogers on the use of self in therapy. In: M. Baldwin and V. Satir (Eds.) *The Use of Self in Therapy*. New York: Haworth Press.

Brodley, B.T. (1988) Responses to person-centred vs. Client-Centred. *Renaissance, 4 & 5,* 12

Brodley, B.T. (1997) The nondirective attitude in Client-Centred therapy. *Person-Centred Journal*, 4 (1), 61–74

Grummon, D.L., and St. John, E. (1954) Changes over Client-Centred therapy evaluated on psychoanalytically based thematic apperception test scales. In: C.R. Rogers and R. F. Dymond (Eds.) *Psychotherapy and Personality Change*. Chicago: The University of Chicago Press.

Natiello, P. (1988) Responses to person-centred vs. Client-Centred. *Renaissance, 4 & 5,* 3

Patterson, C. H. (1984) Empathy, warmth, and genuineness in psychotherapy: a review of reviews. *Psychotherapy, 21,* 431–8

Pörtner, M. (1988) Responses to person-centred vs. Client-Centred. *Renaissance, 4 & 5,* 4

Raskin, N.J. (1947)The nondirective attitude. Unpublished paper.

Raskin, N.J. (1988) Responses to person-centred vs. Client-Centred. *Renaissance, 4 & 5,* 2-3

Rogers. C. R. (1954) An overview of the research and some questions for the future. In: C.R. Rogrs and R.F. Dymond (Eds.) *Psychotherapy and Personality Change* Chicago: The University of Chicago Press.

Rogers, C.R. (1957) The necessary and sufficient conditions of therapeutic personality change. *Journal of Consulting Psychology, 21,* 95–103

Rogers, C.R. (1959) A theory of therapy, personality and interpersonal relationships, as developed in the Client-Centred framework. In: S. Koch (Ed.), *A Study of a Science. Vol. 3. Formulations of the Person and the Social Context*. New York: McGraw-Hill.

Rogers, C.R. (1980) The foundations of a person-centered approach. In: C.R. Rogers *A Way of Being*. Boston: Houghton Mifflin.

Rogers, C.R. (1987) Client-Centred? Person-centred? *Person-Centred Review, 2 (1),* 11–13

Rudolph, J., Langer, I. and Tausch, R. (1980) An empirical investigation of psychological effects and conditions of person-centred therapy with individual clients. *Zeitschrift fur Klinische Psychologie , 9,* 23–33

Contributors

Jacob Belzen trained in social sciences, philosophy and history. He is currently working as a professor of psychology at the Faculty of Humanities of the University of Amsterdam, where 'history and foundations of psychology' and 'religion and mental health' belong to his specialities. A frequent contributor to journals in these fields, he has authored and edited several books, and has served in many international organizations.

Isabel Clarke is a clinical psychologist working for Southampton's NHS Community Trust. She is editor of *Psychosis and Spirituality: Exploring the new frontier*, published by Whurr.

Professor Dr. Petrûska Clarkson is a consultant philosopher, chartered clinical, counselling and occupational psychologist, and is based at the Centre for Qualitative Research in Psychotherapy Training and Supervision PHYSIS, 12 North Common Road, London W5 2QB.

Lorna Hensey is a graduate of Tara Rokpa Therapy training and an experienced workshop leader in its methods. She currently works as a psychotherapist in the NHS.

Judi Irving is a Lecturer in Psychology at the University of Hull and a Chartered Counselling Psychologist with a research interest in personal development.

Edie Irwin studied psychotherapy with R. D. Laing for five years before training with Akong Rinpoche, with whom she has worked since 1979. She has been involved in the development of Tara Rokpa Therapy over the past twenty years.

Simon King-Spooner is a clinical psychologist and psychotherapist currently working at the Scottish State Hospital at Carstairs and in private practice.

Michael Len, MSW, PhD is a Taoist-Quaker psychotherapist in Bristol. He has been a Methodist Lay Preacher, Episcopalian Lay Reader, Eucharistic Minister, Congregational Mission Interpreter (Asia-India), nursing home Chaplain in sacrificial ministry, vowed community member, graduate of CPE and student of interfaith ministries. These and his 'day jobs' in counselling and therapy were in the USA, New Zealand and the UK.

Kate Loewenthal is Professor of Psychology at Royal Holloway, University of London. Her research is focused on religious and cultural issues in mental health, She edits *Mental Health, Religion and Culture*, and has written books and journal articles on these and other topics. She is married and has a large family.

Kate Maguire is a senior trauma therapist for Medecins Sans Frontieres and the founder and director of the EACS in London. She consults on training and treatment of survivors of torture and extreme experiences. She is currently doing a doctorate in *The Language and Concepts of Pain*.

Craig Newnes is a dad and gardener. He is Psychological Therapies Director for Shropshire's Community and Mental Health Services NHS Trust and editor of the *Journal of Critical Psychology, Counselling and Psychotherapy*. With Guy Holmes and Cailzie Dunn he has co-edited *This is Madness: A Critical Look at Psychiatry and the Future of Mental Health Services* and *This is Madness Too: Critical Perspectives on Mental Health Services,* published by PCCS Books.

Brooke Rogers is a PhD student of Psychology at Royal Holloway, University of London. Her research is primarily focused on religion, identity and mental health, including aspects of guilt, shame and forgiveness. She is currently acting as a research assistant for Kate Loewenthal and also lectures at Royal Holloway and the University of Sussex.

Dorothy Rowe was born in Australia in 1930. She worked as a teacher and child psychologist in Sydney. In 1968 she came to England to work as a clinical psychologist in the NHS and to begin her research into depression. She is a Consultant Psychologist and author of numerous books and articles. Her latest books, *Friends and Enemies* and *Beyond Fear* are published by HarperCollins.

David Smail is a retired clinical psychologist and Special Professor in Clinical Psychology at the University of Nottingham. He is author of *How to Survive Without Psychotherapy*, published by Constable.

Arthur Still works as a Counselling Psychologist for the Borders NHS Trust and in private practice, and is an Honorary Research Fellow at Durham University.

Barbara Temaner Brodley has been a client-centered therapist for over forty-five years, and in private practice for the past 34 years. She received her Ph.D. in clinical psychology and human development from the University of Chicago. She teaches CCT at the Illinois School of Professional Psychology and in programmes in Europe. She is also Clinical Consultant to the staff of the Chicago Counseling Center.

William West is a full-time lecturer in Counselling at Manchester University where he directs the Masters in Counselling Studies programme. His book *Psychotherapy and Spirituality* was recently published by Sage.

Dave Williams is a Senior Lecturer at the University of Hull and is a Chartered Occupational and Chartered Counselling Psychologist with a wide range of interests from infertility to the philosophical basis of counselling.

Name Index

Subject Index